LIVING
DEBT-
FREE

LIVING
DEBT-
FREE

The No-Shame, No-Blame Guide to Getting Rid of Your Debt

Shannon Lee Simmons

Founder of the New School of Finance

 Collins

Living Debt-Free

Copyright © 2018 by Shannon Lee Simmons.

All rights reserved.

Published by Collins, an imprint of HarperCollins Publishers Ltd

First edition

HarperCollins books may be purchased for educational, business, or sales promotional use through our Special Markets Department.

HarperCollins Publishers Ltd
Bay Adelaide Centre, East Tower
22 Adelaide Street West, 41st Floor
Toronto, Ontario, Canada
M5H 4E3

www.harpercollins.ca

Library and Archives Canada Cataloguing in Publication information is available upon request.

Typeset by Sam Tse

ISBN 978-1-4434-5759-0

Printed and bound in the United States
LSC/C 9 8 7 6 5 4 3 2 1

For Matt and Bill, my fam. I love you so much.

CONTENTS

Life Happens—and Sometimes Debt Does Too

Debt sucks. No one wants to be in debt. But life happens, and if you've got debt, life has happened to you.

Helping people financially survive real life has been my day job for more than a decade, and I have a secret for you. Most people have debt—even those you wouldn't expect to. Maybe your neighbour does, or your boss, your parents or the person sitting beside you right now. Don't be fooled by appearances or social media feeds. I've been peeking behind the curtain into people's financial lives long enough to know that just because someone has a great job or a nice house doesn't mean they can breathe financially.

You probably have a lot of feelings when you think about your debt. Some days it may be frustration, on others it may be resentment, rebelliousness or guilt. Or maybe you're just so done with feeling blue that you're straight-up apathetic—"It is what it is. Everyone has debt"—which, I can tell you, is the most dangerous.

Here's the thing: whether it's $2,000 chilling on a credit card or $80,000 in line-of-credit debt, I know you have debt not because you have a problem with expensive handbags or Star Wars figurines. It's because life happened, and kept happening, and it took you by surprise.

Trust me, I know that you used debt as a last resort, especially in the beginning, when you first got into it. Maybe it was losing your job, going to university, paying for your daughter's wedding or needing surgery for your cat. Whatever it was, going into debt felt like the only way forward. Then, bit by bit, your monthly income was reduced by new, bigger minimum debt repayments. You still had to financially survive the same things as before, but on less income. It's hard. I hear you, I understand and I know how to help.

Year after year of sitting on the front lines of financial planning, helping real people pay off real debts, has made one thing abundantly clear to me: extreme debt-repayment plans aren't working for most people. Most times, they set you up for failure.

Extreme plans rely on what I call the Debt-Repayment Gospel: reduce your spending as much as you possibly can and pay off your debt aggressively, starting with the highest interest rate first, no matter what your situation. They usually offer mega-promises of financial freedom: *How I paid off $60,000 in three years! Pay off debt fast, even with a low income! How to pay off your debt in 12 months!* Maybe you've come across plans like these on your computer at three a.m., after typing "how to pay off debt fast" into a search engine.

The promise of getting rid of your debt as soon as possible is beyond tempting. It's what you want; it would be such a relief. But extreme debt-repayment plans like these can be a lot like crash dieting. They motivate you with scare tactics: *If you don't do anything, you'll end up paying $3,000 in interest!* And they often force you to reduce your spending to such an unsustainably low level that you can't even grab a coffee without feeling guilty for the rest of the day.

I know that aggressively paying back debt feels good for a while—noble, financially responsible—and it does work at first. Maybe for six months to a year, if you're super diligent or a Virgo. But I can tell you right now, 90 percent of the time it's not going to work for much longer than that. Why? Because *life*.

Let's be honest for a second. It may take you years to pay back your debt. Years—that's a long-ass time. If your debt-repayment plan is supposed to take four years, it's unlikely that you'll be able to put your entire life on hold and be on your best spending behaviour for that long. So instead of pretending that you'll punish yourself by saying no to absolutely everything for the next four years (no birthday parties, no dinners out, only homemade gifts), why not be realistic and brace yourself financially to say yes to some types of spending and no to others. That way you can live with—and stick to—your debt-repayment plan instead of trying to aggressively pay it back, failing and giving up, again and again, getting nowhere fast.

When you fail at a debt-repayment plan, you feel stupid and ashamed and convinced that you are "bad with money." This is a very dangerous mindset. I call it the Shame-and-Blame Mentality. I've seen it enough times to know that the more you fail with your debt-repayment plans, the more likely you'll give up altogether. You've already failed, so why try? And that's when your debt levels *really* start to climb.

This is why extreme debt-repayment plans rarely work. They lead to short-term success but long-term yo-yo budgeting and ever-increasing credit card bills, lines of credit and failure rates. They make it seem as if all you need is willpower and you'll be fine. They perpetuate the detrimental Shame-and-Blame Mentality. When you fail, you feel like an idiot who just can't stop spending irresponsibly.

But that's not you. I'm certain of it. How do I know? Because I've been there, done that and bought the T-shirt that I couldn't afford . . . with a credit card.

Laundry Room Meltdown

"Are you sure you want to make this withdrawal from your RRSP, Ms. Simmons?" the financial advisor on the other end of the phone asked for the second time. "You will have to pay a tax penalty."

"Yes, I know. I'm sure," I said in a hushed tone, even though I wasn't entirely. I was calling from the basement of the rented first-floor flat where I lived, under the guise of doing laundry. I didn't want Matt, my then boyfriend (now husband), to hear.

I hung up the phone and stared at my full laundry bin. I had committed a cardinal sin of personal finance: taking money out of my RRSP before retirement. Worse still, I'd taken money out of my RRSP to pay back $13,000 worth of credit card debt. "I am such an idiot," I said to myself. How could I have let this happen? I knew better. Tears burned behind my eyes and threatened to fall.

"Oh, hey," said the lovely hippie who lived upstairs. "What's up?" He was carrying a large rattan basket filled with laundry.

I was about to give him a smile and say the obligatory "not much, just doin' some laundry," but when I went to speak, nothing came out. The threatened tears and the lump in my throat were blocking my ability to be cordial and get the eff out of Dodge.

I swallowed hard. I'm usually quite friendly, so my lack of response must have given me away. He knew something was up.

"Everything okay?" he asked. We had been neighbours for about two years, but I wasn't sure he knew my name. He was Hippie Neighbour Dude to me. I was probably Perky Girl with Cat to him.

I waved him away without saying anything. The last thing this guy needed was for the girl who secretly moved his laundry from the dryer to the top of the machine after it had been in there for two days to start bawling on his shoulder.

"Whoa! You are not okay," he said, putting down his basket. "Um, ah," he stammered, "I'm not sure what to do. Do you need something? Someone?"

I did one of those loud laugh-cries—you know, when you start to cry while bursting out laughing because you're so embarrassed. Like when you slip and fall on an icy sidewalk and people ask if you're okay. You say yes but it hurts like hell and you're so not okay.

"I'm fine," I blurted out. "Just having a moment." Tears began to fall in earnest. I couldn't stop them; the floodgates had opened. I forced a smile.

"Hey, totally."

We stood there kind of awkwardly. I mean it was really awkward; there I was weeping openly in front of someone I barely knew.

"Well, if you want to talk about anything, you can unload on me. I don't judge and I don't really know you, so I couldn't tell anyone you know even if I wanted to," he joked.

I laughed. I didn't want to tell him what was actually happening. Confess to a stranger that I, a financial planner, had racked up $8,500 worth of credit card debt over 12 months and had just emptied my RRSP to pay it down? Hell no. I'm all for financial honesty, but that would have been just a little too real.

"I just had to make a phone call that I didn't want to make," I said. "That's all."

"Did it work out the way you wanted?" He pushed himself up to sit on the dryer.

"Um, well, it's happening, so that's good. But . . ." I paused. "I guess I'm just upset I had to make the call in the first place."

"Upset at yourself or upset at someone else?"

"Only myself." I pulled myself up onto the washing machine across from him.

"Well, we all do dumb shit sometimes." He shrugged. "It's what makes us human."

I remember thinking that he was so intuitive. *He must have sisters,* I thought, or maybe it was all the Enya I imagined he listened to during sun salutations. Whatever it was, I was glad Hippie Neighbour Dude had showed up for my laundry room meltdown. He was like some sort of fairy godmother with a man bun.

So how did I end up crying over my finances with my neighbour while sitting on top of a coin-operated laundry machine? Let's back up a bit.

Two years before, I had been working a high-rolling Bay Street finance job. At 25 I had paid off $30,000 in student debt, saved up

$13,000 in my RRSP and travelled to Europe with Matt. On paper, everything was great, but I was not feeling fulfilled by my job. The 2008–09 crash had just happened and people were freaking out. Then in 2009 I had a watershed moment that changed the course of my entire career: I realized that, unlike the wealthy Bay Street clients I had been working with, everyday people didn't have anywhere to go to get unbiased financial planning advice, unless they were willing to throw down some serious cash. I wanted to change that.

Inspired and full of purpose, I quit my job to launch a one-year project in which I gave unbiased financial planning advice to 310 women in exchange for bartered goods or services—no money. I was paid with things like two bicycles, ten lasagnas, photography services and even a pie a month for a year. The goal was to make financial planning fun, accessible and affordable. Swoon!

The project was a complete success. It catapulted me into a new career and completely changed who I was and what was important to me. And it showed me that there was, in fact, a business in helping everyday people with their finances—there was demand. It was both the smartest and the stupidest thing I'd ever done. Smartest in the big picture, and stupidest from a short-term financial perspective.

You see, I couldn't pay the rent or my cellphone bill with bikes, photography services or pies (even though I tried). Before I quit my day job, I had saved up $13,220 outside of my RRSP, enough to cover my rent ($10,200 for the year) and my phone ($1,200), plus $35 a week in spending money ($1,820). My assumption was that I'd barter for everything else and spend no money at all. Unrealistic Plan Number 1.

Man, was I ever naive. I blew through the $1,820 put aside for spending money within the first six weeks. I wasn't buying anything excessive. Seriously—groceries, transit, web hosting, a coffee every now and then—I was not living it up. I knew I couldn't touch the rest of my savings because it was for rent and my cellphone.

Paying for things on a credit card is no big deal when you feel confident that you'll pay it off within the grace period. But it's an entirely different thing to swipe your card with the full knowledge that you can't pay it off anytime soon. That's where dread comes in.

The first time I swiped my credit card with the knowledge that I had no way to pay it back, I almost cried—it terrified me. It was for a $24 bottle of wine for the host of a Christmas party. I beat myself up for the entire walk there in the snow, the wine weighing heavily in my knapsack and on my mind. *Don't be so stupid. You can't use credit right now*, I told myself, and I resolved that I wouldn't spend money on anything that wasn't a necessity like groceries or shampoo for the next 10 months. I could do that, right? I mean, I had to. Unrealistic Plan Number 2.

The second time I swiped my credit card came only two days later. My sister was in town and we went out for dinner. I remember the pang of dread when she asked me if I wanted to go out. "Sure," I said. "Sounds great!" When the server brought over the payment machine, I took out my credit card, fearful that the machine would out me as broke. *Excuse me, miss, but your bank account knows you can't pay this off next month, so your card was declined.* But that's not what happened. It went through, no problem. There's no "insufficient funds" warning with a credit card. In those early days of my debt, I was guilt-ridden and fearful every time I spent money.

After a month, my first credit card statement appeared in my online banking. I opened it right away, eager to see the damage. Owing: $350. Minimum payment: $11. *Eleven bucks?* I almost said out loud. *Whoa!*

It was almost exhilarating. Like that IKEA commercial where the people get such a deal that they feel like they're stealing—"Start the car!" I didn't realize it at the time, but that moment was the beginning of the end for my finances over the next nine months. It was a moment that falsely confirmed that I could still live my life, even though I didn't make enough money to afford it.

I hadn't told Matt that I was taking on debt. I had always planned to, but I was ashamed and didn't want him to worry. I mean, I had quit my job and was talking about starting a business after the project was over. I didn't want to freak him out, so I kept convincing myself that I had it under control and that it would all work out somehow.

Within six months I had managed to rack up $3,200 on my credit card and the minimum payment had grown to $125 per month. I had only $5,000 left in savings, with no income in sight for the next eight months at least. I had euchred myself.

You see, the threshold between being a person who does not have debt and being a person who does is a big one. It's scary. When you have zero debt, even a one-dollar jump up is emotionally significant. That's why financial experts always say that it's so much easier to stay at zero debt when you're at zero. But once you break that debt barrier, you become a person who has debt, and the threshold for the next swipe is less scary. The fear becomes normalized. If you already owe $500, what's another $50? If you owe $20,000, what's another $2,000? I was in a Debt Loop. I would spend money that I couldn't afford to spend, owe more money, have less money, then spend money I couldn't really afford to spend. Rinse and repeat.

As the debt mounted higher and higher, something eventually let go. I got really good at compartmentalizing it, ignoring it. It's almost as if the scarier the amount I owed was, the less I thought about it. Weird, right? You'd think the opposite would happen. But in my case, I thought and worried about the debt much more when I felt that it was a manageable amount. When the amount I owed was manageable, I felt guilt about not taking steps to reduce it (because I knew I could), and when I didn't take action, I'd beat myself up. But as the debt grew larger, I genuinely started to believe that I couldn't do anything about it anyway, so why try? The fear of dealing with it was so real for me that I couldn't bear to actually look at it. One time I even held a piece of paper over the bottom portion of my laptop screen when I logged into my online banking so that I couldn't see the balance owing on my credit card. It was self-preservation.

In month nine, Matt got laid off from his job and I reached an "it is what it is" mentality—resignation. I had given up. I had $5,500 on my credit card, with no ability to pay it off or to pay rent. It was going to take something huge to get me back on track. A successful business? Clear out my RRSP? Move to the country and live off the land? Something big and dramatic was necessary. And until that big thing happened, I just kept on spending, except now I was spending on more than just the daily necessities. When you're on thin ice, you might as well dance, right?

By the end of the project, I had maxed out my credit card at $9,000. The jig was up. I couldn't even make the minimum payment. Faced with the horrible reality that I was unemployed and in debt, I had to do something. The "something big" had to happen. Luckily, I had $13,000 in my RRSP. Once I paid the tax penalty, I'd have $9,100 left to bring me back to zero.

That was it. All of my savings, gone. *Poof!* All to pay back the past, not to build something in the future. I was heartbroken and ashamed. And that's how I ended up crying with Hippie Neighbour Dude in the laundry room two months after the project ended.

"Yeah, well, I've got to go confess that phone call to someone right now, and I don't want to," I said.

"If the roles were reversed, would you be pissed off at them?" he asked.

I thought about that. If Matt had quit his job to live out his dream and ended up taking on debt, would I feel pissed? Would I feel betrayed? Would I shame him? No, not in a million years. I believed in him, and I was sure he believed in me too.

"No." I shook my head and smiled. "I wouldn't be pissed."

He smiled and hopped off the dryer. "Well, then, I'm sure you've got nothing to worry about."

Hippie Neighbour Dude was right. I walked upstairs with the laundry that I hadn't even started, ready to confess.

I was nervous as I entered our flat. I was worried that my debt would freak Matt out, but more so that he would be hurt that I hadn't told him about it until then. I cringed inside. How could I have let it go on for so long? I felt selfish and immature.

"Babe, I need to talk to you about something." I was fidgeting with my hands.

"What's up?" He came in from the kitchen.

"Something is going on with me and I need to tell you about it."

"Okay," he said cautiously, and sat on the couch. I could tell I had made him really nervous.

"Crap . . . I don't know how to say this," I said.

"Shannon, you're freaking me out." When Matt uses my full name, I know he's serious.

I took a deep breath. "Okay, I'm just gonna say it. I have debt—lots of it. I just couldn't afford this year." Then it all came pouring out. "Thirty-five dollars a week was just not enough for me to live off. I couldn't barter for what I needed, and I'm so sorry I didn't tell you. I've been so embarrassed. I thought I had things under control." I started to cry. "I'm so, so sorry."

He sat for a moment, then gave a comical "Phew!" and put his hand on his chest. "Wow. You had me scared there for a second."

I was confused. "Wait, my debt doesn't scare you?"

"Well, how much are we talking here?" I liked that he'd asked how much *we* were talking about, not *you* (swoon).

"Nine thousand," I said meekly. "I'm so embarrassed."

"Shan." He got up and came over to me. "You have nothing to be embarrassed about. I'm sorry you didn't feel you could come talk to me sooner. I would have done whatever I could to help." He gave me a big bear hug and I cried even harder, but this time with relief and gratitude for this awesome person who wasn't shaming me or making me feel stupid.

"I didn't want you to worry or think that the project was stupid or that I shouldn't start my business," I said through muffled sobs.

"I would never think anything you do is stupid."

"That's not everything," I said as I wiped my eyes.

"Okay. What else?"

"I pulled all the money from my RRSP to pay off the debt. It's gone—all of it."

"Well, that's okay too. I mean, it's your money. You saved it up."

"It's *our* money. It's our down-payment fund, and now I've just pissed it away."

"Shannon, you are an amazing financial planner. If you think taking money from savings is the best financial move for us, then you have my full support. We'll figure it out. Besides, taking the money from the RRSP has allowed you to survive this year. Think of it as investment capital for your new business."

I can't explain the flood of relief that gave me. The shift in perspective—that I could look at the $13,000 as an investment in my business and not just me being a selfish idiot—made its loss an easier pill to swallow. It saved me from being mired in guilt and shame. It allowed me to move forward.

In hindsight, I wish that I had spoken to Matt sooner. It would have motivated me to not give up. Debt was inevitable, to be sure, but perhaps I would have ended up owing only $4,000 instead of $9,000.

Lessons Learned

That was almost a decade ago, and I'm still uncomfortable remembering that time in my life. But I don't regret it. It taught me some things about debt, things that I use in my practice every day when I'm helping people who are wrestling with debt.

I know that the key to becoming debt-free is threefold. First you have to break the Shame-and-Blame Mentality. That's what caused me to stick my head in the sand and give in to the debt. Second, you have to find motivation beyond debt scare tactics, beyond the math. The fear around the money I was wasting on interest was scary but not enough to motivate me to make better decisions every day. Last, you have to make a realistic plan to dig yourself out. Don't set yourself up for failure the way I did.

Mastering all three will give you a debt-repayment plan that feels safe, happy and doable, one that will keep you motivated long enough to see it through until the very last payment. No shame, no blame, no scare tactics.

Living through spiralling debt made me a better financial planner for anyone carrying debt, because I've been there too. I know how it feels, and that's why I don't judge. I've helped so many people become debt-free. It takes time, stamina and—not to get all woo-woo on you—a lot of self-love. I promise you, it *is* possible to have a life and pay down debt responsibly at the same time. In fact, I know that's the only way your debt plan will actually work, once and for all.

This book will get and keep you motivated. That's the key. Everyone is motivated to pay back debt for the first part of their repayment plan, but *living* motivated is the tough part, where 90 percent of the failure happens. You have to choose to pay down debt and stick to the plan many times.

My goal is to get you to a point where you're not only truly motivated to take action tomorrow but you will also have the tools to execute solid financial decisions, again and again and again, until you're living debt-free once more. In the coming chapters, you'll discover

· How to get out of debt for good.
· How much you can realistically afford to save towards your debt.
· How long it's going to take until you are living debt-free.
· Ways to stay motivated and see your plan through to the end.

You and your debt need to learn to coexist if you're going to see your plan through to the end. Let me open a window so you can breathe. You can do this. You can pay down debt and still live your life. I promise.

▶

Before we get started, I want to be very clear about who this book is for. This book is for anyone who has debt and also has an income or the potential to earn income. You don't need to be a baller, but there needs to be enough money coming in so that you can keep a roof over your head, eat and be safe. If you're currently in a situation where you don't make a living wage, the strategies and advice in this book will still be helpful, but you may not be able to implement all of them until your income is enough to cover your needs. The income ranges in this book reflect those of the people I advise at the New School of Finance, people who make anywhere from $35,000 to $80,000 a year, with most examples based on incomes of $40,000 to $60,000. These are real people, diverse in age, family situation and socioeconomic status. (Everyone's name has been changed, and each has given me permission to tell their story.)

I encourage you to read every anecdote, even if the person it's based on doesn't exactly reflect your life. If you start reading a story and the person has kids and you don't, or maybe you're about to retire and come across a story of a twenty-something with student debt, that doesn't mean there aren't helpful nuggets in there for you too. Read them! Each story is chock full of advice, tips and strategies to help you along the way, regardless of your age, income, family status or type of employment.

Finally, there is a kickass Resource Library in the back of the book that lays out all the nitty-gritty details you'll need to help you create your own debt-repayment plan using the strategies I've laid out.

If you're tired of being in debt and tired of failing at debt-repayment plans, welcome. I'm so glad you found me. The fact that you're reading this book means you're ready to do this once and for all. Take a big breath, my friend, then bust out the calculators and spreadsheets. It's go time!

Part One

Stop the Debt Loop

Oh, hey, you kept on going and turned the page! You're ready to make a change. Yay! The reason I'm being such a Pollyanna cheerleader right now is because making change is hard and debt-repayment plans are intimidating, no matter how much debt you're carrying. You've got some work ahead of you—we both know that. You wouldn't be reading on if you didn't. I'm going to ask you to do some tough stuff. You'll have to tally up your debt, deal with your Financial Tripwires and stop using debt as a go-to financial safety net, and that shiz ain't easy! So I'm going to have your back and be annoyingly happy for you every step of the way.

Part One of the book is how we transform you from a debtor to a saver. We are going to dive deep into the emotional side of your debt—yup, all the feels. Before we can build a plan, you've got to unpack your debt, understand why you have it in the first place and learn how to sidestep it in the future. All the strategies and tips in this book are useless until you deal with the emotional stuff, the root causes of your spending behaviour.

Most debt books skip this crucial step. Many of them jump right into the super-exciting math parts (yes, I said "super-exciting math parts"). But there is so much that needs to happen before that in order to make sustainable permanent changes to your finances. Trust me, I've seen it so many times. If you don't change your spending behaviour permanently and if you don't believe you can truly tackle your debt, you'll never truly stop what I call the Debt Loop.

First you deal with the emotional side of your debt sh*t, then you do the math. I promise, this is crucial. It's like having allergies. Instead of just treating the symptoms—coughing, sneezing, itchy eyes—over and over, you have to figure out the root cause of the allergy and avoid it altogether so you can feel good all the time. No more itchy eyes, ever.

Let's spend some time unpacking how you think and feel about your money. Let's get you to a place where you understand your Financial Tripwires and find motivation beyond the interest your debt is costing you. This is how to stop the Debt Loop forever. Let's ensure that this is the last debt book you'll ever have to read.

CHAPTER 1

Recognizing the Debt Loop

Ah yes, the Debt Loop. The battleground on which you will throw down your enemy (your debt) and smite it to ruin (sorry, I really like fantasy novels). Regardless of your age, type of debt or income level, your Debt Loop will likely continue until you learn how to stop it—forever. In order to stop the loop, first you have to understand what it is, how it works and how it's affecting your daily life. Then you'll stop taking on debt and be in a position to start hammering it down like a boss. This is your first step to living debt-free.

So what *is* the Debt Loop? I'm glad you asked! The Debt Loop is the annoying thing that keeps you owing money.

The Debt Loop

Life throws you curveballs, or as I call them, Financial Tripwires. Things like a friend's wedding, summer camp for the kids, unexpected physiotherapy—expensive things that you didn't plan for financially and that you feel your only option is to pay for with credit. Then you have a new bill to pay: your minimum monthly payment. You have to pay it, whether you like it or not, so now you have less spending money each month but still have to financially survive the same things you did before.

So you make a plan to pay off the debt, but it's probably not all that realistic. You rely on goals like *I won't spend money on clothes for the next six months* or *I'll pack my lunch every day*. But then life throws you another Financial Tripwire. You feel like you have to use credit to survive, and then you end up thinking of yourself as a failure, even though you're not!

This is the Debt Loop. It repeats and repeats until you reach a point I call the F*ck-It Moment. That's when you're just so done with feeling broke and like a financial failure that you simply throw in the towel. *F*ck it. When you owe $5,000, what's another $100. Right?*

The Debt Loop

Financial Tripwire ➡ Debt Happens ➡ Unrealistic Debt-Repayment Plan ➡ Failure ➡ Shame-and-Blame Mentality ➡ F*ck-It Moment

Each stage builds off the one before. The good news is that each stage of your Debt Loop also offers an opportunity to change your behaviour and stop it from looping. That's the beauty of it. The Debt Loop is the problem but also the solution.

Financial Tripwires

Financial Tripwires are spending triggers. Whether it's a weak moment at the sale rack, university tuition for your kids, or a sick parent, life will throw you some financial lemons and opportunities that are ripe for overspending, guaranteed.

There are two types of Financial Tripwires: those you can avoid altogether and those you can't avoid at all. The Financial Tripwires you can avoid are the ones you have control over personally: routine or emotional Tripwires. We break these down in Chapter 3, but essentially routine Tripwires are spending triggers that happen in specific places or during specific events. They are almost habitual. You make spending decisions every day, and some of them happen without a lot of thought or mindfulness. They are just part of your daily life, your routine. Often those routine spending triggers are what's causing you to overspend without even realizing it.

Emotional Tripwires are a bit different. These are familiar feelings that make you want to spend more money than you should; they include both positive and negative emotions. Feeling like crap? Treat yo'self. Out celebrating? "Drinks on me!" Emotional Tripwires are spending triggers that are unique to you.

The Financial Tripwires you cannot avoid are usually something I call setbacks. A job loss, a health scare—some sort of emergency where you have to spend the money whether you have it or not. The only way to protect yourself against setbacks like these is to have adequate insurance or Short-Term Savings such as an emergency account. We break down Short-Term Savings in Chapter 6.

Debt Happens

If luck is what happens when preparation meets opportunity, then debt is what happens when lack of preparation meets a Financial Tripwire. I'm sure you're not stoked when you swipe a credit card or borrow again on a line of credit that you know you can't pay off. But debt happens because, in the moment, it doesn't feel like there's any other choice. That's how Tripwires work. At the time, that swipe felt like the only way forward.

Once you take on debt, there is immediately less money in your pocket, because now you have to deal with minimum monthly payments, either payments on your existing debt that you've increased or payments you've taken on for the first time. The worst part is that in order to pay it back, you'll need to dip further into your spending money so you can not only make the minimum payment but also put money towards the principal. No matter how you look at it, new debt means less money for your daily life. Boo-urns.

This is why debt sucks so much. You still have to financially survive your daily life, but now on less income. In the beginning, the amount of money you had to spend each month in minimum payments was probably nominal. *Oh, it's only fifteen dollars.* But that's exactly what makes it easy to sink slowly into the debt hole.

Every time you overspend, the amount of money you have left over for your daily life is reduced more and more, eventually reaching a point where you're stuck. There's no give in your budget anymore. You can't move, you can't breathe. Like water slowly filling up a room, it's not so scary when it's at your ankles, but without action it will rise up to your chest. That's when it gets terrifying.

Unrealistic Debt-Repayment Plans

This is usually the point at which people start making unrealistic debt-repayment plans. If you type "how to pay off debt" into a search engine, the first thing that likely autofills in the search bar after your question is "fast." Fast, fast, fast. *How to pay off debt FAST!*

I usually hear things like "Shannon, I need to pay everything off in three months." Or "I hear you, but if I don't buy anything for a year, I know I can pay off my credit card." And worse still, "I read about a person who paid off $60,000 in three years. I should be able to do the same!"

Listen, I know you want this debt off your back. You're tired of feeling frustrated and maybe even scared. You want to feel safe, hopeful and in control as fast as possible. But hold the phone. Slow down. When you get spooked by the amount of debt you're carrying, panic sets in, and that is the worst possible time to make a debt-repayment plan. Panic breeds failure.

The problem with overly aggressive debt-repayment plans is that the timeline until you are debt-free is often very short (and arbitrary) and requires you to make unrealistic reductions in your spending. They doom you to fail.

Failure Happens

Failure happens because life happens. If you've reduced your spending money by so much that you have to be on your best spending behaviour all the time, going without even small pleasures day in and day out, failure is a given. Eventually there will come a Tripwire that forces you to spend more than you've allocated and you'll set the Debt Loop into motion again.

Take, for example, my client Shauna, who in six months wanted to pay off $3,000 in credit card debt with an interest rate of 19 percent. With a salary of $30,000 a year, Shauna made $2,040 a month after tax. Per month, her share of the rent was $800, her phone bill was $80, her transit pass was $110, and the monthly minimum payment on her $3,000 credit card was $90. This left her with $960 for any savings and spending money.

Shauna usually spent around $700 a month for groceries, clothes and the rest of her life. If she wanted to pay down her credit card in six months, it would cost her an extra $478 per month on top of the $90 minimum payment. That meant she would have to reduce her spending money to $482. That just wasn't enough for her, given the usual cost of her regular life.

She was able to sustain this level of austerity for three months, but then she had a job interview and needed an outfit. She found one that made her feel really confident and comfortable in her own skin; it cost $65. She purchased it with cash but then didn't have enough for groceries that week. Naturally, she brought out her credit card and swiped. She had failed at her debt-repayment plan.

Of course she failed, but not because she's bad with money, a shopaholic or out of control. She failed because the plan was not realistic for her life. Not someone else's—*her* life. Unrealistic debt-repayment plans and time horizons and spending abstinence lead to failure. I've seen it happen time and time and time again.

The Shame-and-Blame Mentality

The Shame-and-Blame Mentality is the headspace you occupy when you feel like a total failure after your debt-repayment plan falls off the rails. You couldn't pay down your debt or stop using your credit, and you feel like it's all your fault. "I just feel like such a loser," Shauna said, "like I didn't try hard enough."

Shame and blame perpetuate the fear that you will have debt forever, regardless of what you do to stop it. If you tell yourself that you are "bad with money," eventually, over time, you'll start believing it. I think the Shame-and-Blame Mentality is the worst part of the Debt Loop, and I believe it's the main reason why that Loop persists. Shame and blame are not good motivators; in fact, they breed more debt.

Typically, the Shame-and-Blame Mentality leads you to keep secrets, from yourself and from others. The fear of facing your economic reality is so real that often you stop opening your statements or logging in to your bank account, and you never tell anyone you're in financial trouble. Instead you play it down—"Yeah, I've got some debt"—even though you can barely keep it together.

The burden of your debt is strictly yours, and you get pretty good at lying to yourself about the plans you'll make to tackle it . . . tomorrow, after the holidays, sometime before you're 45 . . . 55 . . . 70. You believe that somehow it will work itself out. The Shame-and-Blame Mentality causes the proverbial sticking your head in the sand because you're too afraid and ashamed to deal with your financial reality.

When you feel as if you're doomed to carry debt for the rest of your life, fear and guilt occupy your days. It takes so much mental energy just to deal with that emotional monkey on your back that it interferes with your ability to move forward. You're frozen, constantly worried about the future and constantly feeling guilty about the past.

F*ck It Moment

The Shame-and-Blame Mentality makes you give up. It tricks you into thinking, *What's the point? F*ck it. This is the way things are for you and there is no way forward*. Ignoring debt feels easier, safer and much more comfortable. And so the overspending continues, the debt increases and the dread mounts. You're in the Debt Loop, going around and around and around again.

▶

I get it. If you don't want to give up before you even begin, you need to smash the crap out of the Shame-and-Blame Mentality that's hanging over you like a dark raincloud. The Debt Loop is not inevitable. You *can* stop it, I promise. All the tips and tricks I give you will actually work, and you can learn to break the Debt Loop for good.

The key to taking back your power is to change your behaviour for good. And that starts with reframing your debt, avoiding your Financial Tripwires and finding motivation beyond the math.

CHAPTER 2

Reframing Your Debt:
Beat the Shame-and-Blame Mentality

No one wants to be in debt. In all my years of frontline financial planning, I've never met anyone who said, "I'm so stoked to be in debt" or "Can't wait until I'm in debt!" But, of course, debt happens. Over the years, I've learned that simply looking at a person's balance sheet tells me nothing about them or the reason they are in debt. Behind every credit card statement and every bank overdraft is a very human story, a reason why the Debt Loop began.

When someone walks into my office, whether they're carrying $3,000 on a single card or $90,000 from combined sources, I never assume anything about the person or their situation. The first thing I do is take the time to find out how they got there. I need to know their debt story. What Tripwires happened, what series of events led them to my office? And how do they feel about their debt? I need to know this so I can ensure that it's not affecting how they feel about their ability to make good financial decisions going forward. Here are a couple of examples:

Mateo: I got laid off a few years ago. I only took on about $2,500 of debt during my layoff, and I took the first job I could, out of desperation. It wasn't realistically enough money to afford my life and pay back the debt, which started to climb after that. The debt makes me feel stupid. I mean, I know better. I make okay money and shouldn't be in debt. People have way worse situations than I do. I guess I feel guilty about it. I don't know, I don't really like to talk about it much.

Irene: The first time I remember not being able to pay off my card completely was after I had a big dental bill. I didn't have benefits through work and so I was carrying $1,500 on a credit card for the first time. Then the rest just snuck up on me. It was never anything big—$50 here, $100 there. I'm not a frivolous person, so my purchases never felt irresponsible. Groceries, a birthday gift, a subscription to a new music app—normal stuff. I guess I never really knew what I could and couldn't afford. Turns out I couldn't afford what I was spending, even though nothing was outrageously excessive. That's what frustrates me. You'd think that with $10,000 on a credit card I would have something to show for it. But I don't. It makes me feel so hopeless. I didn't even do anything wild and crazy, but here I am $10,000 in the hole.

Usually when people tell me their debt story, I can see how their debt makes them feel. I watch for the words they use and the body language that goes along with it. Most times the words are negative, words like *angry, resentful, guilty, hopeless, frustrated.* But their body language is even more telling.

Think about your debt for a moment. Now notice what happens in your body when you do. Does your face get hot? Does your stomach flip? Does it make you want to shut your eyes and look away from your banking app—or this book? Super normal. Often when people are telling me their debt story, they press their hands to their chest as if they can't breathe. They don't even realize they're doing it until I point it out. That anxiety, that frustration, that pressure are caused by how you feel about yourself and how you got there, and I know that it dictates how you feel about your ability to succeed moving forward.

The stronger the negative emotions connected to your debt, the more likely you are to fail at your debt-repayment plan. You'd think it would be the opposite, but it's not. How you feel about your debt matters, big time. Feeling negatively about it only makes things worse. Carrying all those negative emotions requires a lot of emotional labour. It gets exhausting after a while. So the stronger the negative emotions a person has about their debt, the more likely they are to keep ignoring it, let it spiral or give up. F*ck it.

Giving up is easier when thinking about your debt brings you so much stress. Ignoring it is a defence mechanism, an escape from the heavy emotional burden you have been carrying every day. That's why you try to not think about it, to push it down, to suppress the stress and divorce yourself from all those negative emotions. That is why you need to reframe your debt story. It will transform the way you see your debt and your ability to succeed at your financial plan. Reframing your debt creates a powerful perspective shift that can give you back hope and allow you to tackle your debt head-on.

You need to acknowledge your story and move to a place of inquiry rather than judgment. You need to ask yourself "What happened?" rather than "How could I?" It's an important distinction. Reframing your debt story can help you to gain a healthier perspective and pull yourself out of the Shame-and-Blame Mentality. It's not about letting you off the hook or rationalizing every swipe of your credit card. It's about showing yourself some compassion so you can shake off the shame and guilt that are keeping you from dealing with it head-on. It's meant to help you pull your head out of the sand and allow you to think positively so you can move forward.

Reframing Your Debt

Over the years, I've learned that a positive perspective is half the battle when it comes to motivating someone to take positive financial action. Perspective may not change the financial outcome or the work required, but it makes the grind of getting the financial work done a lot easier to handle, and therefore a lot more likely to happen. Trust me.

My client Amna is an artist who is also in school doing her master's degree. Last year she made $5,200 from her art business. The rest of her income came from school bursaries and money she was borrowing on a student loan. At tax time she owed $114 and was angry. "I didn't make any money and I'm a student. How can I still owe taxes?"

I understood her frustration. But I pointed out that the $114 she owed was her annual contribution to the Canada Pension Plan (CPP), a very important retirement pension that she will receive one day. She wasn't actually paying income taxes. "This is money going towards your future. You'll see this money again. Imagine if I said, 'Hey, Amna, you need to save $114 at tax time this year for your retirement.' That's what this is like."

She laughed. "That actually makes me feel so much better. I'm more than happy to save for my future rather than pay the taxman." And with that she stopped resenting her tax bill and gladly paid the $114 towards her future self. Perspective, my friends, is everything, especially where money is concerned.

Gary became a new client last year after he had quit his nine-to-five job and struck out on his own. He wanted to do freelance web and graphic design. He had no debt before he quit his job and had saved enough money to launch his new business ($3,000) and pay his bills and eat ($10,000) for the first four months of freelancing. He spent the full $13,000 in the first five months, while the business grew—and it grew fast.

In his first year of freelancing, Gary made $50,000 profit after all his business expenses were deducted. Amazing! Many freelancers take a few years to get to that point. I was impressed.

"I've got a sh*t ton of debt," he said. His frustration was evident.

"So how did you get here?" I asked. "Was it a slow burn or did it all come at once?"

"The taxman killed me," he said and showed me his assessment: $15,000 total, with $12,000 in income taxes and $3,000 in sales tax. It was a doozy. I felt for him.

"Were you able to put aside any savings?" I asked carefully. I wanted to make sure he didn't feel judged.

"I did, but I didn't really know how much I was supposed to be saving. I put some aside—$3,000 for taxes and $2,000 for HST. I didn't expect *this*." He sighed heavily.

"What's that sigh about?" I asked.

"Everyone told me I shouldn't quit my job, that being self-employed is so much more work and unstable. I don't know, I guess they were right. Anyway, I had to fund the other $10,000 owing to the government on my line of credit." He exhaled. "I don't even want to pay it back. It's just so unfair." He was angry.

"What's unfair about it?" I ventured.

"I didn't know I was screwing up. I thought I was doing everything right. I registered my business, I kept good bookkeeping records and I did save money for taxes. I just didn't realize it would be this much money. I worked so hard, for nothing."

"What do you mean, 'for nothing'?"

"I mean I busted my ass all year and all I have to show for it is debt."

I could tell he was irritated by my probing. That was okay. I was happy to hold the uncomfortable space for him, and it was nothing I hadn't dealt with before. Debt is scary, and talking about it can make people really defensive, especially if they feel that I might not be on their side or that I don't get it. But I was on Gary's side and I did get it, so I knew that all would be well between us . . . eventually.

"Okay, Gary, can I offer another perspective here?" I asked.

He shrugged. "Sure."

"The fact that you made a profit of $50,000 in your first year of business is wildly exciting, and so positive. That's not 'working for nothing.' You netted $38,000! [This doesn't include the $3,000 sales tax that Gary had collected and owed.] I don't often see that with first-time free-lancers. It usually takes a couple of years for this kind of growth." I was getting excited.

"Really?" He was surprised.

"Yes! And you need to remember that you pay tax only if you're making money."

"What do you mean?"

"Well, if you hadn't made a lot of money last year, you'd have a loss or a very small profit. In that case it's likely you'd have had a very small tax bill, or none at all. Sure, that would be handy right now, but was making a small profit or a loss really your goal?"

"No, for sure not."

I busted out an income tax calculator (simpletax.ca/calculator) and punched in some numbers. "See? The $3,000 you saved up for income taxes would have been enough to pay your tax bill if you had had a profit of only $20,000. But you made more than double that, which is great! Your goal is to make money from your business and generate a profit, right?"

"Yes."

"Well, you did it. Instead of hating this tax bill, you should be cele-brating it! This tax bill is proof that you earned a profit and that your business is working."

His mood shifted; it lightened. "Ha!" he said. "I guess I didn't think about it like that."

"Well, I sure do," I said. "Your business did not fail. None of your naysayers were right. This tax bill is like a battle wound from a highly profitable first year in business." I smiled. "You literally did everything right. I give you an A plus. The only mishap was that you didn't know what percentage to be putting aside when you got paid. But, Gary, that's an easy fix going forward. You didn't know and now you do. This is not going to repeat itself."

"Thank you for saying that," he said. "It does make me feel better about it."

"Do you want a gold star?" (I keep gold star stickers in my office, and trust me, not everyone gets one. You gotta earn that shiz.)

"For real?" he asked. I nodded and held up the stickers.

"Obviously." He laughed. "Right there." He pointed to the lid of his laptop.

I pulled off a gold star and stuck it on. "There," I said. "Now every time you resent this tax bill hangover, you can look at the gold star and think, *No, I don't suck at running my business. I'm a badass entrepreneur who succeeded well beyond what I expected*—because that's precisely what happened to you."

He breathed a sigh of relief, and I knew we were on track to a debt-repayment plan he would get excited about. Gary and I made a plan to tackle the $10,000 line-of-credit debt and still put enough away for his tax bill for the current year, so he wouldn't get stuck in an income tax Debt Loop.

Did having a $10,000 debt hangover suck after year one? Yes, but reframing it in a positive way gave Gary the confidence to keep going in his business and not feel like a failure. The tax bill was not his fault; it was circumstantial. The $10,000 debt didn't represent his failure but rather his success. The only Tripwire was that he didn't have all the information he needed from the start. If he had known the rules, he wouldn't be there. But now he did, so he could move on both financially and emotionally. Yes, he still had to deal with the debt financially, but it was no longer a representation of his failure. Now he was motivated to pay it back rather than resenting and avoiding it. This shift in mindset is crucial as you get ready to tackle your debt.

Reframing your debt will take you to a more positive headspace and, I promise you, it will make you much more likely to succeed. You will break out of the Shame-and-Blame Mentality that makes you want to give up, stick your head in the sand and keep sinking. It's easier to ignore something that's emotionally draining and negative. But it's also easier to face something head-on when it begins to feel positive.

Without a positive outlook, it's more likely that you'll stay mired in those angry, frustrated feelings that make you want to give up or ignore the debt altogether.

When Your Debt Helped Others

You'd be surprised by how much debt people carry because they helped someone else, someone they loved—a friend, their parents, their kids, their partner. It shows up in many different ways. Maybe it's to pay for a flight so your adult children can come to Florida with the grandkids. You can't really afford it, but you'll be damned if you can't see your grandchildren for six months. Maybe it's taking on more than an equitable share of the rent when your partner goes back to school. Or maybe it's throwing your best friend the most memorable bachelorette party in the world. Whatever the reason, someone else's happiness depended on your willingness to spend money, and that's exactly what you did.

My client Mandi is a great example of this. Mandi was carrying $7,000 between two credit cards, all of it racked up in the previous year after moving out of her parents' house. After graduating from university, Mandi had moved back home to save money. She took a minimum-wage job at a coffee shop while she worked full-time at an unpaid internship to get the experience she needed to start her career in broadcast journalism.

"Everything was going fine when I was living at home. I didn't have any expenses except a little bit of spending money, and I was even able to save $100 a month from my part-time job."

"So how did you get here?" I asked. "Was it a slow burn or did it all come at once?" This is how I always phrase the question to get to the heart of someone's debt story. When someone is telling me their story, of course I'm listening to what they are saying, but even more so I'm listening to how they use that story to shame or blame themselves. I'm listening to hear how their debt makes them feel about themselves and how it's affecting their financial confidence.

"After I moved out, I couldn't afford life. I was working part-time and not making any real money. Rent was 80 percent of my take-home pay. I had to put groceries on my credit card, but I couldn't stay home, so that's what had to happen."

"What had to happen?" I asked.

Mandi sighed. "Okay, you're like the only person I will tell this to. Not even my sister knows." Things were about to get interesting. "I had been living at home for about six months. One day I came home early from work and overheard my parents having an argument. It was about money. Basically, I found out that they have debt and that my dad was worried about getting laid off. The extra cost of having me at home was affecting their ability to pay down their debt and prepare for retirement." She shook her head. "Brutal."

"Yikes, that's heavy," I said.

"Totally. They would be so devastated if they knew I heard that conversation. Anyway, I didn't want to be a financial strain on them; they obviously have their own stuff to figure out. They refused to accept rent from me. They begged me to stay, which was so kind and so selfless. There they were, struggling to make ends meet, and yet they were willing to sacrifice their own financial safety so that I could start my life on the right foot."

"That's love, eh?"

"Totally," she agreed. "But I just couldn't. So I told them that I really needed to live downtown for work, in order to make connections. I found shared accommodation with some roommates and moved out, and that's when the debt started. Small things at first, but then it just built up. I never had enough in my chequing account to pay it down fully each month. Next thing I knew, it was $7,000 and maxed out."

"Let me ask you something. How do you feel when you log in to your online banking?" I asked.

She frowned. "I feel so irresponsible."

"But you're not irresponsible at all."

"Well, what else can you call it? Everyone else thinks I'm stupid for moving out so soon after school, because my parents are awesome and I had a great thing going. So now I feel like they're right. I had no debt when I left school, and now I'm starting my life $7,000 in the hole. I've put myself so far behind. So irresponsible . . . I'm just bad with money."

This debt was robbing Mandi of her financial confidence. Using words such as *irresponsible* and *stupid* to describe herself confirmed that she was deeply mired in the Shame-and-Blame Mentality. In addition, her belief that she had put herself so far behind had robbed her of the hope that she could effect control over her financial future and that there would be an end to this, that all was not lost.

"Can I offer another perspective here?" I asked.

"Sure."

"Okay, so your parents wanted you to stay at home even though it would likely mean more financial troubles for them, because they love you hard. Right?"

She nodded.

"So that's exactly what you did for them in the beginning. I call it setting yourself on financial fire to keep someone warm. You did for your parents exactly what they wanted to do for you. You traded your financial security for their comfort. It's kind of beautiful, actually."

She paused and reflected for a minute. "I never thought about it like that."

"Mandi, you did everything right and you have nothing to be ashamed of. You got roommates and you worked part-time while you were interning as well. That's *so* responsible. You just didn't have the income to make it work right away. If you'd had a job that paid a living wage, you wouldn't have debt. In addition, the fact that you didn't turn a blind eye to your parents' financial needs is something you should be very proud of."

"What do you mean?" she asked.

"I mean the only reason you're in debt is because you had to move out before it was truly financially viable. But you did so because you wanted to help your parents. It's a reflection of how much you love them and how badass you are. This $7,000 debt is like a badge of merit for financial adulting."

She laughed. "I guess you're right, it was pretty badass of me. But I still have $7,000 to pay back, which sucks."

"For sure, but at least when you open up your online banking and you see it, you don't have to feel shame or blame yourself for being financially irresponsible. You were the total opposite—you were *too* financially responsible, and very selfless."

"That definitely makes it easier to swallow." She laughed. "You make me feel like some sort of financial superhero."

I smiled. "You are, and helping people you love is your financial kryptonite."

"Ooh, I like that," she said.

"Me too."

Since the $7,000 was going to hang out there for some time, until she got a job, we made a plan for Mandi just not to take on more debt before she got a full-time job. Once she was being paid a living wage, she would have the confidence that she could pay her bills, live and realistically pay down the debt at the same time.

The key Tripwire here was her parents' conversation that she over-heard. It's what made her move out before she was financially able to afford it, and the debt grew from there. Changing her perspective from a place of shame and guilt to a place of acceptance kept her from spi-ralling down the Shame-and-Blame-Mentality hole and giving up. This new feeling gave her confidence that eventually she would be able to pay it back, that there was hope and that she could be good with money.

I'm not saying that every swipe of your credit card has a deeper meaning. I'm saying that whatever kicked off your Debt Loop in the first place likely happened for a reason. Some Tripwire took you from being a person without debt to a person with debt, and then it built from there, F*ck-It Moment after F*ck-It Moment. The point is that having debt doesn't necessarily mean you're bad with money. It does not mean you can't trust your financial intuition. It does not mean you are doomed to repeat the same mistakes forever.

If you can reframe your debt, you can move on from it emotionally, which is important if you want to break the Debt Loop. If only negative emotions surround your debt, you will get stuck in the Shame-and-Blame Mentality, which is a surefire way to ignore it, lose hope, give up and fail.

How to Reframe Your Debt

Bust out your journals, people. Time to reframe your debt!

- What is your debt story? How did you get here? Was it a slow burn or did it come all at once? Why was spending that money important to you at the time?
- What good came from it?
- What did you learn from that event? Did you learn something about yourself, or how you want to prepare for your life?
- If you had saved money and been able to afford the things you paid for with debt, would you be proud or happy about the money you spent?
- How can you hold on to that pride or happiness? How can you come to embrace that the spending was part of your journey, even if you don't love how you spent the money?

Acknowledging your debt story and reframing it makes it less scary, allowing you to see the humanizing reasons why you're there. It's not because you're bad with money and it doesn't mean you're doomed to be in debt forever. Your debt happened for a reason. It's probably an epic battle wound.

CHAPTER 3

Identifying Your Financial Tripwires

We make financial decisions every day. Think about your day so far. Unless you've been up for only an hour, it's likely you've already made at least five financial decisions. Fill up the gas tank today or wait for prices to drop later this week? Pack the kids' lunch or give them $10? Make coffee at home or grab one on the way to work? These are all daily financial decisions; each one impacts your overall finances.

When you've got debt, you may be living right at the financial edge, with no emergency account. It's likely that you feel guilty or afraid when you spend money. You never really know when spending is okay or when it's going to lead to more debt you can't pay off. When you're living with debt, spending money on your daily life can feel like a balancing act. It's like taking a walk on rocks by the water. You're safe, steady even—until you're not. All it takes is one slippery stone, one Financial Tripwire, and *boom!* You lose your footing and slip, right back into the Debt Loop.

This is why it's important to recognize your Financial Tripwires, both routine and emotional. They are not the same for everyone. Saying no to overspending is not just a simple matter of willpower; it's so much more complex than that. When debt continues to climb, even while you're trying your best to pay it down, it's usually because specific Tripwires happen again and again. When you encounter them, you feel compelled to spend, regardless of affordability. It's a learned behaviour, and before you know it, you're trapped.

If you can identify your Tripwires, you'll be able to see them coming a mile away and avoid them. Knowing your Tripwires is a powerful way to permanently change the root cause of your debt. You need this awareness to sidestep your spending responses and create new habits with your money. This is how you protect yourself against debt. This is how you win.

Routine Tripwires

Routine Tripwires are usually events or places where you find yourself overspending despite your best intentions. Maybe it's every time you're on vacation (*F*ck it, I'm on vacation*), or when you see a sale (*It's such a good price!*), or maybe it's a specific shopping location (*Every time I go into the hardware store expecting to spend $50, I drop well over $100*). The good news is that routine Tripwires are the easiest to identify and to avoid.

My client Lesley kept going into debt. "I'm embarrassed," she said.

"Why?" I asked.

"Because last year we made that whole plan and I still have debt." She looked down. "I'm so sorry."

I laughed. "Don't be sorry. Let's figure out what didn't work last time."

Lesley had come in to see me about a year before with $9,000 on a credit card. At the time I asked her my usual question, "How did you get here? Was it a slow burn or did it all come at once?"

She told me she had maxed out after a bad breakup, an unexpected move and a much-needed vacation, all of which were paid for with credit cards, kicking off a Debt Loop. She had enough cash flow to put $500 per month towards her credit card debt, so she could be paid off in just under two years. It was realistic and doable. She left my office stoked to implement her plan.

So why was Lesley back a year later with her credit card still maxed out at $9,000? I wasn't sure but definitely wanted to know. "Okay, let's dig in," I said.

I had Lesley go through five months' credit card statements with me. I saw that she had been dutifully paying the $500 each month into her card. But every month or two the balance would slowly creep back up to the max. She hadn't had more than one month when the $500 actually lowered the balance. It wasn't big circumstantial events like the breakup or a job loss that kept her in debt. Something was going on in her daily life that was causing her to keep overspending, some routine trigger that I had to find in order to solve the problem for good.

I handed her a highlighter. "I want you to mark any transactions that represent a purchase you wish you hadn't made."

She laughed. "Um, all of them?"

"What do you mean?"

"Well, I have debt. I shouldn't be going out on weekends or taking taxis. That's what you're going to say, right?"

"Not necessarily. There is money in your budget to spend, and how you choose to spend it is up to you. I'm talking about transactions that made you feel really resentful afterwards, the ones you feel you could absolutely have done without and now regret. It's quite likely that some of your expenses don't make you feel bad afterwards. You might even feel proud of the purchase, excited, and you'd do it again—I call this Happy Spending. Other transactions, however, may make you feel blue. They bother you and make you feel guilty, afraid or frustrated—Unhappy Spending. It's different for everyone. Maybe taxis are Happy Spending for you and Unhappy Spending for someone else. Let's find your Unhappy Spending."

I pointed to a grocery expense of $80. "I want you to rate how you feel about the fact that you spent $80 on groceries. Rate it on a scale of one to five, with five being the Happiest Spending and one being Unhappy Spending."

She thought for a moment. "Four. I don't really feel resentful about groceries, and I'm usually pretty mindful about meal prep."

"Great. So that's not a transaction you would highlight." Next I pointed to a monthly music subscription for $10.

"Five. I love music, and this app," she said.

"What about this $45 at a department store?"

She paused. "Okay, this is embarrassing."

"Why?"

"I don't even know what that was, and it was only three weeks ago. Obviously it's not something I needed or really wanted. I'll rate that a one." She highlighted it.

She kept going through the list of transactions. "Three . . . four . . . four . . . definitely five." Then she stopped and highlighted one.

"What did you mark?" I asked.

"That was $10 for magazines and chocolate from a convenience store," she said. "It's a one out of five. I hate it when I spend money on that stuff."

She kept going through the list until she was done. When she finished, we looked at all the highlighted transactions. I was trying to see if I could find a common thread, something that made them routine.

"Where are you when most of these highlighted transactions are happening?"

"Downtown."

I started seeing a pattern. "Most of these charges happen during the week. You don't have weekend spending spikes, and hardly any of your weekend spending is highlighted as Unhappy Spending. Did you realize that?"

She looked over the statements. "Weird. You're right."

"So if most of these highlighted transactions happen downtown and during the week, you're obviously doing it during the workweek. Are they from after work?"

"No. Oh my god, you're right. It's not after work, it's my lunch break!"

She scanned through the pages, noting all the highlighted transactions. "Like 80 percent of these are lunch-break spending."

There it was, Lesley's routine Tripwire. I smiled.

"Lesley."

"Yes?"

"I think you're bored on your lunch break."

She paused for a moment, then laughed. "I totally am. It's my only time away from the office. It takes me only fifteen minutes to eat lunch, but I don't want to go back to the office right away. So I end up just walking around the mall." She sat silent for a moment, staring at the statements. "I can't believe I didn't realize this before."

We went back over the highlighted transactions, and I could see why. There was no specific store or type of purchase such as clothes, entertainment or taxis. The items weren't big deals or massive purchases. In other words, it wasn't a specific type of transaction or place where she spent money; it was the time of day that they all had in common.

Lunchtime boredom was Lesley's routine Tripwire. The good news was that it would be an easy fix. Armed with this new awareness, Lesley could easily sidestep the habit and stop the spending that was leaving her in the Debt Loop. All we had to do was establish a new lunchtime routine.

Lesley felt that it was important to get away from the office for the full hour that she was on lunch, so staying at the office or going right back after eating lunch was out of the question. Also, the mall was warm, and she often didn't want to go outside during the winter months. We made up a list:

- Do not take your credit card with you on lunch break. Debit or cash only; no other access to money. Use debit rather than cash so we can track your expenses afterwards if you end up overspending again.
- Turn on your step counter and try to get in 5,000 steps during lunch break.

- Make a weekly playlist for your lunchtime walk.

While Lesley's usual lunchtime stroll in the mall had kept her out of the cold, boredom had fuelled her routine Tripwire. She couldn't change the weather, but she could give those lunch-hour walks another purpose, keeping boredom at bay and avoiding those Tripwires. She had recently bought a pedometer. Having a lunchtime steps goal gave her another reason besides shopping to be wandering around the mall for 45 minutes. It gave her something to focus on instead of creating errands to reward herself with. In addition, making the weekly playlist allowed her to marry her love of music with her new routine, helping to keep it fun and different each week.

I checked in with Lesley seven months later. "How's the 5,000-step debt-reduction plan going?" I asked.

"Amazing!" she exclaimed. "I've managed to make my $500 payment to the credit card every month without spending more. And I hit my 10,000 steps every workday now!"

I laughed. "That's great! I'm so excited for you and glad we were able to identify your routine Tripwire."

"Me too. I was like a spending zombie, buying things just because they were there and I was there. There were so many purchases that I don't even recall making. I also think I was addicted to buying things and then returning them, just for something to do on my lunch break. I was so bored, I can't even believe."

Identifying Lesley's routine Tripwire allowed her to be aware and mindful of it. Her lunch break was a trigger that used to trip her up. But by identifying it, she is now able to sidestep and avoid it.

Find Your Routine Tripwires

1. Go through your bank statement and credit card statements for three to five months and highlight the transactions that you don't feel good about—the purchases that left you feeling resentful, guilty, frustrated or afraid. This is Unhappy Spending.

2. Remove your credit card information from any apps or online shopping sites where it's automatically populated. Put your credit card away for a week so that you can't use it. Write down each time you feel frustrated that you can't purchase something. Take note of what you wanted to buy, what you were doing in that moment, where you were and what time it was.

3. Examine the transactions that you highlighted or wrote down. What do they have in common? Is it a specific store, a specific time, a specific place? Who were you with? What were you doing? What else was going on during those times? How did you feel when you were about to spend money? Look for trends.

How to Eliminate Routine Tripwires

- If your routine Tripwire is a specific app, take it off your phone. If it's a website or online retailer, remove your credit card information from the site. If it's a particular store or place, stop going there for three months, unless it's a grocery store or somewhere you absolutely need to shop.

- If it's a place where you still need to shop, set your intended spending amount before you go in, and leave your credit cards at home. For example, if it's the hardware store, make a list and set your financial intention before you leave (*I only need to pick up nails for $15*). Don't make credit available to yourself when you are in the places or participating in the events that usually lead to overspending. Use debit so that you're spending your own money, and create that limit for yourself. (In Chapter 9 I provide you with a banking plan that will help support this.)

- If your routine Tripwire is not a specific place or event that you can avoid, it's likely a habit that either chases a good feeling or avoids a bad one. Lesley, for example, was avoiding boredom. Replace your old habitual spending with a new habit. Look for something that gives you that positive feeling or avoids the negative feeling without spending money.

Emotional Tripwires

There are also emotional Tripwires, which may not be so easy to avoid. Emotional Tripwires are familiar feelings that make you want to spend more money than you should. Usually you say "F*ck it" and give in to temptation.

I've been working with people who have debt for a long time. Most times, clients report feeling guilt or anxiety around spending caused by inadequacy or FOMO (fear of missing out)—the main sources of pressure to overspend. *I don't want my kid to be left behind in sports* = $5,000 spent on hockey (inadequacy). *I'm single and I want to feel confident about how I look on a first date* = $100 for a new outfit (inadequacy). *It was my friend's 40th birthday. I didn't want to miss it* = $80 for drinks and dinner at a fancy restaurant (FOMO).

When an emotional trigger is negative, you want to throw money at it to make it go away. I get it. These feelings are utterly human. I'm pretty sure everyone (with the possible exception of Ebenezer Scrooge) has emotional Tripwires that lead to overspending from time to time. The problem isn't that you have these feelings and then overspend. That's life. It's a problem when it happens over and over again, when it becomes a habit. It's hard to point to one transaction on your credit card and say, "Yep, that's the exact transaction that put me into debt." Most times debt is the sum of its parts.

Identifying emotional Tripwires has been one of the most effective ways in which I've been able to help people avoid overspending, stop going into debt and follow their debt-repayment plan right through to the end. The thing is, if you can't identify where you are most vulnerable and most likely to fall off the plan, then you can't avoid it and will end up right back in the Debt Loop.

The interesting thing about emotional Tripwires is that they aren't only negative feelings. Sometimes it's positive emotions that create the pressure to overspend. *We're celebrating? I'm in! And it's my treat!* = $50 on drinks for the table. *Treat yo'self! I worked hard for this. I deserve it!* = $60 at the spa.

When the emotional Tripwire is positive, you want to throw money at it to keep riding that high. This is also completely normal. We're all human. Overspending because of emotional triggers often brings a brief moment of happiness because it either soothes a negative emotion or temporarily sustains a positive emotional high. But on credit, it then becomes a long-term pain in the ass. This is why overspending on emotional Tripwires is not true Happy Spending. The *lasting* impact of your purchase is negative, even though it felt good or easier in the moment.

My clients Marta and Sebastian are great examples of this. They had their first baby, Nikola, last year. The truth is, I usually expect new parents to be a bit of a hot mess financially because so many expenses are associated with a baby: crib, stroller, clothing and diapers, maternity/parental leave and the dreaded daycare years. I often find myself telling clients that their sole responsibility during those financially tough years is to simply break even. If you can come out on the other side of parental leave and daycare without debt, you'll thrive afterwards.

The thing was, Marta and Sebastian were sinking further and further into debt and couldn't seem to figure out what was going on. They had taken on $3,000 in debt during Marta's maternity leave, which was something they felt they could tackle full force when Marta returned to work. Now that she was back at work, they had enough money to put $300 a month towards the credit card, even with daycare expenses. They had planned to pay off the card over the next 12 months. However, six months into their debt-repayment plan, they were in my office, with $10,000 on a line of credit they had maxed out trying to pay down their credit card each month.

"Okay," I said, "how did you get here? Was it a slow burn or did it all come at once?"

"A slow burn, I guess," Sebastian said. "We just don't get it. It's not like we had an emergency or anything."

"We are actively trying to budget and yet we keep sinking," Marta added. "It's so messed up." She shook her head. "We aren't over-spenders! We don't live extravagantly."

"Let's look at your statements," I said with a smile.

I had asked Marta and Sebastian to bring the last five months of spending history with their credit card. I explained Happy versus Unhappy Spending and asked them to rate their spending on a scale of one to five and to highlight any transactions that were a one or two out of five—Unhappy Spending. "I need you both to go through the statements with highlighters, old-school, and mark the transactions you can't remember or expenses that you now regret. Maybe at the time you felt good, but in retrospect you wish you could take them back."

"Ooh, interesting. Can we use different colours?" Marta asked. "I'd like to see my regrets versus Sebastian's."

It was a good call. I handed Sebastian the yellow marker and Marta the blue. Then I said, "Go nuts."

They appeared to be having fun highlighting and discussing. Most times they were fairly aligned on the transactions that they regretted or couldn't remember.

"Okay, done!" Sebastian said.

"Let's have a look." I scanned the highlighted Unhappy Spending transactions. There were two very distinct trends: takeout and baby gear. "Marta, why does the takeout bother you more than some of the other expenses?" I asked.

"Because it's so expensive," she said. "But after I race home from work, I want to spend as much time with Nikola as possible, getting her dinner going, starting bath time, bedtime, et cetera. The last thing I want to do is cook. By the time Sebastian gets home, we're both starving, and we probably didn't have time to do a proper grocery shop. So we end up ordering in. It's so bad."

"Sebastian, how do you feel about it?" I asked.

"Actually, I care less about the takeout. We're new parents who both work full-time, and I think we need to cut ourselves a bit of slack. Getting takeout buys us that extra time with Nikola and also allows us to just sit for maybe five seconds at night—we're exhausted."

"You're right," Marta said. "I guess I feel like I'm supposed to feel guilty about it. I mean, we do have debt, so isn't spending money on takeout stupid of us?"

"Not if it's Happy Spending. You just need to make room for it by decreasing expenses that are truly Unhappy Spending. Then you cut from the expenses you don't like to make room for the ones you do like." I brought their attention back to the statements. "The other thing I'm noticing here is the baby gear. You've both highlighted a lot of online purchases. What do they have in common?"

"Oh my god, the gear," Marta said. "It's so expensive."

"I get things on sale," Sebastian explained, "but it adds up. Kids cost money."

"So why do you regret these?" I pointed to the online purchases. "Why are they highlighted as Unhappy Spending?"

"We don't need all of it," Marta said. "We have so much junk in our house, with nowhere to put it."

"So what's happening in those moments when you purchase it? What's the driving force?" I asked.

"I have this sense that we need it. For Nikola," Sebastian said.

"Why do you think that?" I asked, and pointed to a $60 purchase from an online retailer that they both had highlighted. "Tell me about this one. What did you buy? Where were you? Why did you think it was important at the time?"

"That's the walker," Sebastian said. "We bought it a few months ago, online from home. Our friends' baby is only five days older than

Nikola, and she was already cruising and walking around using one, so we thought maybe a walker would help Nikola too. And it was on sale."

"Did it help?" I asked.

"No." They both laughed. "She never really had any interest in it. She walks now, but she used the walker maybe five times. It just wasn't her thing," Marta added.

"Okay, what about this one?" I asked and pointed out another high-lighted transaction from the same online retailer. "Tell me about this purchase. What did you buy? Where were you? Why did you think it was important at the time?"

"Books. Online, from home. My friend sent me a link to a 50-percent-off sale of kids' books and I was worried that Nikola was getting bored with her existing ones."

"Was this the same friend?" I asked.

"Yes. But it's not like she made me buy them," Marta said, a bit defensively. I was pretty sure she could see where I was going with this.

"Okay, last one. Tell me about this one. What did you buy? Where were you? Why did you think it was important at the time?"

They were both getting a little uncomfortable. I could tell that they weren't finding the game fun anymore. But my job wasn't necessarily to make friends. My job was to get to the root cause of their overspending so they could avoid it.

"Okay, online again," Sebastian said, sounding a bit deflated. "A swing for the baby."

"And why did you think that was important at the time?" I asked.

They looked at each other.

"What?" I asked.

Marta sighed. "We tried it out at our friends' house and Nikola loved it, so we bought one too."

I opened my mouth to ask a question, but Sebastian answered it before I had a chance.

"Yes," he said, "the same friends."

"So why do you regret it now?" I asked.

"Because we were too late with it," Sebastian said. "Nikola was already a bit too old. We used it a few times and now we're just hanging on to it in case we have a second child."

"Totally," Marta agreed.

"How do you think your friends are influencing your decisions to overspend on baby gear that you later regret?" I asked. It was a hard question. I wasn't entirely sure how it would land.

"Obviously negatively," Sebastian said. "But it's not their fault. It's our fault."

"So what's going on when you come home from a visit with them and find yourself purchasing baby gear? How are you feeling in those moments?" I asked.

"Usually a bit guilty and worried, to be honest," Marta said.

"About what?" I asked.

"The fact that we didn't research the best gear out there." Her eyes welled up. "I just want to do right by Nikola, you know? I hate that I'm back at work now. I barely get to see her, and I feel like it's my fault that somehow she won't develop as quickly because I'm not home and she doesn't have all this helpful stuff." Tears fell in earnest now. "I hear myself saying it and know it sounds ridiculous, but that's how it feels."

"Mom guilt," I said, and handed her a tissue. Sebastian put his arm around Marta and gave her a squeeze.

She dried her eyes. "Totally."

"Marta," I said, "you're a good mom and Nikola will be totally okay, even if she doesn't have the best swing in town. Evolution has ensured that." I was trying to get her to smile.

She laughed a bit. "I know. Nikola is perfect and she's doing just fine. I'm just having a hard time adjusting."

"Sebastian, how do you feel about this?" I asked.

"Is dad guilt a thing? It should be, because I have it."

"Parental guilt," I said.

"Exactly. I also feel bad that I hardly ever get to see Nikola. Sometimes she's in bed before I'm even home."

Parental guilt. It's real, and it was the emotional Tripwire that had tripped up both Marta and Sebastian. It made them feel that they had to spend money on baby gear so they would feel better about not being home during the workday, and to relieve their fear that Nikola wasn't developing as fast as their friends' baby. Guilt, fear and inadequacy were the root causes of the overspending that was keeping them in their Debt Loop. It wasn't the takeout, which is typically what everyone points to. The takeout was actually helping them to not feel the parental guilt. The real culprit was the baby gear.

"How do you think your parental guilt led to the debt's climbing?" I asked.

"I guess I just normalized it," Sebastian said. "I mean, we'd research for deals, so I always thought I was doing my best to save money. Everyone just kept saying that kids are expensive. So I guess I thought we were just normal and it was okay that we were overspending, y'know? Even though we were sinking."

"What needs to happen for you to avoid parental guilt without overspending?"

"I need to be home to do bath and bedtime every night," Marta said.

"And I need to make sure I'm around on weekends and in the mornings to spend some time with her," Sebastian said.

"How can you use this information to get control over your cash flow?" I asked.

"Well, the debt is making my parental guilt worse," Marta said. "Now I feel like I'm not around enough and also that I can't save for the future, so I'm stressed out. I'm beginning to realize that I'm spending money I don't have on things I don't need because I'm feeling guilty and not good enough. No more overpriced baby gear or expensive Pinterest crafts!"

"Also, we need to stop comparing Nikola to Ophelia for development cues and just trust our guts and the pediatrician that Nikola is happy, healthy and developing perfectly. I hadn't realized that I always leave our friends' house a bit anxious if Ophelia is talking, walking or hitting some other milestone before Nikola. Most of these Unhappy Spending purchases were an attempt to make sure we aren't screwing up Nikola for life," Sebastian joked. "So it feels easy to stop, now that I realize why we were doing it. Those purchases weren't for Nikola, they were for us."

We made up a new routine to help them sidestep their emotional Tripwires.

- They took their credit card credentials out of all the online retail sites so that they would have to enter them physically every time. This made it harder to spend in low or weak moments.
- They asked friends not to alert them to sales on baby gear unless they specifically asked for it.
- When they did want to purchase something, they wrote down why they thought they needed the item for Nikola and then placed a 24-hour embargo on buying it. If they revisited their notes the next day and still wanted to buy it, they could, as long as they made reductions elsewhere in their spending.

I checked in with Marta and Sebastian seven months into their plan. "How's it going?" I asked.

"Good," Marta said. "We've managed to put the $300 towards the line of credit every month and not rack it back up again. It's coming along."

"Awesome!" I cheered. "And how's the parental-guilt avoidance going?"

"Better," Sebastian said. "We still feel it all the time—not sure if it will ever go away—but the 24-hour spending embargo has been our financial saviour. I think we actually went through with a purchase only twice out of 12 potential ones. That's how much our guilt was wreaking havoc with our finances before."

"I'm so glad," I said. "It sounds like you're both more mindful now.

The guilt and fear may never go away, but now you recognize how those emotions were affecting your finances and can sidestep that knee-jerk reaction to spend money."

"Totally," Marta said. "It's been really eye-opening and empowering. We've placed the 24-hour embargo on other things too, like clothes or electronics for ourselves. Just taking a moment to check in and ensure that we actually want to buy something, not just throwing money at it to absolve ourselves of negative emotions. It's been a really helpful tool."

"That's amazing. You two are a great team."

Emotions have a powerful impact on how we spend our money. They can hijack our logical brains and make us feel as if we *must* spend money, regardless of affordability. That's why it's important to identify any emotional Tripwires that may be causing you to consistently over-spend and leaving you full of regret.

Find Your Emotional Tripwires

Identifying your emotional Tripwires is a process quite similar to iden-tifying your routine Tripwires. But instead of scanning your Unhappy Spending transactions for trending places or events, you're scanning for the emotions you were feeling just before you spent that money. Follow the instructions on pages 41–42 to identify your Tripwires.

How to Avoid Emotional Tripwires

1. The next time you have the urge to overspend, check in. What are you feeling?
2. Write down three reasons why you think the specific item, service or experience is an important purchase.
3. Place yourself under a 24-hour spending embargo for that expense.
4. Revisit your list the next day. If you still agree that it's a good idea, make a plan to reduce your spending elsewhere to make room for the purchase. (Check out the banking plan in Chapter 9 for help with knowing what you can and cannot afford.)

▶

Identifying your Tripwires, both routine and emotional, is one of your most powerful tools when you take on your debt once and for all. Now that you know some of the root causes that make you want to overspend, you can sidestep them. You can see them coming, acknowledge them and choose to act differently. This will help you break the Debt Loop so that you can actually start paying down debt and get control over your cash flow. You are now one step closer to living debt-free.

CHAPTER 4

Getting Motivated

When someone comes into my office ready to make a plan to pay down debt, they are super motivated. They are ready. Everyone feels driven to take on their debt in the beginning, and the first few months can be so exciting. But if it's going to take you a few years to pay down the debt, what will happen to that energy by Month 19 or Month 30? Will you still be driven? What will happen when the grind of daily life sets in and sticking to a financial plan becomes tiresome, annoying, frustrating? If you're not properly motivated, you'll give up, and why wouldn't you? Your debt-repayment plan will start to feel oppressive, and that is when hopelessness sets in. That is why most debt-repayment plans fail. If you've tried to pay down debt before and failed, you were likely not properly motivated.

Usually something I call "debt scare tactics" are used as the sole motivation to get people on a debt-reduction plan. Debt scare tactics include pointing out the "math facts" about your debt. The interest you're paying—it's so expensive! The length of time you'll be paying it down—it's going to take forever! The money you're losing each month to minimum payments—what a waste! I think people use debt scare tactics with good intentions; they are meant to motivate you to take action *today*. Think of the interest you'll save!

The problem is that using scare tactics as the sole motivating factor almost always leads to failure over the long run. I've been on the front lines of financial planning for a long time, and I know that they are simply not enough to keep you motivated throughout the entire debt-repayment period. Sure, everyone knows that paying interest is bad, and of course you want the money that's going to minimum payments to be back in your pocket as soon as possible. But if you're locked in a serious battle with debt, the interest you're paying can become just another number on your credit card statement. It doesn't feel real. The monthly minimum payment morphs into just another bill you need to pay, like rent or your cellphone. And the four years until you are debt-free feels so long that it might as well be 24 years.

Over time, the promises of "interest saved" and "less money wasted" pack less of a motivational punch. The threats become less and less potent, which makes it so much easier to give up midway through your plan and wind up right back in the Debt Loop. In order to truly succeed over the long haul of your debt-repayment plan, *I have to*—driven by interest costs, time horizon and financial stress—must become *I choose to*, which is driven by all those financial things and more. That's the ticket to real success. I don't want to sound trite, but you have to *choose* to do this. And you'll have to choose to do it again and again and again, because life is messy. Tripwires will happen. Because life.

When it comes to paying down debt, maintaining your willpower is a matter of constant cost-benefit analysis that answers the question "Why am I doing this again?" If you don't have a good enough reason, you're more likely to give up. I've talked to so many people with debt. When they succeed at their repayment plan and are finally debt-free, I always take the time to ask, "What clicked?"

What clicked for them? What took them from knowing they should pay down debt to actually wanting to do it and making it happen? Truly wanting to make that change and choosing to do so again and again, even when it was really hard and choosing to stick to the plan felt frustrating. What clicked for those who managed versus those who failed? The answers, I can tell you, have absolutely nothing to do with interest and everything to do with something I call your Financial Touchstone.

Your Financial Touchstone

Your Financial Touchstone is the reason you want to be debt-free that goes far beyond how much interest you'll save. It's the thing that clicks, the reason that will help you choose to stick to your plan even when you don't want to. Even when all the debt hacks fail and motivation is low, you still choose to stick it out. That's motivation. That's how to ensure that you can make a plan and see it through until the very last payment.

My client Elizabeth had $50,000 on a line of credit that was charging 6 percent a year and she made a $500 monthly payment. She lived in Calgary, was 60 years old and had two adult children. Her line of credit had shot up after a messy divorce five years before our meeting. Since that time, Elizabeth had been able to save $400 a month towards her retirement. When I asked her what she wanted to get out of our financial session, she wrote "retirement planning and clarity around whether I invest $400 a month in an RRSP or TFSA." She didn't mention the $50,000 debt, which was interesting to me.

We met in person when Elizabeth was in Toronto visiting her kids. When she came into my office, I asked her, "What's important to you about this meeting?"

"I don't want to be screwed in retirement," she said. "If I can even afford to retire."

"What does being able to afford to retire mean to you?" I asked.

"Well, I'd like to stop working at 65. I'm tired, and my best friend is also single and we'd like to travel together once we're both retired. My parents passed away young, so I would love to stop working and enjoy my life while I'm still here and healthy. But I've accepted the fact that it's not possible. I'm going to have to work forever." She sighed.

"What makes you say that?"

"I don't think I have enough money in my retirement accounts, so I want to keep putting $400 a month into my savings."

Again no mention of the $50,000 debt. Before our meeting I had been nerding out on her file. I knew that if she directed the $400 a month towards her debt, she would be debt-free in five years, by age 65. That's retirement planning at its best, no?

"Let me ask you something. Why wouldn't you want to direct that $400 a month of savings to your $50,000 line of credit?"

"Huh, I thought you might bring that up. Yeah, I just don't really think about it. If I die before it's paid off, the equity in my home will cover it and my kids won't inherit the debt. So why would I rush to pay it off?"

It was an honest question. At her current monthly payment of $500, Elizabeth would have the $50,000 paid off when she was 71 years old. She would spend just under $20,000 in interest over the next 11 years.[*]

I had to ask the math-fact question. "How do you feel about the $20,000 in interest you'll pay over the next 11 years if you make only the $500 payments?"

"The interest is only $250 a month right now. I pay $500 a month [$6,000 a year] and I've kind of accepted that. It's just another bill to me. Plus I got an 8 percent rate of return on my investments last year," she said. "So why would I bother paying down the debt when it's charging me only 6 percent?"

Fair question, but I had the answer. "For starters, the 8 percent rate of return is not guaranteed. Investment markets come with risk. It's possible that the return will be 8 percent again next year, or maybe

---

[*] Check out the "Debt-Payoff Calculator" in the Resource Library (page 300).

more. But it's also possible that it will be much less, even negative. That's a normal part of investing. The 6 percent interest on your debt, however, is guaranteed. It's a sure thing. If I said, 'Hey, Elizabeth, do you want to get a 6 percent guaranteed rate of return on the dollar?', wouldn't you say yes?"

"Yes, I suppose I would."

"Well, the 6 percent interest you're being charged on your line of credit is like getting a rate of return of 6 percent. Guaranteed."

She thought about it for a moment. "But I won't ever get to feel or see that $20,000 I'm paying in interest. It's an abstract concept. It doesn't really affect me daily. Seeing the balance rise in my savings accounts does. It's money I can see and use. It's tangible."

This is really common. It feels so much better to see your assets going up as opposed to your debts going down. It feels real, safe and financially responsible, which is way more fun. Paying down debt can feel thankless because it doesn't give us the same boost of confidence as seeing the balance grow in your account.

It was clear to me that Elizabeth needed to be motivated beyond the cost of interest. I could sit there and crunch numbers for her all day, but if she wasn't truly emotionally motivated to pay down her debt, the math wouldn't matter. I needed something to click for her.

"How do you feel about your debt?" I asked carefully.

"What do you mean?" She was slightly defensive.

"When you think about your debt, how does it make you feel?"

"I don't know. Frustrated? Angry?" Her body stiffened. I knew I was edging close to a pain point.

"It sounds like you don't enjoy having debt," I tried.

"Of course I don't like having debt. Who does?"

Things were getting a bit tense. That was okay. Debt brings up so many things for so many people.

I leaned in. "Elizabeth, what do you think your debt is costing you, besides the $500 a month?" I asked gently.

"Okay, stop." She waved me away. "I know what you're getting at." Her face was flushed.

I pressed further. I knew I was close. "What am I getting at?"

"That I'm stupid for not paying it down, that this debt is the reason I have to work forever!" And with that, Elizabeth unloaded on me. "That's what the debt is costing me—my sanity and my ability to retire when my best friend is retiring. That debt means I'll have to work until I'm 70 years old, wasting my healthy years when I could be travelling." She paused for a moment. "I'm sorry, I didn't mean to get so angry. I'm not mad at you, just at the situation." Her voice wavered, and she was on the verge of tears. "It's just really emotional, you know? It's hard. This is not where I thought I'd be at 60."

I squeezed her hand and let us hang out in silence for a moment.

Time to lighten the mood. "So, what if paying off your debt would allow you to retire earlier than 71?"

She looked up from her hands. "What? Is that even possible?"

I showed her the Debt-Payoff Calculator. "If you direct the $400 a month to the line of credit instead of savings, you'll be debt-free in five years. And I think you may be actually able to retire at 65 by freeing up the $500 that has to go to the line of credit each month."

"Really? How?"

"Well, once you retire at 65, you'll be debt-free. Your government pensions (Canada Pension Plan and Old Age Security) and retirement savings (your RRSP and Tax-Free Savings Account) wouldn't be enough to sustain the cost of the extra $6,000 a year in payments until age 71 and also your travel expenses. But once you are debt-free you won't owe those payments anymore! You can retire safely and put that $6,000 a year that used to go towards the line of credit towards travel. You don't need to wait until you're 72."

She studied my screen in disbelief. "Oh my god, you're right. I didn't think about it that way. I thought I just needed more savings."

Elizabeth hadn't realized that she could be debt-free by age 65.

The $50,000 felt insurmountable. In addition, she hadn't thought about the fact that being debt-free meant her pensions and existing savings could cover her cost of living. Freeing up the $6,000 per year ($500 per month) that used to go towards the line of credit would give her money for travel instead. She didn't need more savings to retire; she just needed her life to cost less. Paying down debt would do that.

"This is your Financial Touchstone, Elizabeth. Paying down the debt will allow you to retire at 65 and travel while you're still young and healthy enough to enjoy it with your best friend. How's that for motivation?"

"Very motivating!" She laughed.

"How do you feel about your debt right now?" I asked.

She sighed. "I never thought about paying down debt as a form of savings, but this feels good. I feel better, motivated. Excited, even."

I smiled. "Good."

Now that Elizabeth had found her Financial Touchstone, she just needed to create a physical manifestation of it. Then she would have something concrete to remind her about her plan and the motivating factors that had spurred her into action and made her excited about paying down debt. We came up with a plan. Elizabeth was going to put 60 pink Post-it notes on the wall in her bedroom. Sixty Post-its because there would be 60 months (five years) during which she had to stay motivated until she could retire debt-free.

I checked in with Elizabeth after 22 months to see how she was holding up. "How's the pink Post-it plan going?" I asked.

"Brilliant. Debt is at $36,000 now and I've stayed motivated the whole time. No joke!"

"Sounds like you're still jazzed about your plan," I said.

She laughed. "Yep! Thirty-eight Post-its left to go. Every month I yank one off the wall. 'Another one done!' I say, and call my best friend. I've got her doing it now too. She doesn't have debt, but she's yanking pink Post-its with me. We're both counting down."

"How has your Touchstone helped you stay motivated in those moments when you want to give up?"

She answered right away. "Looking at the Post-its makes me smile, every day. When I see them on the wall, I anticipate how good it's going to feel to pull off the next one at the start of the month. They remind me that I'm that much closer to being done. It's so freeing. It puts me in a good mood even on a bad day, and it makes me want to stick to the plan."

We had done it. Elizabeth had found her Financial Touchstone—a reason to tackle her debt that went beyond how much interest she would save. She had found a way to stay motivated that not only lasted far beyond the first few months of her plan but would also see her through the entire 60 months, until the day she could retire safely with her best friend.

A few months ago I received an email from Elizabeth. The subject line read, "Pulled the last Post-it." The attachment was a photo of her in Texas with her best friend.

I smiled and wrote back, "Awesome. You deserve this."

When It's Not Just about You

I know you're motivated to make changes. You may even be excited. But if you've tried to pay down debt before, only to get lost along the way, it's likely that you just haven't experienced that *click* yet. You haven't found your Financial Touchstone and so you haven't been able to call on it to motivate you to keep making the harder choice: debt repayment.

Take my client Devin. Devin was struggling with his credit card debt. At the time of our meeting, he had $12,000 on a credit card that charged 19.99 percent interest. He had been yo-yo budgeting for years, paying down his credit cards by a few thousand dollars and then racking them right back up again. Up and down his balance went, making him feel frustrated and tired.

"It keeps going up," he said. "I've pretty much stopped trying."

"Hmm. I wonder what's been holding you back from sticking to the plans you made before."

"It feels like I have more pressing things to do with my money in the short run. When something comes up, I usually just go for it."

"And fear of the interest you're going to end up paying or the minimum payments you're losing doesn't freak you out?"

"It used to. But I've been in debt for so long it actually feels like normal now. I'm so used to money leaving my chequing account to go towards debt that it doesn't rattle me anymore."

Devin needed to get motivated beyond the math. It's not that he liked losing money to interest and debt, it was just that he had grown so accustomed to it that he wasn't afraid of it. This is something that people who have never had consumer debt don't understand, and why it's so much easier to stay at a credit card balance of zero when you're already at zero. I call it the "diminishing marginal return of fear." If you don't have debt, the idea of wrecking that pristine credit card balance is intense. The threshold is large; it feels really significant to go from a place of no debt to a place of debt, even by $100. And if you're not used to paying interest, it feels like the rip-off that it is. But if, over time, you end up where you've had debt for some time—be it $3,000 or $30,000—you become comfortably numb to it. If you're already at $8,000, what's another $1,000? You still owe thousands at the end of the day. This is what had happened to Devin. He was motivated by the math but never enough to actually get to zero, because he wasn't motivated enough to see the plan through to the end.

"Why do you think that is?" I asked.

"Since debt seems so normal to me, a balance around $5,000 feels low." He chuckled. "Ridiculous, right?"

"Not ridiculous. I've seen this before. What's your usual yo-yo pattern with your credit card?" I asked.

"Well, I aggressively pay down my debt until my card gets to $5,000, and then it's almost like the debt doesn't scare me anymore. Then I rack it back up again. It's as if I trick myself into thinking that I'll always be able to pay it down eventually if I really, really try. But I don't think that's true; I'm never actually able to pay it down. I haven't been debt-free for more than a decade."

"It's like $5,000 is your new zero," I said.

He laughed. "Totally."

"So why are you here? Why now?"

He grinned from ear to ear. "We're expecting a baby."

"Aw! Yay!" I exclaimed and jumped up to give him a big hug. "Oh, Devin, congratulations!" I was so excited for him.

We both sat back down. "Can I ask you something?" I asked.

"Shoot."

"How do you feel when you think about your debt?"

He sighed. "Bad. I mean, I obviously don't want to be in debt. I sort of oscillate between feeling angry and then apathetic and then hopeless. Like, I'm dumb."

"Dumb?" I asked.

"Yeah. I mean, I have a decent job, and I know better. All my friends seem to be managing just fine, yet here I am carrying debt from month to month and just ignoring it until the payment is due."

"What do you think your debt is costing you, besides the interest?" I asked.

He let out a deep breath. I could tell I was making him feel really exposed. "Take all the time you need."

After a moment he said softly, "My debt stresses out my wife, and that bums me out."

"What about it bums you out?" I asked gently.

"I want to be a good father. I don't want my wife to think I'm a flake, and I feel like my debt makes it seem that I'm irresponsible." *Boom!* Devin's Financial Touchstone.

"How would paying down your debt help?"

"It would show her that I'm reliable and that she can trust me."

I so appreciated his vulnerability and honesty. Pretty brave. "I agree," I said. "And I know without a doubt that you absolutely can do this. The thought that you're paying it off for your family is so much more motivating than the interest you're being charged every month."

"For sure," he agreed. Devin's Touchstone was wanting to prove to his wife that he could be trusted, that she could rely on him to be a good husband and father.

"When do you think you'll need to draw on this motivation the most?" I asked. "When are you most likely to give up on your debt-repayment plan?"

He gave it some thought. "I don't think there's a specific time or item. It's more just mindfulness around whether I can actually afford to buy something or not. Basically, every time I spend money."

He thought he was making a joke, but I saw a solution. "That's great," I said.

"What's great?"

"We just need to find a way to remind you of your motivation, your Touchstone, when you're about to spend money."

First I had Devin delete from his phone all the apps and browsers that stored his credit card information. He would not be able to spend money on credit unless he had to physically take out his credit card. That was key.

Then I suggested that he tape to the front of his credit card a small handwritten note from his wife that said either *I love you* or *I trust you*. He chose *I trust you*. That way, every time he wanted to swipe his credit card, he'd see that loving, reassuring note from her. He'd be reminded that he wanted to pay off his debt for reasons that were bigger than what-ever he wanted to purchase in that moment. He didn't want to let his family down.

Every time Devin pulled out his card, it was a beautiful reminder that, while he was sacrificing in that moment, he was doing it for his family. It wasn't for him and it wasn't to save interest. It was for them.

That was his Financial Touchstone, and it was enough to keep him motivated again and again and again—all the way through to the end.

I got a call from Devin about a year after our meeting. "I did it!" he exclaimed. He was a new dad and debt-free.

"Wonderful! So why do you think it worked this time?" I asked.

He laughed. "I guess I just needed you to kick my butt into gear."

"I disagree," I said. "You needed to kick your own butt into gear."

"I guess, but I never really felt motivated enough until after our meeting. Putting that note on my credit card worked so well. I couldn't have done it without you, for real!"

"All I did was ask a few questions. You did all the work. I'm proud of you."

"Me too," he said, and I could tell he was smiling on the other end of the line.

Finding your Financial Touchstone is crucial to breaking the Debt Loop once and for all. You need something to click. It's the perspective shift that will move you from a place where your motivation to pay debt is *I have to* or *I should* to *I choose to* and *I want to*. That is the only way to stay motivated long enough to see your debt-repayment plan through to the end. You must be motivated by something beyond financial gain. Sure, that's important too, but what's truly at stake for you?

Find Your Financial Touchstone

It's journal time again. Here's a little bit of woo-woo that will go a long, long way. Answer these questions for yourself. Really think about them. I want you to be living debt-free one day, and staying motivated for the right reasons is crucial. Hopefully these questions will help you find your Touchstone, the motivation to stick to your debt plan that has nothing to do with your finances.

Step 1: Write down the answers to these questions.

- What does your debt cost you besides interest?

- What's at stake in your life if you don't pay it down?
- How will paying down your debt make your life better?
- What will being debt-free allow you to do that you cannot do now?
- What's important for you to remember during tough times, when you want to quit?

Step 2: Look for similarities or themes.

Once you've written down your answers, look for a common theme. What's the reason, besides interest paid, that you want to be debt-free? Is it a feeling of freedom? Is it more self-confidence? Is it a trip? Your own home?

Step 3: Create a physical manifestation of your Touchstone.

Once you've found your Financial Touchstone, you need a physical representation of it that helps to make your plan real. It must be tangible—you need to be able to see it and touch it. This Touchstone represents the pact that you have made with yourself to stick to the plan. It will help you to stay motivated even when sticking to the Debt Game Plan is hard and inconvenient.

This reminder will be totally unique to you. To help you find it, here are some examples of tangible reminders that clients of mine have used over the years to help keep them motivated during their Debt Game Plan.

- Small sticker on the front of a credit card to act as a reminder when you're about to swipe. I've seen stars, happy faces, emojis and notes from loved ones, like Devin's.
- Small sticker on the front or back of your cellphone.
- A specific piece of jewellery. One client wore a band on her engagement finger as a reminder that she was trying to pay down debt before her wedding.
- Post-it note countdowns. I've seen this done on a monthly basis

(as with Elizabeth) and I've seen people use a small Post-it daily, setting them up each month.

- Inspirational photo in the wallet. One client kept a photo of an open window in his wallet; it represented the sense of freedom and possibilities that being debt-free would bring.

- Crystals in the wallet. One client kept a piece of jade in her wallet, which reminded her that she wanted to attract good money vibes.

- Something on the purse zipper. A client of mine attached a small black pompom to the zipper of her purse, where she stored her money, to represent being "in the black."

- Countdowns. Whether they use Post-its, a calendar or some other sort of tracking device, countdowns can be a great way to stay motivated. One of my clients put a loonie in a jar every day during a four-year debt-repayment plan (1,460 days) and then celebrated with a trip that cost exactly $1,460. The jar sat at the front door of their apartment; they put in the loonie at the end of the day, but only if they'd succeeded at following their budget. You can also do something like this with chocolate coins, except that you eat one each day instead, like a Debt Game Plan Advent calendar!

Paying down debt is tough and you may have a long road ahead of you. A physical representation of your Financial Touchstone will help make that road easier. It will be there as a reminder of how you're kicking ass on those days when you feel really great about your plan, and it will pick you up and keep you motivated on days when it feels really hard to keep pushing down the road. Whatever form it takes, it's just for you. No one else has to know what it represents—an intimate relationship with a promise to yourself and the plan that will get you there. You can do this. *I* believe you can. You just need to believe that too.

▶

Here you are, ready for Part Two. Ready to make a plan. Ready to take action and ready to change yourself. You know how to break the Debt Loop once and for all. You have hope that you can do it, you know how to avoid your Tripwires, and you understand your motivation to do so. You've built the foundation you need to do this, for real. The only thing left is to math the sh*t out of this debt-repayment plan! It's spreadsheet time.

Part Two

Your Debt Game Plan

Now that you're in a place where you want to take action, you need tools and strategies to implement a plan. You are about to create your Debt Game Plan. In this part of the book, you'll calculate how much you can realistically put towards your debt and how long it will take to get rid of it. Oh yeah, we're going deep.

If you feel a bit scared right now, that's okay, normal even. It's like when you watch a scary movie and the anticipation of the monster is so much scarier than the monster itself. Once you finally see the monster, it's not so scary. It's almost cheesy, in fact, especially in movies made before CGI effects. That's what creating your Debt Game Plan is like. It's a lot scarier when it's all in your head, no plan has worked so far, and your only reference is a statement that says it will take 90 years to pay down. But once you lay it all out on the table and make your plan, you'll see that it's not so bad. In fact, you'll be pleasantly surprised.

In the next section you're going to map out your debt, calculate what you can realistically afford to put towards what's owing, and learn how to pay it off as fast as possible while still having a life. Ready? Let's go.

CHAPTER 5

Map That Debt

Okay, here comes the hard part: tallying up your debt. It's time to open up those statements, log in to those accounts, run a credit report and get on the phone. If your stomach just flipped, that's okay. Just breathe.

If you've ever gone to an aesthetician for, say, a bikini or back wax, you may have been nervous. You may have felt compelled to say to your service provider, "Eep! It's bad. I'm so sorry!" But the aesthetician will always wave your worries away. "I've seen it all. Trust me, this is nothing." Well, that's what I'm like, only with debt. I've seen it all. Trust me, this is nothing.

You can't make your Debt Game Plan until you know where you're at and where you're going, financially speaking. If you're going to attack your debt like a boss, you need to map out what you owe and how much you're currently paying each month. You may have debts in different places—a student loan, a department store card, a line of credit with the bank. If you've got multiple debts, it can be easy to forget how much you actually owe altogether, what the different interest rates are, and how much you're paying into each debt every month.

The problem is, when you don't know exactly what you owe and how much it's costing you, it can make you feel scattered, frustrated and disorganized, because there's no game plan, reinforcing your worst fears that you are bad with money. This is why mapping out your debt is empowering. Is it also a bit scary? It can be, if you haven't been logging in to your accounts or you're not entirely sure how much you owe right now. But let's rip off the Band-Aid together.

Your Debt Game Plan starts here. Mapping out your debt will get you organized and then you'll feel more in control, aware of and on top of your money!

Taking Stock of Your Debt

Meet Paul. Paul lived in a suburb outside Toronto and had some debt: two credit cards, a personal loan, a line of credit and a partridge in a pear tree.

"So tell me," I said the first time we met, "how much debt are we talking about?" He hadn't filled out his Debt Map for me, so I didn't know exactly how much he owed.

Paul took a big breath. "I've got a personal loan of about $8,000 and I pay $100 or so each month. I also have a line of credit; it's maxed out at $10,000. I don't know what the interest rate is, but I think I pay around $200 a month. My mortgage is about $200,000 or so and I pay $500-ish biweekly. My credit card has about $12,000 on it and I think the rate is 18 percent, or something like that."

This is how most people describe their debts to me before we map everything out. The *I think* and *approximately* and *sounds about right* are usually said very quickly, disjointedly and in spurts, as if to say, *I don't really know and I don't want to talk about it.*

If you've got more than one type of debt, when you start naming them, it's easy for it to feel like a laundry list of crimes. When there's more than one debt, information is often stored in different places, making it inconvenient to pull together, and if you've had debt for some time, you may not have looked up the balance owing in a while. The problem is that you need to know how much you have to pay down before you can officially start. It could be better than you think. Maybe you're overpaying; maybe you're underpaying; perhaps the interest rates aren't as bad as you recall. The point is that whatever the outcome, mapping your debt and getting organized are key to feeling in control again.

Without a Debt Map, the disorganization can make you feel scattered, as if you're a hot mess with your money and that's why you are in debt. But you're not. You just need to take stock and get organized. Feeling on top of your money will help to keep you motivated and reduce anxiety.

At this stage of our meeting, Paul's anxiety was evident, so I made sure he understood that my office was a safe financial place. "I know it can feel overwhelming," I said, "but is there any way we can get the exact amounts owing and find out what the minimum payments are each month?"

He turned a bit red in the face. "It's kind of all over the place. Nothing is with the same bank and I'm not sure where to find everything." He looked down. "Sorry."

"Not to worry," I said cheerfully, trying to lighten the mood. "The best way to get started is to run a credit report. You can do that for free."

"Isn't it bad to run a credit report?" he asked. "Doesn't it hurt your credit score?"

"Great question, and the answer is no. Running a credit check for yourself is called a soft credit check. It doesn't hurt your credit score. If you apply for credit with a financial institution or lender, they will check your credit, and that is called a hard check. A hard check *could* ding your credit score."

He shook his head. "Why do they make it so complicated?"

I laughed.

I showed Paul a few sources where he could get a credit score, both paid for and for free, and he ran a report in my office. From his report we were able to see his score and, more importantly, how many debt accounts he had open and if any of them were past due.[*]

---

[*] Be sure to check out "Your Credit Score" in the Resource Library (page 300) for more information on your credit report.

None of Paul's accounts were past due (yay!) but it turned out that he had another debt he had forgotten about—$5,350 owing on an old credit card. "Oh sh*t!" he said and put his hand to his forehead. "I totally forgot I had that card from a business I used to run." He looked sheepish. "So sorry."

"It happens. The good news is that now we know."

Paul's Revolving Credit Accounts		
Personal loan	$7,800	Bank 1
Line of credit	$10,000	Bank 1
Credit card A (old)	$5,350	Bank 2
Credit card B (current)	$12,000	Bank 1

But we weren't done there. Not all loans or debts may show up on your credit report, since it depends on which bureau you get the report from and what type of debt you've got. When you're taking stock of your debt, be sure to think about all types of debt, even the ones that may not be on your credit report, to ensure that you haven't missed one. Here's a list of potential debts that you may have.*

- taxes owing to the government (personal taxes or for sole proprietors)
- payday loans
- overdrafts
- credit cards
- unsecured personal lines of credit
- personal loans (such as consolidation loans)
- student lines of credit
- secured loans (such as car loans)

---

* For more information, check out "Debt Types" in the Resource Library (page 301).

- secured lines of credit (such as home equity lines of credit, or HELOCs)
- student loans (non-government)
- government student loans
- loans from family or friends

"Do you have anything from this list that didn't show up on your credit report?" I asked.

Paul scanned the list of debts. "Well, there's my mortgage."

"I don't want to include your mortgage on your Debt Map."

"Why not?" he asked.

"Because, unlike credit card debt or a line of credit, I consider paying down a mortgage above the minimum payments as long-term saving, almost like retirement savings." (We'll touch on this more in Chapter 8.)

"Okay. So that's everything, right?"

"Nope. Now we need to figure out how much you're being charged in interest for each of these debts, and the monthly minimum payments."

Once you've written down every debt you have and how much is owing, you either check your statements or get in touch with the appropriate financial institution to confirm the interest rate, the monthly minimum payment and the payment date for each of your loans. We knew that Paul had three of his debts with his current bank, Bank 1, so it was just a matter of logging in to his online banking to have a look. He simply downloaded the statements for each loan to record the information we needed.

As for the old credit card with Bank 2, Paul had no idea how to access that information electronically. "It was so long ago, I don't know my password," he said. So we got on the phone. After ten minutes of hold music, two customer service reps and one identification questionnaire, we finally got the info we needed. It turned out that, even though Paul had forgotten about the credit card at Bank 2, he hadn't missed a monthly minimum payment. It was automatically coming out of a small amount of cash left in his old business chequing account. Phew!

"How much did they say is in there now?" I asked.

"A hundred and fifty dollars," he said. We had caught it in the nick of time!

Here's what we confirmed using the information from Paul's credit report, his online banking and the phone call:

Debt	Amount Owing	Interest Rate	Minimum Payment
Personal loan	$3,500	5.60%	$70
Line of credit	$10,000	4.00%	$35
Credit card A (old)	$5,350	19.99%	$160
Credit card B (current)	$12,000	18.00%	$360

We had done it—we had taken stock of Paul's debts! But that was only the beginning. Now we had to organize everything by setting up his Debt Map. That would help him feel less scattered and totally on top of his money game.

Your Debt Map

Now that you know your total amount of outstanding debt, the interest rates you're being charged and the monthly minimum payments, why do you have to organize it? Because you will not only see the total amount of debt, but (and more important) you'll be able to calculate the total monthly minimum payment.

You may find yourself asking, "But Shannon, why should I care about my total monthly minimum payment?" Which is a great question, and here's the answer: your total monthly minimum payment is the sum of all your minimum payments smushed together. It's what you have to pay towards your various loans each month, whether you like it or not. *Whump. Whump.* This is so important to know, both from a cash-flow-management perspective and from a motivational standpoint. This is the amount of money that will eventually be yours again! Future you will have this money back in your pocket!

Let's use Paul as an example. I organized Paul's Debt Map with the highest interest rate at the top. You should do the same for now. In Paul's case, his forgotten business credit card had the highest interest rate, at 19.99 percent. His other credit card came in second, with $12,000 outstanding at 18 percent interest, followed by his line of credit and then his personal loan. After we organized his info, his Debt Map looked like this:

Paul's Debt Map				
Debt	Amount Owing	Interest Rate	Minimum Payment	Payment Date
Credit card A (old)	$5,350	19.99%	$160	21st
Credit card B (current)	$12,000	18.00%	$360	20th
Personal loan	$3,500	5.60%	$70	13th
Line of Credit	$10,000	4.00%	$35	25th
Total	**$30,850**		**$625**	

Paul's total debt was $30,850, and now he knew that his monthly minimum payments added up to $625 per month.

"How does it feel seeing it all laid out like this?" I asked.

"That $30,850 scares me," he said. "It didn't feel like that much in my head."

"That's pretty normal, but it's okay. We haven't even started to make our awesome plan yet," I said, hoping to reassure him (this is a tough moment for anyone with debt). "How do you feel about the $625 per month?"

"Surprisingly, that feels low to me. I used to think I was paying more than a thousand towards debt each month."

"Well, you were, but that amount wasn't all minimum payments.

You see, if you put $1,000 towards your total debt each month, $625 was the minimum amount you had to pay, like a bill. You had no choice. But the extra $375 was by choice. In fact, it was a form of savings."

He chuckled. "Well, at least that feels good."

"Totally. And there's more where that came from. The point of mapping your debt like this is to make sure you know exactly what your starting point is and the amount of money you *must* pay each month versus the amount you *choose to* pay each month. That's where the magic happens."

"It will feel so good to reclaim that $625 a month," he said.

"Hells yes, it will! That's an amount of money that won't be a bill forever. It will go away soon, unlike your mortgage, your phone bill and your life insurance—unless you cancel those services or sell your house in the short run. So your monthly minimum payments are bills that will not be bills for a long time."

"I actually feel a bit relieved," he said.

"How so?" I asked.

"I guess it's just good to get it all down on paper. To see it, acknowledge it. It makes it real. Sometimes I'm so overwhelmed that it doesn't feel real to me, and thinking about the $625 as a bill that won't last forever is exciting. Like, it would change my life to have that money back in my pocket."

"Totally."

And that's the power of the Debt Map. Taking stock of and organizing your debt is a crucial step to creating a sustainable, realistic Debt Game Plan. You need to know how much you owe, what you're paying in interest, and how much your total monthly minimum payment is. This will give you control, putting you back in the driver's seat again. Now you know the who, what, where and when of your debt. No more eyeballing it, no more assuming or guesswork. It is what it is. What a relief to know exactly where you stand—good, bad or ugly, this is you sitting in your financial truth, and there's something really empowering about that.

Take a moment to pat yourself on the back. Regardless of how scary this part may have been, understand that no one actually takes this step unless they are absolutely serious about making change and paying down debt. So if you're tallying up your debt right now, that means you don't want to be a person who sticks their head in the sand. You don't want to ignore it. You want to face it head-on. I love it.

How to Create Your Debt Map

Step 1: Make a list of all your debts. You can do this by logging in to your bank, calling your financial institution or running a credit report. Remember, some debts may not be on a credit report. Here's a reminder of the types of debt:

- taxes owing to the government (personal taxes or for sole proprietors)
- payday loans
- overdrafts
- credit cards
- unsecured personal lines of credit
- personal loans (such as consolidation loans)
- student lines of credit
- secured lines of credit (such as home equity lines of credit, or HELOCs)
- secured loans (such as car loans)
- student loans (non-government)
- government student loans
- loans from family or friends

Step 2: Confirm exactly how much money is owing for each account.
Step 3: Confirm the minimum payment for each debt.
Step 4: Confirm the day of the month that your payment is due, so you don't miss a payment.

Step 5: Organize all this information in a Debt Map grid so that you can see it in one spot.

Step 6: Prioritize your debt by interest rate, with the highest first.

Step 7: Calculate your total debt.

Step 8: Calculate your total monthly minimum payment.

CHAPTER 6

Your Magic Amount: How Much to Put Towards Debt

Now that you've drawn your Debt Map, you need to calculate how much your daily life costs. Only then can you start to calculate what you can realistically put towards debt on top of the total monthly minimum payment.

Most times people come into my office and want to pay their debt off as soon as possible. Like yesterday. Maybe they've seen those extreme debt-repayment plans on the Internet and are now super motivated to try to live frugally—*I can eat beans for six months* or *I won't buy anything new for a year*.

But the average person who comes to my office has not been able to give up every expense and live on a shoestring budget for any length of time, and it's probably the same for you. Maybe you couldn't pack your lunch every single day. Living like that may not be realistic. For many people, as they get older, the frugal approach gets harder and harder to maintain. Maybe you had a bar mitzvah to attend, a broken microwave, a child's swimming lessons, a friend visiting from out of town, a leaking bathtub. You know, a life.

Let's say you wanted to be debt-free by the end of the year, 12 months from now, and it would take $1,000 a month in addition to your total monthly minimum payment to accomplish that. If you made $3,000 a month after tax and your portion of housing bills was $1,700, your phone $100, and your total monthly interest payment $100, your total Fixed Expenses would be $1,900, leaving $1,100 left over for everything else, like groceries, gas, food, clothes, maybe a coffee. If you put $1,000 towards your debt in addition to the $100 minimum payment, you would have just $100 left over each month for you to eat and live your life.

I'm going to take a shot in the dark here and say that $100 for everything in your life, including food, is not enough money for most people. Such a short timeline and extreme budget will inevitably lead to "re-borrowing" on your line of credit to make ends meet, making you fail at your Debt Game Plan and ultimately perpetuating your sense of failure.

Enough already! Figure out what you've got coming in and what you've got to spend in order to live your life sustainably. Then we can talk about your Debt Game Plan.

What Does Your Life Cost?

First things first. You may be expecting me to start working out a budget for you. Well, in a way I guess I am. But I'm going to let you in on a little secret: I don't like budgets. I don't think they work— traditional budgets, that is. You know the ones. You sit down with an epic spreadsheet, spend an entire Friday night poring over bank and credit card statements, categorizing your spending into micro categories such as groceries, coffee shops, takeout, clothes, house shopping, gifts, bills, housing and (my personal favourite) "misc. shopping." It's bananas!

Then you set your spending targets with what you think/hope will happen over the next month and do your best to spend and live within the confines of the budget. But what if one week your family comes over for a barbecue and you overspend by $30 on groceries because you need to buy salad fixings, condiments and veggie burgers for your vegan cousin? Well, you'll just "borrow" $30 from your $50 clothes budget, leaving $20 for clothes that month. But then, a week later, you need a new shirt for work and have to spend $35, so now you've overspent there too.

Maybe you even have one of those apps that alerts you to your failure. *Buzz—you overspent! Beep—oops, you did it again! Ding—are you some kind of financial failure? Get it together!* On and on it goes, "borrowing" from one category to make good on another. It's exhausting.

Most people don't live their lives in such predictable ways. Your life changes from week to week, and those kinds of budgets don't leave any room for flexibility. This is why I've found that most people who attempt these rigid, overcategorized budgets inevitably end up failing, validating their gut concern that they're bad with money. If you've got debt and you want to get on top of it, the worst possible thing is to fail at budgeting. If you're already in a vulnerable headspace when it comes to how you feel about your money, failure compounds those concerns about your financial responsibility. But it's not you. It's the budget! Those types of budgets are outdated, unrealistic and far too constricting for regular life. They set you up to fail.

Now I'm not saying that you can just spend all your money willy-nilly, but instead of 30-plus categories that you have to try to live within, I use only four: Fixed Expenses, Meaningful Savings, Short-Term Savings and Spending Money. That's it. All of your money belongs to one of these four categories. Doesn't that make your shoulders want to drop down from under your ears? How much more chill is four types than 35? Let's break them down.

Fixed Expenses is money you must pay every month (or year) whether you like it or not. The job of this category is to pay your bills and meet any other obligations such as support payments, housing, cellphone, ongoing gym memberships and so on. This is money you *cannot spend on anything else* in each pay period. Your total monthly minimum payment is included in your Fixed Expenses. For example, if your minimum payment on a loan is $350 but you pay $500 per month towards that debt, only $350 is included as a Fixed Expense, because $350 is the amount of money you *must* pay. It's fixed. The additional $150 goes into the Meaningful Savings category, because it's money you *choose to* pay. You're choosing to better your financial situation.

Meaningful Savings is money set aside to improve your finances. This category has the job of increasing your net worth. That's why, in our example, the additional $150 you put towards your debt is considered Meaningful Savings. I call this your Magic Amount—the amount of money you choose to add to your total monthly cost of debt so that you can pay it off faster. Your Magic Amount works to reduce the amount of debt that you carry, which improves your net worth. It's where the magic happens in your Debt Game Plan. Without it, you're simply making minimum payments and getting nowhere fast.

Other types of Meaningful Savings include saving for retirement, a down payment or your kids' education. The question of whether all your Meaningful Savings should go towards debt is a big one. We'll tackle that throughout the book. For now, let's assume that it all goes towards your Debt Game Plan in the form of a glorious Magic Amount, so you can just hammer it down! Meaningful Savings is money you *cannot spend.*

Short-Term Savings is money set aside for big purchases and emergencies. The job of this category is to keep you out of debt by protecting you against large spikes in your spending. A big purchase could be a vacation, a couch or a replacement for a lost cellphone. Emergency savings cover home repairs, car repairs and job loss. This is also money that you *cannot spend* in each pay period.

Spending Money is what's left over. After you've put aside money for your Fixed Expenses, Meaningful Savings and Short-Term Savings, the money left over is your daily Spending Money. It's yours. This category has only one job: to ensure that you're living life—being fed, having fun and getting around. This is money you *can spend* every pay period! Woo-hoo!

You need to calculate how much it costs for you to pay your bills (Fixed Expenses), live realistically (Spending Money) and protect yourself against future debt (Short-Term Savings) in order to make sure that anything you put towards your debt that is above the minimum payment is realistic and sustainable. This is how you calculate what your life costs and how you figure out the amount of money you can put towards debt. Excited? You should be.

Calculating How Much Your Life Costs

Step 1: Calculate Monthly After-Tax Income

First things first. How much money is coming in? This is the first order of business for any Debt Game Plan. In order to make your plan, you need to know your after-tax monthly income, also called your take-home pay. This is the amount of money that actually drops into your chequing account.

If you're an employee, this is fairly easy to figure out. When you open up your bank statement, you'll see the amount of money you earn after all the deductions. This is your net paycheque.

If you're paid bimonthly, you'll receive money twice a month—that's 24 paycheques a year. In order to figure out your monthly after-tax income, multiply your net paycheque by how often you're paid each month. For example, if your net paycheque is $1,500 and you're paid bimonthly, your monthly after-tax income is $3,000.

There may be some variance in your paycheques. Maybe benefits come out of one but not the other. Or perhaps you max out your Canada Pension Plan (CPP) and Employment Insurance (EI) contributions in the first part of the year, so your net paycheque increases in the latter part of the year. Whatever the variance is, my advice is to use the amount from when your net pay is at its lowest. Build your Debt Game Plan around that. Then, for paycheques that come in with a higher amount, consider that "bonus money" that you can use to top up your Debt Game Plan and get debt paid faster.

If you are paid biweekly (every other week), you'll receive 26 paycheques a year. However, I still suggest that you multiply your net paycheque by two, using 24 paycheques instead of the 26 to calculate your monthly after-tax income. Why? Because for 10 months of the year you will get only two paycheques per month. If you use 26 paycheques, you may risk overestimating how much money you'll have to live off.

For example, my client Karen was paid $1,200 biweekly, receiving 26 paycheques a year. If she set her budget based on her annual take-home pay of $31,200 ($1,200 x 26), she might think that she had $2,600 a month to live off, because $31,200 divided by 12 months is $2,600 per month. Let's say that she budgets her life like this, based on $2,600 per month:

Fixed Expenses	$1,300
Meaningful Savings	$350
Short-Term Savings	$200
Spending Money	$750
Total	**$2,600**

The thing is, for 10 months of the year she gets only two paycheques a month. At $1,200 per paycheque, that would add up to only $2,400, making her $200 short every month. Instead, Karen should budget as if she receives only two paycheques every month, living within $2,400 a month so she doesn't set herself up to fail.

Like Karen, it's best for you to calculate your monthly after-tax income by assuming 24 paycheques a year (two per month) and using the additional paycheques you will get for Short-Term Savings. (We will deal with how to handle extra paycheques in Chapter 9.) Similar issues can arise if you're paid weekly or if you have bill payments that come out biweekly. We will handle that in Step 2.

For now, here are the four ways that you can calculate your monthly after-tax income, based on how often you are paid. Assume that the net pay is $1,500 for those who are paid bimonthly or biweekly, $3,000 for those paid monthly and $750 for those paid weekly.

Pay Frequency	Net Pay	Cheques/ Month	Monthly After-Tax Income	Additional Cheques/ Year
Bimonthly	$1,500	2	$3,000	0
Monthly	$3,000	1	$3,000	0
Biweekly	$1,500	2	$3,000	2
Weekly	$750	4	$3,000	4

If you're self-employed as a sole proprietor, there's a bit more work involved, because you're going to have to forecast what your income will be. Think about what you can *realistically* earn in the next 12 months—not your best-case and not your worst-case scenario. Then deduct what you'll pay for business expenses, sales tax and income taxes. For example, if you think your annual revenue or sales will be $60,000 (not including sales tax) and you anticipate $13,000 in business expenses, you will have a taxable income of approximately $47,000 per year.

Use an online tax estimator to figure out roughly how much federal and provincial income tax and Canada Pension Plan (CPP) contribution you'll need to put aside to pay your tax bill.* Here, for example, is how it would work if you lived in Ontario:

Estimated revenue (excluding sales tax)	$60,000
Estimated expenses (excluding sales tax)	$13,000
Estimated income before income tax and CPP	$47,000
Estimated income tax	$10,920
Estimated annual after-tax income	$36,080
Months in the year	12
Monthly after-tax income	**$3,006**

---

* See "Tax Estimator" in the Resource Library (page 301).

Step 2: Add Up Fixed Expenses

Fixed Expenses are those that you must pay every month, quarter or year. The amount you have to pay is predictable and doesn't fluctuate much. Fixed Expenses are the easiest type of expenses to plan for. Include your total monthly minimum payment. Here are some examples of other predictable Fixed Expenses:

- total of monthly minimum debt or loan payments
- mortgage payments or rent
- utilities
- daycare fees
- consistent monthly pet-walking or boarding fees
- condo fees
- insurance (car, home/renters')
- property taxes
- consistent transit costs (such as a monthly pass)
- car loan or lease payments
- life and living insurance (such as disability or critical illness)
- spousal and/or child support
- consistent gym membership fees
- subscriptions (cable, apps, print media)
- regular monthly charitable donations
- bank fees

Basically, a Fixed Expense is anything that doesn't fluctuate by much each month. A lot of times people think the term means "not optional," so you may be confused about why I include things like gym memberships but not groceries or gas. It's not that the latter are optional, but the amount you need each month may fluctuate a lot from week to week and month to month. For example, one month you may spend $600 on groceries and the next $750. It's the same with your transportation costs. Sometimes it takes $50 to fill up the tank and the next month $60. You still have to pay for gas, but the cost varies.

When deciding which of your expenses are Fixed Expenses, think about the nature of the expense. I always tell people it's about predictable versus unpredictable; it has nothing to do with important versus unimportant. Your fluctuating but necessary expenses such as groceries, gas, toiletries and transportation are dealt with in Step 4. For now, focus on figuring out your Fixed Expenses—those that are predictable and guaranteed.

A few things to note when you're calculating your monthly Fixed Expenses: Sometimes expenses come out of your account at different times. Some may come out monthly and others biweekly, or even annually or quarterly, depending the expense. Your job is to calculate how much you need *annually* to cover all of your Fixed Expenses and then divide by 12.

Let's use a simple example. Imagine that the following are transactions from your bank and credit card statements.

Monthly Transactions		Timing	Nature
Phone	$50	monthly	predictable/ guaranteed
Rent	$1,250	monthly	predictable/ guaranteed
Groceries	$200	monthly	not predictable/ guaranteed
Clothing	$50	monthly	not predictable/ not guaranteed
Cable/Internet	$49	monthly	predictable/ guaranteed
Loan payment	$100	monthly	predictable/ guaranteed

Life insurance	$25	monthly	predictable/ guaranteed
Parking	$10	monthly	not predictable/ not guaranteed
Bank fees	$5	monthly	predictable/ guaranteed
Gas	$75	monthly	not predictable/ guaranteed
Other Irregular or Regular Transactions			
Gym membership	$28	biweekly	predictable/ guaranteed
Renters' insurance	$180	annual	predictable/ guaranteed
Hydro	$100	every other month	mostly predictable/ guaranteed

Utilities like hydro and gas may fluctuate seasonally. The best way to handle utilities that fluctuate is to estimate the annual amount that you need and then divide by 12. Be conservative. Look at what you spent in a previous year or estimate what you think you'll spend. Let's say that you spent $600 for hydro last year, with some payments of $150 and others of $75; you'd treat this as $50 per month ($600 ÷ 12 months). For the first year this may take a bit of finessing to ensure that you have estimated properly.

Next, you remove all the expenses that are *not* predictable/guaranteed so that only the predictable costs remain. Then you tally up the annual amount that goes towards predictable/guaranteed Fixed Expenses. As you'll see from the following example, the annual total is $19,245. Therefore, the amount of money that must go towards your total monthly Fixed Expenses is $1,603.75 ($19,245 ÷ 12), which we will round to $1,604.

Fixed Expense	Nature of Expenses	Annual Amount
Phone	predictable/guaranteed	$600 ($50 per month)
Rent	predictable/guaranteed	$15,000 ($1,250 per month)
Cable/Internet	predictable/guaranteed	$585 ($49 per month)
Loan payment	predictable/guaranteed	$1,200 ($100 per month)
Life insurance	predictable/guaranteed	$300 ($25 per month)
Bank fees	predictable/guaranteed	$60 ($5 per month)
Gym membership	predictable/guaranteed	$720 ($28 biweekly)
Renters' insurance	predictable/guaranteed	$180 (per year)
Hydro	predictable/guaranteed	$600 (per year)
Total		**$19,245 (per year)**

Usually, as a rule of thumb, these expenses should be 55 percent or less of your after-tax monthly income in order to be considered affordable. In our example, your after-tax monthly income is $3,000. Your monthly Fixed Expenses of $1,604 come to 53.47 percent, so you'd be living within your means. This is powerful information, because your Fixed Expenses represent the money each month that is already owed to someone else. It's not yours! So if more than 55 percent of your income is going to someone else, that means the money left over for spending and saving will be tight. When your Fixed Expenses are over 55 percent, it can feel as if you're suffocating.

If you're in a position where your Fixed Expenses are higher than

55 percent, don't worry. It's okay. Most people who are trying to pay off debt usually have high Fixed Expenses. Want to know why? Because the minimum payments they have to make towards their debt are Fixed Expenses that push the percentage higher and higher. Try this: remove the monthly minimum payments from your calculation of Fixed Expenses and see what your affordability percentage would be without them. In our example, the total Fixed Expenses would become $1,504 after removing the $100 minimum loan payment. This means that Fixed Expenses would drop to only 50.13 percent, which means you'd be living well within your means. What a relief! Once you are debt-free, whatever that percentage is will be how you will live all the time. Woot!

Step 3: Work Out Short-Term Savings

Short-Term Savings are the best (and only) way to stay out of debt permanently. Usually it's one of two things that really rocks someone's finances and throws them into a Debt Loop: a spike in spending or an emergency. Both of these can wreak havoc on anyone's finances. Fortunately, Short-Term Savings work to prevent both of them from throwing you off course financially. That's why Short-Term Savings are the best.

I've seen this many times over the years: someone is following their Debt Game Plan without having Short-Term Savings and everything is okay . . . until it's not. All of a sudden something happens—a tax bill, a dental bill, whatever—and they have to pay with credit. There is nothing more discouraging than having to rack up debt midway through your plan, just when you were starting to see some progress. That's why having Short-Term Savings is so important, even if you have debt.

Yes, I just said that. You should be putting money into Short-Term Savings even if you have debt.

But wait! you say. *Shouldn't all my money be going towards my Debt Game Plan?* The answer is "not always." Yes, you need to put money towards your debt to pay it down—your Magic Amount (we'll deal with this in Step 5). But even as you tackle your Debt Game Plan, you should try to simultaneously build up some Short-Term Savings. Don't confuse Short-Term Savings with Meaningful Savings. This is money you're setting aside today in case you need to spend it tomorrow. This money will help to keep you from slipping back into the Debt Loop.

If your Debt Game Plan will take less than 12 months, it's okay to skip this step. Full steam ahead to debt repayment, no Short-Term Savings! But if your Debt Game Plan will take longer than a year, you should make every attempt to pad your pockets with some sort of emergency account. Even a little bit.

Maybe you're thinking of your line of credit as your emergency account. Well, I don't agree. I still suggest saving up. I understand that, if you look at the math, the money you might be sending to Short-Term Savings could help to pay off debt faster, and if there's no emergency you won't need to spend anything on the line of credit. But I don't believe you can put a price tag on motivation. There's something deeply upsetting about having to bail yourself out of an emergency situation with debt while at the same time paying debt back. It's like kicking yourself while you're down. People often give up entirely when this happens; I've seen it many times. That's why I recommend putting even a small amount towards Short-Term Savings while you pay back your debt, so you can avoid bailing yourself out of a financial pickle with more debt. It will help you stay motivated.

As I mentioned, there are two types of Short-Term Savings: savings for spikes in spending and savings for emergencies. Predictable spikes in spending include things like vacations, kids' summer camp, furniture, weddings, unicorns. Emergency savings, however, cover things like home repair and maintenance, health-care emergencies, car repairs and maintenance, and job loss.

In order to figure out how much you need to put towards your Short-Term Savings, you have to identify the almost guaranteed spikes in spending that will come down the pipeline and separate them from the emergency savings. Predictable spikes in spending are relatively easy to forecast, because you're already planning for them and you've probably got some choice. For example, you can choose how much you'll spend over the holidays versus what you must pay for new brakes. You can set limits, based on what you want to spend and what you think is reasonable.

For spikes in spending, you need to set aside enough money each month to accomplish the goal within that timeline. For example, if you have a destination wedding coming up in 13 months and you've already RSVP'd and you know it's going to cost you $1,105, then you need to put aside $85 each month for the next 13 months. Or if you know you'll need to buy a new bike in eight months' time and it will cost you $800, you'll need to put aside $100 per month.

For our example, let's say that the month of May brings Mother's Day, four family birthdays and your wedding anniversary. You usually end up having to shell out $360 over two weekends, which would typically go straight onto a credit card. Imagine how great it would be if on May 1 that $360 was already sitting in a Short-Term Savings account, armed and ready to be spent, helping you avoid debt, guilt and anxiety. Brilliant!

In order to do this, every year you need to put aside $30 per month. If it's already October, you have to put aside $60 a month for the next six months. After that you can reduce it to an ongoing $30 a month. This spike in spending is for sure going to happen. Instead of pretending it's not, plan for it. Put the money aside and breathe a little bit easier because of it.

Emergencies are not as predictable or easy to plan for, but short-term emergency savings are very necessary. When planning your emergency account, you need to take four things into consideration:

- **Home repairs** do not include decorative renovations, furniture or fun projects. Those would be spikes in spending. I'm talking leaks, a broken furnace, insect invasions and other expensive surprises that come with home ownership.
- **Car repairs** are fixes and maintenance that will keep your car on the

road. They do not include new 36-inch rims or rad flame decals.

- **Health care** means thinking about how a medical emergency could impact you financially, including treatments not covered by provincial or private insurance plans. This doesn't mean a massage at the spa (that would be Spending Money). I'm talking about health-care *emergencies*.
- **Job loss** is last but definitely not least. As much as we don't like to think about this, you should aim to have at least three months' worth of living expenses saved. Five months' worth if you're self-employed or in an industry where finding a position will be difficult if you're laid off.

The only way to set a savings target for an emergency account is to work out an average based on your spending history. For car-repair, health-care and home-repair emergencies, looking at the amounts you had to spend over the past two or three years can be a good indicator of what's to come. For example, if you spent about $6,000 over the past three years on home repair and maintenance, $2,000 a year is a good estimate for annual home-repair emergencies, unless that $6,000 included fun things or one-offs that are unlikely to happen again over the next three years. For example, if you've just replaced the roof, you likely won't need to budget for that over the next three years.

As for job loss, you need to first figure out how much a month you need to keep your financial head above water. I call this your "Crack-the-Nut" number. Your Crack-the-Nut number is the sum of your Fixed Expenses plus your basic life costs: groceries, necessary transportation and limited spending money. If you're an employee, you need to work towards saving up enough survival money to make your Crack-the-Nut budget for three months. If you're self-employed, work towards five months.

In our example, your monthly Fixed Expenses are $1,604. Let's say that you need $600 for basic life ($300 each for basic groceries and daily spending). If you lost your job, you would need a minimum of $2,204 ($1,604 + $600) every month for at least three months. That means you'd need a total of $6,612 ($2,204 × 3).

In the event of a job loss, one thing to keep in mind is that this amount could potentially be reduced by money that you'd still be able to collect—things like your partner's income, government pensions, spousal or child support or Employment Insurance (if you qualify). For our example, let's assume that you qualify for $1,300 per month in Employment Insurance and that you have been laid off from your job. Your emergency savings for job loss can be reduced from $6,612 to $2,712. While your Crack-the-Nut number is $2,204 per month, $1,300 will be covered by Employment Insurance, so you'll need to cover only $904 each month. For three months that would come to $2,712. Employment Insurance can take several weeks to drop into your chequing account, though, so just take note of that! To build up your savings towards job loss over a year and have $2,712 in your emergency account, you will need to put aside approximately $226 per month.

In our example, then, your total Short-Term Savings would be $256 per month. This includes $30 per month for your annual May spending blowout and $226 per month for job-loss emergencies.

Step 4: Calculate Spending Money

When it comes to your Debt Game Plan, I am very sure of one thing: you must be realistic. Not you on your worst spending behaviour or at your best—just you, living your life like a normal person. This is key to a sustainable Debt Game Plan. No more yo-yo crash budgets!

Your Spending Money is the only part of your income that's for you to enjoy your life. Everything else has a job—paying bills, saving for the future, or protecting against debt. Spending Money is the flexible money you need to live your daily life. These expenses include groceries, gas, clothes, shopping, takeout, movies, books—things that make life worth living! They're not bills (Fixed Expenses) and not money earmarked for spikes in spending or emergencies (Short-Term Savings). This money is meant to be spent, so it's not increasing your net worth (Meaningful Savings). This is the only money that doesn't have any rules imposed on it.

You deserve to have a realistic amount of money to spend each month. Calculating your typical monthly Spending Money *before* you make your Debt Game Plan allows you to stress-test your strategy; this will help protect yourself against making unrealistic budget limitations that doom you to fail. By determining your typical Spending Money, you can ensure that you aren't tempted to reduce your Spending Money beyond what's sustainable. Plans like *Yeah, I can live off $35 a week for one year* may not be realistic. Trust me.

Let's dig in. Download your credit card or debit statements for three months of the past year that are the most reflective of your normal life. Don't pick a month where you were on a no-spending kick and don't use the credit card bill from just after the holiday season. That's not self-love. Neither of those extreme scenarios reflect the real you on a day-to-day basis.

Once you've got your transactions laid out, remove those amounts that should be included in your Fixed Expenses, Short-Term Savings or Meaningful Savings. We want to get to your Spending Money only. Average out the expenses that are left over into a monthly amount and then take the average of the three months.

Let's look at a simple example, as shown in the Average Monthly Spending chart that follows. In our example, your typical monthly Spending Money is $900. Sure, in some months it was a bit below or a bit more than $900. But, on average, if you had approximately $900 to spend, your lifestyle wouldn't change so drastically that you would inevitably fall right back into another Debt Loop.

Average Monthly Spending				
Category	April	July	October	Average
Groceries	$250	$260	$280	$263
Toiletries	$20	$25	$15	$20
Transit	$50	$55	$30	$45
Entertainment	$200	$250	$300	$250
Self-care	$100	$120	$80	$100
Takeout	$65	$80	$70	$72
Shopping	$150	$150	$150	$150
Total	**$835**	**$940**	**$925**	**$900**

Step 5: Calculate Your Magic Amount

Without making any cuts to your average spending, the amount left over after you deduct your Fixed Expenses, Short-Term Savings and realistic Spending Money equals the amount of money you can comfortably put towards your debt-repayment plan as a form of Meaningful Savings. The amount that you put towards your Debt Game Plan on top of the minimum payments is the amount that actually improves your financial situation. It pays down principal on your debt. I call it your Magic Amount because it's the one where all the magic happens.

Take a look at the Financial Snapshot I've included for you. In our example, your after-tax monthly income is $3,000. With $1,604 set aside for Fixed Expenses, $256 for Short-Term Savings and $900 for Spending Money, your Magic Amount is $240. That's the amount of money you can use to move the dial towards becoming debt-free. Your monthly minimum debt payment is $100 towards a credit card each month (Fixed Expenses). Now the amount you can start putting towards your debt can be $340: the $100 minimum plus the $240 Magic Amount.

Financial Snapshot	
Monthly After-Tax Income	**$3,000**
FIXED EXPENSES	
Rent	$1,250
Phone	$50
Cable/Internet/subscriptions	$49
Renters' insurance ($180 ÷ 12)	$15
Bank fees	$5
Gym membership ($720 ÷ 12)	$60
Life insurance premiums	$25
Hydro ($600 ÷ 12)	$50
Minimum debt payment: personal loan	$100
Total Fixed Expenses	**$1,604**
SHORT-TERM SAVINGS	
Spikes in spending: annual May blowout	$30
Emergencies	$226
Total Short-Term Savings	**$256**
SPENDING MONEY	$900
TOTAL COST OF LIFE	**$2,760**
Meaningful Savings (Magic Amount)	**$240**

This is powerful information. Your Magic Amount is the amount of money that's going to change your life. If you've calculated it this way, you know it's realistic, sustainable and doable.

Putting Your Magic Amount to Work

The above is a critical step to figuring out your realistic Debt Game Plan. Start from what you can afford rather than when you want to be done, and see where that gets you first. Let's say that putting an extra $240 towards your debt is realistic and results in a three-year Debt Game Plan. Compare that to a repayment plan to get you debt-free in two years, but one that requires you to put an extra $400 towards debt each month. This is potentially setting yourself up to fail before you even start. Four hundred dollars is much bigger than $240. Sure, the realistic plan may take longer, but take a breath, check in. Are you setting yourself up to fail? If your plan is realistic, you are so much more likely to succeed, even if it takes longer.

My client Dianna lived in Vancouver. She was battling expensive rent and expensive credit card debt. When we met, she told me she wanted to pay off $10,000 of her debt within a year.

"So, how much should I put towards my credit card in order to pay it off this year?" she asked.

"Well, it's not about what you *should* put towards your debt. It's about what you *can afford* to put towards your debt."

"Okay," she said, a bit doubtful.

"Let's calculate how much you can afford to put to your debt without making massive adjustments to your lifestyle."

"Why wouldn't I change my lifestyle? I have debt—aren't I supposed to live frugally and put as much as possible towards it?" The old debt-repayment-as-punishment way of thinking.

"I know this seems like the opposite of normal debt plans," I said, "but let me ask you something. Have you tried to pay down this debt before?"

"Yes. One hundred percent."

"Did it work?"

She laughed. "Obviously not."

I smiled. "Well, maybe it's because you were calculating incorrectly how much to put towards your debt. Instead of letting the timeline drive your plan, give your realistic finances a chance to drive it and show you what's possible, and—more important—what's sustainable."

"Hmm . . . okay. I've never really thought about it like that," she said. "I always rush to figure out the time I want the debt gone by and then try to cram my finances into accommodating that."

"Totally. That's how most people approach debt-repayment plans. It usually means an unrealistic budget, which sets them up to fail. So let's look at your realistic numbers and go from there. If you don't feel the debt-repayment plan is fast enough, we can always go back and make changes."

Dianna had $10,000 on a credit card that was charging 19 percent interest, with a $300 minimum monthly payment.

"Right now, if you keep paying $300 per month and no Magic Amount, you'll be debt-free in approximately four years and you'll pay approximately $4,329 in interest.* Does that feel like a good enough time horizon?" I asked.

"Hell no! I can't stomach the idea of having this debt for four years. No. Gross. No." She shook her head emphatically.

I chuckled. "Okay, okay. Four years is no good. I agree. So, let's see what your finances would naturally have you put towards your debt before we start making mega reductions."

We went through her statements to calculate her Magic Amount.

Dianna's Financial Snapshot	
Monthly After-Tax Income	**$3,400**
FIXED EXPENSES	
Rent	$1,700
Cellphone	$100
Subscriptions	$40
Minimum debt payment: credit card	$300
Renters' insurance	$25
Transit pass	$135
Total Fixed Expenses	**$2,300**
SHORT-TERM SAVINGS	
Big purchases	$100
Emergencies	$100
Total Short-Term Savings	**$200**
SPENDING MONEY	$700
TOTAL COST OF LIFE	**$3,100**
Meaningful Savings (Magic Amount)	**$200**

---

* To see how I figured this out, go to "Debt-Payoff Calculator" in the Resource Library (page 300).

"So your original Magic Amount is $200. How does that feel?"

She sat up taller and leaned closer to her screen, clearly engaged and curious. "What will that do for my Debt Game Plan?"

I used the Debt-Repayment Calculator to see how much time a Magic Amount of $200 would shave off the four years. With an additional $200 per month towards her credit card, Dianna would be debt-free in two years. I shared my screen with her.

"Two years," I said.

"Shut up!" she said enthusiastically.

"I'm serious. Look. Twenty-five months, $2,120 in interest."

Her eyes widened. "Holy sh*t!"

I laughed. "That feels good?"

"Yes!"

"So originally you asked me how to pay it off within a year. This is two years, but you seem very excited. Why is that?"

"Well, I thought I was going to have to live off beans and spend zero dollars in order to make a dent in my debt. The $200 Magic Amount feels so doable, because I know it's reflective of what I actually spend. Also I'll know that I'm tucking money away for emergencies. I feel safe. It's relieving."

"Yes. You're totally cool to eat beans, but you can eat other things too if you want," I joked.

If you've got only one outstanding debt, you can figure out how fast you'll be debt-free fairly easily, using the Debt-Payoff Calculator in the Resource Library. If you've got multiple debts, it's a bit more complex. But hang tight; we will tackle that in Chapter 8. For now, follow the instructions for one single debt. Use your debt with the highest interest rate and see the difference between paying the minimum and paying the minimum plus your Magic Amount. Pretty exciting stuff!

If you've just calculated your Magic Amount and you feel like it's too much, or maybe not enough, don't worry. That's up next. The original Magic Amount that you calculate is like ground zero. It's how much you could put towards your debt with no major changes to your life. I like to think of your original Magic Amount as a starting-off point for negotiations.

The power of your Magic Amount is incredible. It can drastically reduce how long it's going to take to repay your debt. In addition, calculating your Magic Amount based on what you can realistically afford rather than letting an arbitrary timeline drive your Debt Game Plan is extremely important. You will know without a doubt that you can sustainably pay down the debt without major, potentially self-defeating lifestyle changes while still protecting yourself against future large spikes in spending or emergencies. It feels like magic . . . because it is!

CHAPTER 7

Being Realistic about Spending

Part of staying motivated to pay down debt is seeing the light at the end of the tunnel and truly believing you can get there. That's why calculating your Magic Amount is both fun and freeing. It's the amount of money you can safely and happily put towards your debt without unrealistically reducing expenses and setting yourself up for failure.

But what happens if your original Magic Amount isn't so magical? What if the amount you're supposed to put towards debt each month feels ridiculously high and unrealistic, despite what the numbers are saying? Or what if the repayment period and interest paid are still too long and too high for you to feel excited? Neither of these are motivating scenarios. As I said earlier, I like to think of your original Magic Amount as a starting-off point for negotiations. You can always tone it down or crank it up, as long as it's realistic for you, not someone else. That person isn't you.

Permission to Enjoy Your Life

If you've just calculated your original Magic Amount and it makes you afraid that you can't actually swing it, that's probably because you think it's quite a large amount of money to pay each month. You may find yourself thinking, *I don't have this much free cash each month. If I did, I wouldn't be in debt!*

If you're feeling like that, it's likely because you didn't properly estimate your spikes in spending for Short-Term Savings. Since your Fixed Expenses are what they are, it's unlikely that you miscalculated them, and since your Spending Money comes from your spending history over three average months, it's likely that you didn't miscalculate there either. The problem probably lies in your Short-Term Savings forecast. You may need to revisit it.

Underestimating what you think you'll spend in spikes is very common. *I won't go on a trip for the next four years; I'll give only handmade gifts*—promises to yourself that you vow to live by in order to keep those spikes in spending under control. But, like Spending Money, your Short-Term Savings forecast has to be realistic. Short-Term Savings are basically Spending Money: you're saving today to spend tomorrow. Don't set yourself up to fail.

People give up on their Debt Game Plan if the plan doesn't feel doable. I've seen it again and again and again. But if you know that you can pay off debt and still enjoy life, you're way more likely to stick it out until the end. *I can't do this* becomes *I can try*, because it feels possible and not punishing. My client Kathleen is a perfect example of this.

Meet Kathleen

Age: 38

Relationship status: married

Kids: 2, ages 2 and 4

Annual gross household income: $45,000 (Kathleen) + $55,000 (her partner) = $100,000

Assets: house valued at $400,000

Liabilities: $240,000 mortgage; $4,000 credit card debt

Kathleen lived in a small town near Lake Huron and had been in and out of debt for a few years. This wasn't our first appointment; she had been to see me a year earlier. At that time she had debt: $4,000 on a credit card that charged 18 percent interest, with a minimum payment of $120 per month. Although Kathleen was married, she and her partner operated their finances separately. They shared all the household bills equitably, but otherwise they each did their own thing. Back when we met the first time, we made a plan for Kathleen; it obviously hadn't worked, because there she was back in my office.

Here's a snapshot of where her finances were a year ago:

Kathleen's Financial Snapshot from Our First Meeting	
Monthly After-Tax Income	**$2,970**
FIXED EXPENSES	
Mortgage (her share)	$700
Utilities (her share)	$200
Home insurance (her share)	$50
Property tax (her share)	$150
Car lease payment (her share)	$175
Car insurance (her share)	$90
Cellphone	$80
Cable/Internet/subscriptions	$80
Minimum debt payment: credit card	$120
Total Fixed Expenses	**$1,635**
SHORT-TERM SAVINGS	
Gifts, holidays, big purchases	$100
Emergencies	$200
Total Short-Term Savings	**$300**
SPENDING MONEY	$745
TOTAL COST OF LIFE	**$2,670**
Meaningful Savings (Magic Amount)	**$280**

During our first meeting, Kathleen had told me that her lack of emergency savings made her really nervous. She was a self-employed photographer, and winters were slow. We dedicated $200 a month to her emergency fund to help protect her against dips in income during her slow season. In addition, she had estimated that she would need about $1,200 per year to handle spikes in spending such as the holiday season and birthdays. At the time I had asked her, "Are there any other types of expenses that spike your spending in a big way and wind up on credit?"

"Clothes. But I've got everything I need. I don't need new clothes," she said, very matter-of-factly.

"We all need pants at some point," I said. "You're wearing pants right now. Putting no money aside for clothes doesn't feel right to me."

"No, the amount I have for flexible spending money will cover it," she assured me. "I'm good."

And so I calculated her Magic Amount. "You've got $280 a month to put towards your debt each month."

"Really?" She was surprised.

"Look." I showed her my screen. "If you add this to your monthly $120 minimum payment, you'll be putting $400 a month towards your debt. This will have you paid off in 11 months versus 42, and you'll reduce the amount of interest you pay from $1,586 to $366. Which is amazing!"

She beamed. "Oh my god, that's so exciting!"

But I still had my doubts. "Are you sure this feels realistic and doable?"

"One hundred percent," she said.

Kathleen had left our session with a plan to be debt-free before the end of the year. So why was she back a year later, with more debt than before? Now she owed $4,500 on her credit card, and the monthly minimum payment had risen to $135.

"So what happened?" I asked.

"I suck."

"You don't suck," I said. "The plan obviously sucked. I want to know what we missed."

"I feel like I'm trying so hard to pay it off, but I can't get it to come down."

"Sounds like you've got a bit of Debt Creep," I suggested.

She lifted an eyebrow. "A bit of what?"

"Debt Creep. It's when your credit card balance keeps going up even though you're actively trying to pay it down. It means you're overspending somewhere. It also means we missed something in your spending last year."

I opened her file. "After you left here last year, you were supposed to add $280 a month to your $120 minimum payment for a $400 payment to the credit card. Why do you think that was tough to do?"

She slumped. "When you told me $280 last year, I was excited. But that night I remember thinking that it felt like a lot."

"Why didn't you speak up?" I asked. "We could have lowered it."

"I was so excited by the prospect of being debt-free in 11 months. I wanted that to be what happened. So I didn't bother to tell you how I actually felt once I got home."

"How did it feel?" I asked.

"Scary! That $280 felt like a lot. It worked for a couple of months and then all of a sudden I would feel so broke. I'd have to borrow again, and then the whole cycle repeated itself."

I smiled. "Sounds like our plan wasn't realistic."

"I guess not." She also smiled, putting on a sheepish expression.

I laughed. "Sometimes it's a process. Not to worry—we'll figure this out."

I had Kathleen go through the same exercise we had done the previous year. This included downloading three average spending months from her credit card history to examine her spending.

Her average Spending Money had been $846, over $100 more than the $745 we arrived at based on her statements from the same times the previous year. As I looked over her history, something stood out for me—her clothes. "Which of these expenses look like a spike in spending to you?" I asked.

Kathleen's Average Monthly Spending				
Category	May	August	November	Average
Groceries (her share)	$290	$300	$285	$292
Toiletries (her share)	$50	$80	$60	$63
Personal clothes	$300	0	$30	$110
Kids' clothes (her share)	$20	$80	$60	$53
Entertainment	$200	$250	$300	$250
Pet care (her share)	$20	$25	$15	$20
Takeout	$50	$65	$60	$58
Total	**$930**	**$800**	**$810**	**$846**

She looked over the chart. "Actually, only the $300 in May for clothes. The rest is just normal stuff, day-to-day life. I have a spending problem."

"I don't think it's a spending problem at all. Watch this." I deleted the $300 May purchase from her spreadsheet (oh man, I love spreadsheets). "If I take out that $300 spike, your average spending goes down to $746, which is pretty much the $745 average from last year. This means your daily spending has remained relatively stable."

"So I have a shopping problem then?" she asked.

"Not a shopping problem. A Short-Term Savings problem. It's a spike in spending that we didn't realistically prepare for last year."

She sat back. "Ugh, I know! I know I shouldn't be spending $300 on clothes when I have debt and kids and a mortgage. But I started feeling like I'd gone so long without, and then I cracked, and next thing I knew I'd added $300 to my credit card and I couldn't pay it off. It's a whole thing."

"What's important to you about having new clothes?" I asked.

She looked at me, a little taken aback by my question. "Um, I'm not sure."

"Tell me about this shopping spree in May."

"Well, it was the first spring I'd been through in ages without having an infant or a toddler. I'm not having more kids and they're in school or daycare now. Nothing fit me anymore, and my clothes were all so raggedy from being the mom of two kids under three. I felt washed up, invisible. So, I don't know, I needed to buy some new shirts for spring, and one thing led to another." She sighed. "Three hundred dollars later, I had a great new wardrobe for summer but couldn't pay for it."

"Before you had kids, how did clothes fit into your life?" I asked.

"I had a killer wardrobe. Not expensive, just well put together. Thoughtful outfits. I had time to shop and think about what I wanted to wear." She looked down. "Sounds kind of shallow, doesn't it?"

"Not at all," I assured her. "Obviously fashion is fun for you—a hobby, part of your identity. It's no wonder you keep coming back to it, especially now that you've had kids and your clothes literally don't fit. I wish I had known this in our meeting last time. We need to include a budget for clothes."

"What?"

"You heard me. Let's not pretend that you're not going to spend money on clothes. Let's be realistic and see what would happen if you gave yourself permission to enjoy your life a little while you pay down debt."

"Okay, but I feel like it must be some kind of trick."

I laughed. "No trick, just real life. We have to be able to spend money on things that we enjoy, even while paying back debt. It makes the plan more palatable, realistic and motiving. So how much would you need to spend on clothes every year to feel that you're still able to have some fun with fashion?"

"I'd love to be able to buy things seasonally and keep my wardrobe fresh, especially now that I'm working with clients again."

"Great. What's an amount of money that would allow you to do this each season while still reining it in?"

"Well, obviously I'd love to spend thousands on clothes, but that's not a thing." We both laughed. "I think, realistically, I could truly feel like me again with $300 a season. That feels so good. Even a bit luxurious."

"Great. So that would be $1,200 a year. If you set aside $100 per month in Short-Term Savings for your clothes, it will build up so that every three months you'll get to blow $300 on clothes—guilt-free!"

"Yeah, but what about the debt?"

"Let's see." I said. I tweaked her spreadsheet by adding the $100 to Short-Term Savings and reducing her original Magic Amount by $100.

Kathleen's New Financial Snapshot	
Monthly After-Tax Income	**$2,970**
FIXED EXPENSES	
Mortgage (her share)	$700
Utilities (her share)	$200
Home insurance (her share)	$50
Property tax (her share)	$150
Car lease payment (her share)	$175
Car insurance (her share)	$90
Cellphone	$65
Cable/Internet/subscriptions	$80
Minimum debt payment: credit card	$135
Total Fixed Expenses	**$1,635**
SHORT-TERM SAVINGS	
Clothes	$100
Gifts, holidays	$100
Emergencies	$200
Total Short-Term Savings	**$400**
SPENDING MONEY	$745
TOTAL COST OF LIFE	**$2,770**
Meaningful Savings (Magic Amount)	**$180**

"Nothing has really changed since last year," I said. "Fixed Expenses are the same, even though your minimum payment went up by $15 with the higher credit card balance."

"Yes, but my cellphone bill went down by the same amount because I got a new plan."

"Great. Also, if we take clothes out of the equation, we know that your daily Spending Money is the same as it was last year, $745. By adding $100 to your Short-Term Savings, we've increased it from $300 to $400 per month, and that will decrease your Magic Amount to $180 from $280."

I started number-crunching. With the clothes budget added, Kathleen could put only $315 ($180 Magic Amount + $135 minimum payment) towards her credit card. So what would be the cost of this more realistic plan?

	Plan with Clothes Budget	Plan without Clothes Budget
Monthly payment	$315	$415
Time to pay debt	17 months	12 months
Total interest paid	$602	$448

"Without a clothing budget, you'd take 12 months to be debt-free, versus 17 months. Plus you'd save an extra $154 in interest." I showed her the Debt-Payoff Calculator. "How does that feel?"

She paused and thought about it for a long time. Then she said, "The idea that I will have this for a year and a half versus a year feels disappointing."

"For sure," I said. "And it's up to you to decide which plan is more motivating. From a financial planning perspective, you're out $154. So let's start with that. Is paying $154 worth it to you to be able to spend $300 a quarter on refreshing your wardrobe?"

She responded quickly. "Yes. I'm totally fine with the $154 in interest. It feels like a small price to pay for self-confidence."

"Great, so you're not worried about the financial side of things. But the emotional side of things may be more complex. Tell me how the extra five months is making you feel."

"If I'm honest, I don't really care. But I feel like I should care."

"Who's making you feel guilty?"

She laughed. "Everyone! It feels weird to be spending money on myself when I have debt. Some people make me feel like that's selfish and stupid."

"So why do you think I'm actively promoting it?" I asked. "What's at stake here if you don't give yourself permission to spend money on some personal happiness?"

"I think I'll keep failing," she said.

"I agree. You tried the clothes-abstinence thing and it didn't work. Cut yourself some slack and be realistic. You're not out of control, you're not a shopaholic, you don't live extravagantly. Clothes are your hobby, and that's okay. For some people it's yoga, for others it's hosting gourmet meals. Whatever it is, we all have a thing. If you give yourself permission to enjoy some small pleasures, you're much more likely to stick it out and pay back the entire amount of debt, even if it takes a bit longer."

"You're right. I don't want to hate my life for a year, and I'd likely end up buying clothes anyway and failing again." She laughed, and I knew she'd had a breakthrough.

"This plan is solid," I assured her. "You are being realistic and now you're making an informed decision."

I checked in with Kathleen 14 months later, and she was right on schedule.

"I haven't had any spending spikes that I wasn't prepared for, and I absolutely don't feel upset about the plan. In fact, as soon as I'm done with the debt, I'm going to roll the $315 I used to spend on debt into my savings. I'm so used to not spending that now I know I can finally start saving, for the first time in a long time."

I was so happy. By giving herself permission to be realistic about how she lived, Kathleen had been able to stick to her Debt Game Plan for the first time.

I'm not saying that you should abandon your Debt Game Plan in the name of spending sprees. Spending money on anything and everything you want will get you nowhere fast. I am advocating for you to give yourself permission to have a realistic plan, one that reflects you and what's important to you. It's the compromise between happiness and financial responsibility. You have to find the sweet spot. This is how *This doesn't feel good* becomes *This feels right*, which means that you're much more likely to follow through on your plan all the way to the end.

When a Debt Game Plan feels right, you are much more likely to stick to it, because you don't resent the plan. A good Debt Game Plan is equal parts emotional and financial; you have to be motivated by both. It has to feel good while still packing the punch of financial success. Play with your Magic Amount. If it feels too high and unrealistic, it's okay to reduce it. Sure, this may drag out your timeline and increase the interest paid, but now you can make an informed decision. You're choosing long-term motivation over the quick fix that's likely to fail. Staying motivated is how you start living debt-free.

When You Need to Spend Less to Pay Down Debt

Meet Jake and Jill

Ages: 28 and 30

Relationship status: common-law partners

Kids: 0

Annual gross household income: $55,000 (Jake) + $50,000 (Jill) = $105,000

Assets: $2,000 in emergency savings; house valued at $500,000

Liabilities: $380,000 mortgage; $12,500 credit card debt; $17,000 in car loans

Jake and Jill's Debt Map			
Debt Type	Amount Owing	Interest Rate	Minimum Payment
Joint credit card A	$7,000	19%	$210
Joint credit card B	$5,500	19%	$165
Car loan 1	$5,000	8%	$400
Car loan 2	$12,000	8%	$400
Total	**$29,500**		**$1,175**

Jake and Jill were frustrated. "We've been maxed out for almost two years now and I just can't handle it anymore," Jake said.

"Tell me about the debt," I said. "Has it been a slow build or did it all happen quickly?"

"Various things over the years," Jill said. "Our friends' wedding, for starters. We were both in the wedding party and the ceremony was out of town. Then there were a few vacations and I had to get a new bike. Just normal life stuff that never got paid off. Always one thing after another."

"Are we the worst?" Jake asked. "Like, we make good money. I don't get how other people do it. Does everyone just have debt?"

"Lots of people do," I told them. "But let's focus on how this affects you."

"It's definitely stressing me out," Jill said.

"Why do you think that is?" I asked.

"Because I feel like we're doing everything right and living normal lives and yet we're just never ahead of the game. The debt makes me feel like I'm always struggling and we can't get ahead."

"Same," Jake said.

"Let's have a look at what's going on and see what we can do to get you out of this Debt Loop," I said.

Here's a snapshot of their finances:

Jake and Jill's Financial Snapshot	
Monthly After-Tax Income	**$6,335**
FIXED EXPENSES	
Mortgage	$1,980
Utilities	$300
Property tax	$280
Home insurance	$85
Joint car insurance	$155
Cellphones	$200
Cable/Internet/subscriptions	$70
Gym memberships	$110
Minimum debt payments:	
Car payment 1	$400
Car payment 2	$400
Credit card A	$210
Credit card B	$165
Total Fixed Expenses	**$4,355**
SHORT-TERM SAVINGS	
Big purchases	$0
Emergencies	$0
Total Short-Term Savings	$0
SPENDING MONEY	$1,980
TOTAL COST OF LIFE	**$6,335**
Meaningful Savings (Magic Amount)	**$0**

Jake and Jill's Average Monthly Spending				
Category	May	August	November	Average
Groceries	$650	$700	$680	$677
Gas	$250	$300	$200	$250
Toiletries	$80	$60	$60	$67
Clothes	$80	$80	$60	$73
Grooming	$50	$140	$50	$80
Health care	$80	$160	$110	$117
Hockey league fees	0	0	$300	$100
Entertainment/ dining out	$302	$355	$405	$347
Coffee/takeout	$50	$65	$40	$52
Parking	$40	$40	$40	$40
Gifts	0	$200	0	$67
House stuff	$120	$130	$80	$110
Total	**$1,800**	**$2,300**	**$1,995**	**$1,980**

As it currently looked, there was nothing left over for anything to go towards debt.

"I feel as if all our money is spent before we even get it in our chequing account," Jill said.

"Well, it kind of is," I said. "Sixty-eight percent of your after-tax monthly income goes to Fixed Expenses—your bills. That's pretty high. I usually don't get fussed until they go over 55 percent."

"It's so expensive living in the suburbs," Jack said. "Everyone thinks it's cheaper, but we have two cars, the property tax is actually really high, and we have to drive everywhere, so we spend a ton on gas."

"I know," I assured him. "There are lots of hidden costs, whether you're living in the city, the suburbs or even the country. Life is expensive, no matter which way you slice it."

"I just feel like we're always broke," Jill said. "Then when we finally get a grip and start tackling the debt, *boom!* Something comes up."

I motioned to the list. "One thing I'm seeing is that you don't have anything going towards Short-Term Savings, yet you've got a bunch of spikes in your spending. It looks like your hockey league fees and gifts probably wind up on credit cards."

"They do," Jake said. "It's so annoying, because we know we have a wedding in August, but the $200 gift still feels frustrating when it happens. Plus, with hockey, I pay $300 twice a year, and it always catches me off guard, even though I know it's coming."

"Okay, so how much is coming up for gifts in the next 12 months?" I asked.

"We have one more wedding, in eight months. It will cost around $200. Then I think all our friends and family will finally be married off," Jill said with a laugh. "Of course, then the baby showers will start. Ay-yi-yi!"

"I hear you," I said. "So let's look at hockey fees and gifts. What would make them feel less stressful?"

"If we had the money set aside, for sure," Jill said. "I wouldn't resent them as much, because they wouldn't wind up on credit cards."

"Totally," Jake agreed.

"Okay, so what if we put aside $100 a month for Short-Term Savings? That would give you $600 a year for hockey fees and $600 per year for gifts. It would also get you to $800 over eight months, so you'd be prepared for those two spikes."

"That would actually be great," Jake said. "But it still doesn't solve our problem. I feel that we can't reduce our spending any more than it already is."

I looked at their spending again.

"You're probably thinking that we have loads of places where we can reduce," Jill added. "But we've tried and tried and tried, I swear. Life is so expensive."

"I'm not thinking that at all," I told her. "But that's interesting. Tell me what you think I would point to as places where you could reduce."

She indicated their entertainment costs and then Jake's coffee shop spending.

"Go out less, reduce entertainment . . . give up all joy," Jake said with a wry laugh.

"Not if it's not realistic for you both," I offered.

"What do you mean?" Jill asked.

"I mean I won't ask you to reduce spending in a way that is unrealistic," I said. "Because that will set you up to fail. Let's just take a look at the entertainment. What do you think makes it cost so much?"

"We don't have kids yet," Jake said. "We're foodies and we love to try new restaurants. We also love going to the movies. It just adds up."

"So you both like spending money on those things," I said.

"Yeah, for sure," Jill said. "They're our hobbies."

I sat back. "How would you feel if I told you that you couldn't do those things anymore, because you need to pay back your debt?"

They stared at me for a moment, unsure of exactly how to respond. "I think that's what I expected you to say," Jake said at last. "But, obviously, that would be awful."

They both laughed nervously.

"Do you think you'd still go out for dinner anyway, after today?" I asked. "Still see your friends, go to a movie?"

"Yes, probably," Jill said. "We have to live life."

"Exactly," I said. "So what's the point in pretending you wouldn't? If that's the type of spending that makes you feel like you're living your life, I don't want to reduce it to nothing. It's not realistic."

Making a Debt Game Plan isn't about me pointing to the places where you spend the most money. Usually if someone spends the most money on a certain type of expense—be it takeout, coffee, dining out, clothes, whatever—it's probably because that item is really important to them. Maybe the takeout saves them a lot of time; maybe that morning coffee sets up their whole day for success. Who knows? Certainly not me. That's why I didn't know what expenses Jake and Jill should cut back on. Only they did.

If you're trying to reduce expenses in your Spending Money, be sure not to fall victim to the "I should" trap. That's where you think you should cut back in certain areas, not because you genuinely want to but because other people shame you into thinking that way. You know the old chestnuts: bring your lunch; shop thriftily; make coffee at home; easy meals for a family of four for $100 a week! If you're a person who can't feed your family on $100 a week, or if you love your morning takeout coffee, you're shamed into thinking that's the reason you're in debt. That's why you're bad with money. Those are the things you can easily cut out to get your finances in shape—tomorrow!

I call bullsh*t. There is no quick and easy fix for finances. That's why the plan needs to be realistic, so that you can keep making your payments every month, again and again, and not feel like you won't be able to live your life until it's over.

"Then what do we do?" Jake asked. "Something has to give, right? We can't just keep paying the minimum amounts. We have to do something."

"Absolutely," I agreed.

If you're in a situation where your Magic Amount is zero and you need to reduce expenses, try to reduce Fixed Expenses first, *before* reducing your Spending Money. You'll get a more sustainable, more realistic bang for your buck. This is probably the best tip out there if you've got debt. While everyone else is pissed off about how you use your Spending Money on takeout, I'm over here being like "Let's reduce your Fixed Expenses where we can!"

Spending Money is tough to navigate. It's hard to cut back, hard to enforce, and hard to plan for. Life changes from week to week. Making cuts to Spending Money should be your last resort, because the expenses rarely happen consistently. Everyone starts with the best intentions, but it's hard to maintain.

On the other hand, making permanent reductions to your Fixed Expenses is wonderful. If you are used to paying $1,500 in rent and you reduce it to $1,400, that's $100 that will consistently be available to you, month after month. If you usually pay $100 for your cellphone and manage to get it down to $80, that's $20 that you can consistently save, month after month. Look for consistent reductions, even minor ones, because they become sustainable ongoing savings. Reduce a bill to make room to save like a bill. That's how you pay yourself first. *Boom!*

The problem with reducing Fixed Expenses is that they tend to be harder to give up without a lifestyle change and require administrative work to reduce. It's harder to cut $100 from rent or bills than to vow to not spend money on lunch out, but you probably won't end up reducing your lunch money by $100 for long. If you put the work into raising money each month by reducing Fixed Expenses, you will create sustainable savings towards your debt. It will feel so much easier once it's done.

Jake and Jill's Fixed Expenses	
Mortgage	$1,980
Utilities	$300
Property tax	$280
Home insurance	$85
Joint car insurance	$155
Cellphones	$200
Cable/Internet/subscriptions	$70
Gym memberships	$110
Minimum Debt Payments	
Car payment 1	$400
Car payment 2	$400
Credit card A	$210
Credit card B	$165
Total Fixed Expenses	**$4,355**

"What if, instead of trying to reduce your Spending Money, we look to your Fixed Expenses instead," I suggested. "Are there any reductions that you could make?"

They scanned them together. "I don't know," Jake said. "I can't see anywhere to make a change."

They looked at me expectantly.

"Let's go one by one," I said, "starting with the house. Are you able to reduce your payments from biweekly to monthly any time soon?"

"We renewed just six months ago," Jill said. "And we're so careful with water and electricity already. I feel like our hands are tied there."

"What about your cellphones?" I asked.

"No. We both need the data for work," Jake said with a sigh. "Last time we went below the unlimited plan we ended up with way higher bills every time."

We continued through the list. With every entry I asked, "Does this expense give you a high enough emotional return to keep it the same?"

To the cellphones, they both said yes. To the car insurance, Jake said, "No, but I have to pay it and it's the lowest it can go."

Cable and Internet? "Yes," Jill said. "It's as low as I can reduce it while still getting what we need. And we love our music subscription."

Then we reached the car payments and I swooped in. "How do you feel about having two cars?" I asked.

"Ugh. I hate that we have two cars," Jill said. "It's so expensive."

Excellent. "Tell me about the car loans," I said.

"When we moved out there from the city, we had one car, which we bought used for $20,000 six years ago. There's $5,000 left to pay on that loan. We bought the second car about a year ago. We still have $12,000 to pay on that over 34 months. We found the logistics of the morning commute getting really stressful with only one car. 'Who's picking up who?' 'Who has the car today?' 'I need it for work.' That kind of thing."

"Does the second car give you a high emotional return on investment?"

"No. We hate it," Jill said with a laugh. "But I worry about how we could live with one car. We've talked about this a lot."

"What's possible with one car?" I asked.

"Well," Jake said, "I could go into work earlier so I could drop you off on the way, and then leave earlier to pick you up."

"But what if you get called into a meeting or something?" Jill asked.

"Well, that happens only two or three times a month, realistically. So if you took a taxi home those three times, that would be like $100 for cab fares—still cheaper than the $400 for the car loan, insurance and the extra $50 in gas."

Jill tapped her nails on the table. "I guess. But I'm not super comfortable yet," she said. "I'm still worried that it's not realistic to go down to one car. I feel like there's always a time when we both need one. There's a reason we got two, you know."

I thought for a moment. "Okay, so how about this? What's the second car worth right now?"

"Probably $14,000," Jake said.

I did some quick head math. "Do you think you guys could get a car that makes you feel safe that will last for the next five years for $11,000, including sales tax?" I asked.

They looked at each other and thought about it. "I think so," Jill said. "We don't drive far. Why? Wouldn't that mean we still have two car payments?"

"Well, if you traded in the newer car for $14,000 and paid off the $12,000 car loan, you'd have $2,000 left over for a down payment on a cheaper used car. Then if you took on a new car loan of $9,000 at the same rate ($11,000 – $2000), you'd be done in 34 months, but your monthly payment would only be $300 per month instead of $400." I was starting to get excited.

"So we would still have two cars but would pay $100 less each month?" Jill asked.

"Oh, I get it," Jake said.

"Yes!" I said excitedly.

Jill turned to Jake. "Babe, I think that might actually work."

"It's going to be a pain to get all that going for only $100," Jake said. "We could just consolidate all our debt on the mortgage when we renew in three years."

"For sure," I said. "But then you're rolling your debt into the mortgage, which is helpful in the moment but doesn't do anything for your overall net worth or retirement preparation. I know you guys don't want to retire with a mortgage. So let's see what $100 does to your Debt Game Plan for the credit cards in 36 months, which is when you renew."

Using the Debt-Payoff Calculator, I worked out how much they'd pay in interest and how much would still be outstanding on their credit cards when they renewed their mortgage. The car loans would be done with before Month 36, but I wanted to show them the powerful effect $100 could have on their credit card debt, regardless of car payments.

Jake and Jill's Credit Card Debt at 36 Months— Magic Amount 0 (no change)		
	Outstanding	Paid in Interest
Credit card A	$2,237	$2,797
Credit card B	$1,758	$2,198
Total	**$3,995**	**$4,995**

"Brutal," Jill said. "That's basically half the equity we built up over a year, just gone." She slumped in her chair.

"What happens if we reduce the car payment by $100?" Jake asked.

"If you reduced the car payment, your Magic Amount would be $100. So the payment on your first credit card would be $310—the $210 minimum payment plus the $100 Magic Amount. Let's see what that would do." I busted out the Debt-Payoff Calculator again.

Jake and Jill's Credit Card Debt at 55 Months— Magic Amount $100 (from reduced car payment)		
	Paid Off By	**Paid in Interest**
Credit card A	Month 29	$1,731
Credit card B	Month 35	$2,280
Total interest paid		**$4,011**
Debt added to mortgage	0	

"Do you see?" I showed them my screen. "A hundred dollars goes a long way. It reduces the amount you need to roll into your mortgage by almost $4,000 and saves you almost $1,000 in interest. Just from reducing your Fixed Expenses by $100 a month!" (Note that I used a technique called debt stacking to calculate this. We'll tackle that in the next chapter.)

Jake looked at me, then the screen, then me again, and smiled. "No sh*t."

"A hundred bucks makes all that difference?" Jill said. "Really?"

"Yes, look!"

They both smiled.

"You seem happy," I said.

"Of course. I mean, I usually discount an amount like $100 when it comes to bills. Housing, cars . . . what's $100 in the grand scheme of life, ya know?" Jake said.

"I can't believe that $100 can make that much of an impact," Jill said.

"It does. And just remember that while you're being incredibly inconvenienced by the amount of time and paperwork you'll have to do to get your car payment down to $300. Just keep reminding yourself that it's worth $4,000."

"Totally," Jill said. "It's going to suck, but it's basically going to take me only five hours to save four grand. An hourly rate of $800 is pretty decent."

"I love that," I said. They were motivated, I could tell. When they left my office, I had no worries that they wouldn't succeed.

Reduce Your Fixed Expenses and Add to Your Magic Amount

If you're looking to reduce expenses to increase your Magic Amount, try to reduce Fixed Expenses first. Chances are, if you're in debt, your Spending Money is already as low as it can possibly go, with the exception of a few slips, spikes or sprees. If you look to your Fixed Expenses, you'll create Meaningful Savings that are sustainable and predictable. That's what it takes to hammer down debt: sustainable, predictable payments above the minimum, month after month. Save like a bill, right? So let's look to your bills to see where the savings are and remember that $25, $50, $100 makes a huge difference in your Debt Game Plan if you can consistently do it. It's all about consistency.

1. Calculate your Fixed Expenses.
2. Go through the list and ask yourself if you're getting a high enough emotional return from each expense to keep it the same. For those that you feel resentful of or frustrated by you can reduce and still be happy!
3. See how you can possibly reduce your Fixed Expenses on an ongoing basis, even if it's only by five dollars!
4. Add up the reductions. For example, $30 from a cellphone plan + $10 from a video-on-demand subscription + $15 from bank fees = $55 to sustainably boost your Magic Amount every month.
5. Use the Debt-Payoff Calculator in the Resource Library to calculate how many months it would take to pay off your debt using your current plan, and how much interest you'd pay.
6. Add the new Magic Amount to your monthly payment and then compare the timeline and interest paid. I bet you'll be pleasantly surprised!

CHAPTER 8

Debt Stacking:
The Fastest Way to Pay Down Debt

If you've got more than one debt, this chapter will change your life. Perhaps you've heard of debt stacking before. It's a tried-and-true method of paying down debt that works to keep your cash flow consistent and help you stay motivated along the way. It's a debt-repayment strategy that is hella effective.

I often see people with multiple debts: credit cards, lines of credit, bank loans. Each debt has its own minimum monthly payment. If a person has a Magic Amount of $300, I often see them spread that out across their debts every month—an extra $150 to the credit card, $50 to the loan, $100 to the line of credit. It's like Oprah giving away free cars: "*You* get a car, *you* get a car, *you* get a car!" Only instead of cars, it's Meaningful Savings being doled out.

This typically happens when you're not sure what's the most effective way to pay down your debt, so you try to hit all of them. It makes you feel financially responsible to know that you didn't just make the minimum payments on your debts. But even though your attempts to be financially awesome feel good, they aren't actually having the biggest impact on your finances. And if you've got debt, you probably want it to be gone as soon as possible. There is a better way—it's called debt stacking. I love it, and here's how it works.

The first step to debt stacking is building your Debt Map. Recall how you took stock of and organized your debt into a Debt Map in Chapter 5. Let's use Paul's Debt Map to refresh your memory.

Paul's Debt Map				
Debt	Amount Owing	Interest Rate	Minimum Payment	Payment Date
Credit card A (old)	$5,350	19.99%	$160	21st
Credit card B (current)	$12,000	18.00%	$360	20th
Personal loan	$3,500	5.60%	$70	13th
Line of credit	$10,000	4.00%	$35	25th
Total	**$30,850**		**$625**	

Paul's total debt was $30,850—the maximum amount he needed to tackle. In addition, now Paul knew that his monthly minimum payments added up to $625 per month. This is your starting point.

Debt Stacking

Step 1: Prioritize Your Debt

Right now Paul's debts are prioritized, or "stacked," in order of interest rate, from highest to lowest. This is the standard order of operations: use your Magic Amount to attack the debt with the highest interest rate first. You want to ensure that you're getting the biggest bang for your buck, right? By paying the highest-interest-rate debt first, you pay the least amount of interest overall.

Basically you want the debt you need to pay off first to be at the top of the stack. Here's how I generally prioritize debt, from highest priority to lowest. (This isn't an exhaustive list; it's possible you may have a debt that is really unique and not seen here.)

- payday loans
- income taxes
- overdrafts
- high-interest credit card debt
- unsecured personal lines of credit
- personal loans (such as consolidation loans)
- student lines of credit
- secured lines of credit (such as home equity lines of credit, or HELOCs)
- secured loans (such as car loans)
- government student loans
- family loans

You'll notice that the list generally goes from highest interest rate to lowest interest rate. However, there are two potential exceptions: income taxes and government student loans.

For income taxes, the interest rate that you're charged can vary widely, depending on whether you filed late, if there are penalties, and how long the taxes have been outstanding. It's unlikely, however, that the rate will be higher than that for payday loans, which can be as high as 60 percent. You may also be wondering why I have listed government student loans as a lower priority than, say, a secured line of credit such as a car loan. We'll get to that in the next chapter.

You will note that mortgages are not listed. I look at your mortgage as a cost of living, like rent. Sure, I absolutely recognize that it is debt and that you are paying interest, but a mortgage tends to have the lowest interest rate of all debts, and there's forced savings in the payments. In other words, the part of your payment that goes towards principal is a form of savings.

This is why I usually don't include someone's mortgage in their Debt Map until they are entirely debt-free otherwise and getting ready to retire. That's when hammering down that mortgage becomes a priority over other financial goals. Until then, treat it as a bill and focus on more important and more expensive debt.

Step 2: Apply Your Magic Amount to the Highest-Priority Debt

If Paul's Magic Amount was $300, that additional $300 would go to the highest-interest debt first. He would basically ignore all the other debts, with the exception of their minimum payments.

Paul's Debt-Stacking Plan, Prioritized by Interest Rate ($300 Magic Amount)					
Debt	Amount Owing	Interest Rate	Minimum Payment	Magic Amount	Payments Made
Credit card A	$5,350	19.99%	$160	$300	$460
Credit card B	$12,000	18.00%	$360		$360
Personal loan	$3,500	5.60%	$70		$70
Line of credit	$10,000	4.00%	$35		$35
Total	**$30,850**		**$625**	**$300**	**$925**

In other words, you make a full-fledged attack on one debt and pay only the minimums towards the other, less expensive debts. Paul has a $925 Debt-Stacking Plan. That's his total monthly cost of debt plus his Magic Amount. The point is that he will never spend more than $925 a month towards debt, and that amount will take care of all of his debt.

Step 3: Apply Your New Magic Amount to the Next Priority Debt

Let's see how this would play out. On January 1 of Year 1, Credit Card A has $5,350 outstanding. Paul will put $460 a month towards it ($160 minimum + $300 Magic Amount) and make only the minimum payments on his other debts until Credit Card A is completely paid off.

Using the Debt-Payoff Calculator, you can see that Paul will pay off Credit Card A in 14 months. This frees up $460—the $160 minimum from Credit Card A plus his $300 Magic Amount. The $460 that used to go to Credit Card A is now the new Magic Amount. See? Magic! Since the other debts have been getting only their minimum payments, the amounts owing on them may have changed as well, so it's helpful to make an updated debt-stacking chart 14 months in.

Paul's Debt-Stacking Plan, Prioritized by Interest Rate ($400 Magic Amount)					
Debt	Amount Owing	Interest Rate	Minimum Payment	Magic Amount	Payments Made
Credit card A	0	19.99%	0		0
Credit card B	$9,218	18.00%	$360	$460	$820
Personal loan	$2,725	5.60%	$70		$70
Line of credit	$9,974	4.00%	$35		$35
Total	$21,917		$465	$460	$925

You'll note that the total amount owing has decreased to $21,917 (down from $30,850). Total minimum payments have decreased to $465 (down from $625), but the total actual payments made will remain the same ($925) throughout the whole plan.

The new $460 Magic Amount is now applied to Credit Card B, making each actual payment $820. That's huge! This is when it starts to feel like an avalanche. As you finish off each debt, you pick up the old Magic Amount plus the minimum payment to make an even larger payment on the next debt each month.

With a payment of $820 each month on the $9,218 still outstanding on Credit Card B, the starting balance would be paid off over 13 months. With 14 months to pay off Credit Card A and 13 months for Credit Card B, that's 27 months to completely get rid of Paul's credit card debt.

Step 4: Repeat Step 3 Until All Debts Are Paid Off

For Paul, this is how his debt stack played out:

Debt	Paid Up By	Interest Paid	Money Freed Up for Payments
Credit card A	Month 14	$646	$460
Credit card B	Month 27	$3,212	$820 ($360 + $460)
Personal loan	Month 30	$1,516	$890 ($70 + $820)
Line of credit	Month 41	$1,196	$925 ($35 + $890)

Using debt stacking, Paul would be entirely debt-free in under four years (41 months) without ever saving any more than the $300 original Magic Amount. See "Debt Stacking" in the Resource Library for step-by-step instructions on how to use the Debt-Payoff Calculator to create your own Debt-Stacking Plan.

Step 5: Redistribute the Debt-Payment Amount to Savings

Now Paul has freed up $925 per month! If he wants to build up emergency savings and other Short-Term Savings very quickly, he can. This would help ensure that he never goes into debt again.

If Paul needs to replenish $7,500 in Short-Term Savings—$5,000 in an emergency account and $2,500 set aside for large purchases and spikes in spending—he can accomplish this only eight months after being debt-free ($7,500 ÷ $925). Then the $925 can be applied to Meaningful Savings such as retirement, down payments—the sky's the limit.

How to Implement Your Debt-Stacking Plan

You can apply the debt-stacking method to your debts at any time. You can start tomorrow! This is how debt stacking works: it's a bit slow in the beginning but builds and builds over time. This is how you strategize to tackle your debts one at a time, systematically paying them down.

1. Take stock and organize your debt into a Debt Map (Chapter 5).
2. Stack your debt according to priority (highest interest first).
3. Calculate a sustainable but impactful Magic Amount (Chapters 6 and 7).
4. Pay down debts one at a time. Add your Magic Amount to the highest-priority debt first and pay it down completely while making only minimum payments on your other debts.
5. Repeat with each debt until debt-free. (See "Debt Stacking" in the Resource Library for more.)
6. Redistribute the monthly debt payments to savings once you are debt-free.
7. Party!

CHAPTER 9

Strategic Spending: How to Pay for Life When You Have Debt

You've got the plan and you've got the motivation. Now comes the final thing you need to ensure that you can not only start your Debt Game Plan but sustain it. Otherwise, all this juicy, wonderful planning will be for naught. We can't have that—I will lose sleep. And so I give to you one of my single greatest gifts.

That gift is a strategic banking plan. This is the key to killing your debt without hating your life. I promise, it will make your Debt Game Plan feel easy. It will lift the burden of endless budgeting off your shoulders. It will allow you to spend money without guilt, even while you have debt—a crucial step towards living debt-free.

One of the main reasons people can't get their Debt Game Plan off the ground or wind up back in a Debt Loop is the fact that they have no cash-flow strategy. Sounds boring, right? But *how* you spend money is a big deal! It's not just about *what* you spend it on.

Let me say that again. How you spend your money is a big deal. Sometimes you pay with debit, sometimes with credit, sometimes with cash. Maybe your rent or mortgage payment is due with one paycheque, so you scrimp until the next cheque and then you feel like a baller. It's constant feast or famine, and it creates anxiety. And if all your money goes in and out of one chequing account, it's really hard to know when you're safe to spend money and when you're not.

I call this the Spending Vortex. The Spending Vortex robs you of your ability to know when you can or cannot afford something. When you feel as if your paycheque goes into your bank account and it's already spent before you even get to debate ordering a pizza. *Poof!* Gone. Usually you're left feeling broke, that you've overspent and must depend on credit to survive until the next pay period.

Without a spending strategy, you won't know what you can or cannot afford to spend safely each pay period. You may find yourself stuck in a Debt Loop for a long time, even though you don't want to be there. It's not so much that you're overspending; it's just that you may not know exactly where the line in the sand is between the money you can spend and the money you cannot. Then, at the end of the month, you can't pay the balance on your credit card or you have to borrow on a line of credit. It's exhausting.

A strategic banking plan is a cash-flow strategy that will fix this right up. The key is to separate the money you *can* spend from the money you *cannot* spend each pay period, creating a line in the sand that I call your Hard Limit. Know your Hard Limit and spend within it. It's your green or red light, your stop or go, your spend-or-say-no indicator of affordability.

So how does it work? Let me show you.

The Strategic Banking Plan, or How to Spend Money Without Going into Debt

Let's continue with our simple example from Chapter 6. We calculated your financial snapshot as follows:

Financial Snapshot	
Monthly After-Tax Income	**$3,000**
FIXED EXPENSES	
Rent	$1,250
Phone	$50
Cable/Internet/subscriptions	$49
Renters' insurance ($180 ÷ 12)	$15
Bank fees	$5
Gym membership ($720 ÷ 12)	$60
Life insurance premiums	$25
Hydro ($600 ÷ 12)	$50
Minimum debt payment: personal loan	$100
Total Fixed Expenses	**$1,604**
SHORT-TERM SAVINGS	
Spikes in spending: annual May blowout	$30
Emergencies	$226
Total Short-Term Savings	**$256**
SPENDING MONEY	$900
TOTAL COST OF LIFE	**$2,760**
Meaningful Savings (Magic Amount)	**$240**

Step 1: Rename the chequing account where your paycheque or income from sole proprietorship is deposited as "Bills and Savings."

Your existing chequing account (where your paycheque is deposited) is no longer what you spend money from. Say what? It is now a holding tank for money that is *not yours to spend*. This is where the money earmarked for Fixed Expenses, Short-Term Savings, Meaningful Savings, including your Magic Amount, will live. Basically, all the money you are not allowed to spend on daily living remains in this account.

In our example, the following expenses would come from the Bills and Savings account:

Rent	$1,250
Phone	$50
Cable/Internet/subscriptions	$49
Renters' insurance ($180 ÷ 12)	$15
Bank fees	$5
Gym membership ($720 ÷ 12)	$60
Life insurance premiums	$25
Hydro ($600 ÷ 12)	$50
Personal loan minimum payment	$100
Spikes in spending (gifts in May)	$30
Emergencies	$226
Magic Amount	$240
Total Money You Cannot Spend	**$2,100**

Step 2: Automate all bills and automatic savings so they debit from your Bills and Savings account.

One of the key things that messes people up with their Debt Game Plan is that some bills automatically charge to their credit card. So, while you're busy paying down debt, you are still forced to use it. For example, if you owe $3,000 on a credit card that charges 19 percent interest and your Debt Game Plan has you putting $300 ($100 minimum + $200 Magic Amount) towards it each month, you'd expect that by the end of the month the balance on your credit card would be $2,747.50 ($3,000 + $47.50 in interest – $300 payment).

But if you also have your $50 phone bill charged to the card, as well as your $10 video-on-demand subscription, your balance will be $2,807.50 ($2,747.50 + $50 + $10). Yes, you could move $60 from your Bills and Savings account to pay them off as you use them, but if you've got a lot of subscriptions and automatic payments—gym fees, music streaming subscriptions, hydro charges, recurring donations—all coming through at different times, it's going to feel like a hot mess.

Did you actually even hit the principal with your $300 payment? It will feel impossible to know.

I suggest that you remove as many subscriptions and recurring expenses from your credit cards as possible. I'm not saying that you need to get rid of those expenses or services, but pay as many as possible from your Bills and Savings account instead of charging them to your credit card. You can set it up so that they are automatically debited from the account, so you don't have to pay them manually.

While you're at it, unsubscribe from any service you don't use. Check out your credit card statements. Where are the recurring transactions? If you haven't used a service you're paying for in four months, get rid of it. I was subscribed to an online fitness website for a year and used it precisely twice. Every month I'd be like, *I need to cancel that*, but then I'd get distracted—*Oh, look! A butterfly!* Don't be like me.

We are living in a micro-transactions era—$5 here, $9.99 there. Sign up here, free trial there. Our credit cards are hooked up to apps and online retailers that make it ridiculously easy to spend money without thinking for a moment. Take your credit card information out of those online sites, clear your cache and delete any apps that force you to spend on your credit card. Make it a little harder for you to use credit.

There may still be some transactions that must go through your credit card, even though they are Fixed Expenses. Okay, I relent, but you'll have to stay on top of it. When a Fixed Expense must be charged to your credit card, you can either manually move the money from your Bills and Savings account every month, on the same day as the charge, or set up an automatic payment to your card in the same amount, again on the same day that the bill is charged, so that it doesn't mess with your Debt Game Plan.

You'll notice that I call it the "Bills and Savings" account. The "Bills" part is fairly straightforward: it covers, well, your bills. All your

Fixed Expenses. The "Savings" part of the account is the amount earmarked for Short-Term and Meaningful Savings, including your Magic Amount. This doesn't mean that your Bills and Savings account is where you keep your savings, but you should have the money earmarked for Short-Term Savings and Meaningful Savings automatically withdrawn each month from the Bills and Savings account and moved to the appropriate destinations. For example, if you have $200 per month earmarked for emergency savings, a $200 automatic withdrawal should be going from your Bills and Savings account each month into your emergency savings account.

You should have two Short-Term Savings accounts, minimum. One is for spikes in spending like vacations, big purchases, gifts and so on. You should also have a second Short-Term Savings account that is for emergencies only—home, car, health and job-loss emergencies. Why? Because if the money you've put aside for vacations gets mixed in with your emergency money, you'll never really know what you can afford to spend safely, or if you're truly covered for an emergency. Separating them means you have an immediate indicator of affordability.

"Can we afford to go to our friends' cottage next weekend?"

"What's in the vacation account?"

"Three hundred dollars."

"Yep!"

Or: "Can we afford to go to our friends' cottage next weekend?"

"What's in the vacation account?"

"Nothing."

"Nope!"

If that $300 were in the same savings account as your emergency money, you'd run the risk of believing you were in a position to afford the trip, when really you weren't, since you'd be eating into your emergency savings.

Make sense? The Bills and Savings account is just a holding tank for the money you cannot spend each month and the money earmarked for Short-Term Savings and Meaningful Savings.

138

One last thing. Your Magic Amount should be automatically applied to your Debt-Stacking Plan. Call your financial institution and have them put your Magic Amount on your debt on the day the minimum payment is due. If you can't do that, you'll have to put a reminder in your calendar so that when the minimum payment comes out, you pop the Magic Amount onto your debt as well.

Step 3: Open a second chequing account, with your debit card attached to it, as your primary chequing account.

This is your new Spending Account, probably the greatest gift I'll give you. Your very own Spending Account—ooh la la! You want to open a chequing account that is separate from your Bills and Savings account because the Bills and Savings account has all the money you *cannot* spend in it, all the money that's going towards Fixed Expenses, Short-Term Savings and your Magic Amount.

This new chequing account is your Spending Account, and only your Spending Money goes into it. By isolating all your Spending Money in its own chequing account, you give yourself permission to spend that money to zero without worrying that you're using money earmarked for bills or savings. No more wondering if you can actually afford something. Every dollar in that account is safe to spend. No anxiety over what bill comes out tomorrow.

Step 4: Move your Spending Money into the Spending Account every pay period.

On payday, move your Spending Money into your new Spending Account. In our example, with a paycheque that comes twice a month, this would be $450. Your $1,500 paycheque comes into your Bills and Savings Account twice a month. Every payday, you would move $450 to your Spending Account and leave $1,050 in your Bills and Savings Account.

This is so powerful. By isolating your Spending Money each payday in a separate chequing account, you know exactly what you can and cannot afford to spend during the pay period without risking going into debt or overspending. If it's the day before payday and you have $30 in your Spending Account, you know you have $30 available to spend before tomorrow. *Can I afford a pizza tonight?* you might think to yourself on a Thursday night. Now your thought process will be: *What's in my Spending Account? Thirty dollars? Yep, pizza it is. Just keep it under $30.* No guilt, no shame, no worries. No debt.

Being able to log in to your banking and see exactly the amount of money you can safely spend between now and your next pay period will feel like someone opened a window, allowing you to breathe. It stops you from feeling guilty and afraid every time you spend money, because you know this is an amount you can safely spend without risking running out of money to pay your bills or overspending and winding up back in the Debt Loop. What a relief!

There are other ways in which you might get paid. Maybe it's monthly, biweekly or weekly. Simply divide the amount of Spending Money you're allotted each month by the number of paycheques you get for most months of the year, per the chart below. If you're paid biweekly or weekly, there are times when you will get "extra" paycheques. See "Extra Paycheques" in the Resource Library for how to manage those extra pay periods.

How Much to Move to Your Spending Account			
Pay Frequency	Monthly Spending Money	Cheques/ Month	How Much to Move
Bimonthly	$900	2	$450 ($900 ÷ 2)
Monthly	$900	1	$900 ($900 ÷ 1)
Biweekly	$900	2	$450 ($900 ÷ 2)
Weekly	$900	4	$225 ($900 ÷ 4)

Step 5: Use credit cards wisely, when you must.

You may be wondering about using credit while you're paying down debt. I get this question all the time: "Do I leave my credit card at home?" You don't have to. For the record, paying with debit is ideal, but I recognize that people still like to use their credit card. So, here's how to use it alongside your strategic banking plan.

Use your credit card only for the type of spending that would be paid from your Spending Account—fluctuating expenses. No Bills or Savings if you can help it, as I said in Step 1.

If you do use your credit card to pay for something that would normally come from your Spending Account, move the corresponding amount of money out of your Spending Account *that night* so your Spending Account always represents what you have to spend to zero until the next pay period. For example, if you just went out for dinner and it was easier to use your credit card, log in to your online banking or banking app that night, look at the pending transactions, and manually move the money from your Spending Account to the credit card. (It's helpful to have your bank accounts and credit card at the same financial institution, if possible, so all this can be done with one app or one login.)

If you put a big purchase on your credit card, say, a couch for $700, it should hopefully already be saved up for in your Short-Term Savings account for spikes in spending. You swipe for the couch, then move $700 from your Short-Term Savings account to your credit card that night. This is the only way to safely use credit cards while you're repaying debt. It ensures that the minimum payment and the Magic Amount are actually doing the work.

Again, you're welcome to use credit. You don't need to cut up your cards or put them in the freezer, but you must create a new habit of moving money onto them so that you're never spending beyond what you've allotted, and so that your Spending Account reflects the money you can safely spend to zero before the next payday. I do this every night while I'm brushing my teeth before bed. It's part of my routine.

In order to do this effectively, you'll need to ensure that your banking plan allows you to do many transactions (preferably unlimited) from the new Spending Account. This is so you can use debit as much as possible and, if you do use credit, you can transfer money between your Spending Account to your credit card that day. Yes, you may have bank fees to contend with, but I've been doing this for a long time.

This strategic banking plan works. It really does. It will give you peace of mind, clarity about what you can afford, and guilt-free Spending Money. It's a gift. If your banking fees come to $10 a month, ask yourself this: would you subscribe to an app that charged $10 a month for peace of mind and a sense of control over your money? I sure would, again and again. If you can find fee-free banking, that's even better!

Let's walk through a simple example of how your strategic banking plan would play out in real life, using my client Jessica.

Strategic Banking in Action

Meet Jessica

Age: 31

Relationship status: single

Kids: cat

Annual gross household income: $70,000

Assets: $4,000 in emergency account

Liabilities: $10,000 credit card debt

Jessica's Debt Map			
Debt	Amount Owing	Interest Rate	Minimum Payment
Credit card A	$10,000	18%	$300
Total	**$10,000**		**$300**

"I just can't get my money sh*t together," Jessica told me.

"How so?" I asked.

"I feel like money comes in and out and I have no control over it. I'm trying to pay down my debt, but every month I'm right back where I started. I make decent money. I shouldn't be scrambling like this," she said.

"Well, let's have a look," I said.

Jessica's finances weren't a disaster, but how she spent money was. Her credit card had a bunch of subscriptions and some bills and apps set up on it. She used debit 40 percent of the time and would occasionally take out cash from ATMs. All this activity on one chequing account and a credit card.

"I feel like the extra $300 monthly payment I make to my credit card isn't actually doing anything. Then I get frustrated at the lack of progress I'm making and end up doing that thing you told me not to do," she said, making a sheepish face.

I laughed. "What thing?"

She laughed too. "Putting almost all the money from my paycheque onto my credit card to pay it down."

"Nooooo!" I cried dramatically. "That's the worst! Nothing sets up people for failure more than that."

"I know. I fail every time. I obviously end up needing to use my credit card, feeling like garbage about it and then just saying, 'Screw it.'" She shook her head. "Help!"

"I get you. You need a strategic banking plan," I said.

"Do you mean like a budget?"

"No, I mean a cash-flow strategy that will help you live within your means without hating your life."

She laughed. "Sign me up!"

I looked at her most recent month of transactions.

Monthly Transactions: Chequing Account			
Transaction	Out	In	Date
Phone	$100		June 1
Rent	$1,750		June 1
Grocery store	$80		June 1
Clothing store	$50		June 3
Grocery store	$80		June 5
ATM withdrawal	$100		June 8
Car insurance	$125		June 12
Payday		$2,000	June 15
Money to emergency savings	$200		June 18
Credit card A minimum	$300		June 20
Gas	$75		June 22
Parking	$10		June 22
Car Payment	$255		June 25
Takeout	$30		June 25
Bank fees	$5		June 30
Payday		$2,000	June 30
Magic Amount	$300		June 30

Monthly Transactions: Credit Card			
Transaction	Out	In	Date
Clothes	$150		June 8
Cable/Internet	$100		June 10
Grocery store	$100		June 13
Wine store	$15		June 16
Gift	$40		June 16
Renters' insurance	$25		June 17
Grocery store	$90		June 17
Minimum payment		$300	June 20

Takeout	$35		June 20
Yoga subscription	$10		June 22
Ride share	$15		June 24
Gas	$75		June 25
Ride share	$10		June 25
Magic Amount		$300	June 30

"Okay," I said. "It's no wonder your money makes you feel all over the place. You've got money going out from all directions."

"Is that wrong?"

"No, no. *Wrong* isn't the right word. It's not wrong, but it makes feeling in control of your money much harder. You know how some people have a savings strategy?"

"Yes."

"Well, people also need a *spending* strategy to back it up. Basically, your spending strategy is how you set up your banking so you can spend money within your means and not overspend on credit. When you're trying to pay down debt, it's imperative, so that the money you're putting towards your debt has a chance to actually pay it down."

"Okay, so what do we do?" she asked.

Step 1: Rename the chequing account where your paycheque or personal business income is deposited as "Bills and Savings."

"The chequing account that you currently run all your money through is going to be renamed 'Bills and Savings,'" I told her. "And all the money that you have earmarked to pay bills or go towards savings is going to come from that account. Nothing else—no spending money."

"Money that I can't spend," she said.

"Exactly. Fixed Expenses, Short-Term Savings and Meaningful Savings, including your $300 Magic Amount."

We went through her accounts and pulled out all the items that could be considered Fixed Expenses and Meaningful Savings.

Money Jessica Cannot Spend Each Month		
Monthly After-Tax Income		**$4,000**
FIXED EXPENSES		**Source**
Rent	$1,750	chequing account
Phone	$100	chequing account
Cable/Internet/subscriptions	$100	credit card
Renters' insurance	$25	credit card
Car insurance	$125	chequing account
Credit card minimum payment	$300	chequing account
Car payment	$255	chequing account
Bank fees	$5	chequing account
EMERGENCY SAVINGS	$200	chequing account
MAGIC AMOUNT	$300	chequing account
Total		**$3,160**
Amount available for spending		**$840** **($4,000 - $3,160)**

"You can't spend $3,160 of your $4,000 monthly after-tax income," I said.

"Wow," Jessica said. "That feels like a lot. I guess I always just thought money I can't spend is for things like my rent and car payment. But it's so much more than that."

"Knowing what you can't spend each month is so important. But though you *can't* spend $3,160 every month, you now know you *can* spend $840."

"And that's for everything? Like, all of life?" she asked.

"Yes, everything that is not a bill or savings," I said. "I call this your Hard Limit. Within your Hard Limit, you can spend money on anything you want."

"Anything?"

"Yep. I don't care if it's takeout, coffee, clothes, taxis, gas, groceries—

whatever. You don't need to budget it. As long as you're fed, safe and having fun, spend your money on whatever you want to."

"Oh, I like that."

Step 2: Automate all bills and automatic savings so they debit from your Bills and Savings account.

We went back to Jessica's transaction list. "One of the things that's making you feel like you never know where money is coming from or how much you've actually spent is the fact that you're spending money from so many different places."

"It's a hot mess."

I laughed. "It's normal. That's why I have a job. In your case, your renters' insurance, cable and Internet subscriptions should be debited from your Bills and Savings account and taken off the credit card."

Step 3: Open a second chequing account, with your debit card attached to it, as your primary chequing account.

"The third change," I said, "is opening a second chequing account and calling it your Spending Account."

"A second chequing account? Why?" she asked.

"This is what you will spend money from—hopefully using only your debit card—so that you don't have to use credit while you're paying it down. By isolating the amount of money you have before each payday to spend to zero, you can safely spend within your Hard Limit without worrying about overspending or blowing through money that's needed to pay bills."

Step 4: Move your Spending Money into the Spending Account every pay period.

"Since you're able to spend $840 a month," I continued, "you'll need to separate it so you know what you can spend to zero each pay period. Because you're paid twice a month, you're able to spend $420 ($840 ÷ 2) every 15 days."

"So on payday I move $420 to my new Spending Account," she said.

"Yep. Two thousand dollars comes into your Bills and Savings account and you move $420 to the Spending Account. This will leave $1,580 in your Bills and Savings account to cover the money you can't spend."

"Will the $1,580 be enough to cover all the transactions when they come out?"

"Let's map out your next month. Right now you've got $2,000 in your Bills and Savings account."

Expense	Out	In	Date	Balance
				$2,000
Phone	$100		June 1	$1,900
Rent	$1,750		June 1	$150
Cable/Internet	$100		June 10	$50
Car insurance	$125		June 12	– $75
Payday		$1,580	June 15	$1,505
Renters' insurance	$25		June 17	$1,480
Money to emergency savings	$200		June 18	$1,280
Credit card minimum payment	$300		June 20	$980
Car payment	$255		June 25	$725
Bank fees	$5		June 30	$720
Magic Amount	$300		June 30	$420
Payday		$1,580	June 30	$2,000

"As it stands," I told her, "you'd be in overdraft by $75 with your car insurance payment. So you need to top up your Bills and Savings account by this amount before you start the banking plan next month.

You can use $75 from your emergency savings to bring the starting balance in the Bills and Savings account up to $2,075. Then you'll never run out of money as long as the bill and income amounts remain the same."

"Will I have to move $75 every month?" she asked.

"Nope, just to kick off the plan," I said.

Like Jessica, you need to map out your Bills and Savings account to see if you could end up in a situation where there isn't enough money because of when the transactions come out. There will be some Fixed Expenses or automated Short-Term or Meaningful Savings withdrawals where you can control when they come out. Move automated transactions to as close to the end of the month as you can. If you've mapped out your transactions like this and are diligent about setting them up, you won't go into overdraft, because only the transactions you've planned on will come and go from your Bills and Savings account. There shouldn't be any transactions coming from this account that are unplanned for or that fluctuate a lot. If you're in a situation where you could go into overdraft, move money from Short-Term Savings to kickstart your strategic banking plan by the amount of potential overdraft. If you don't have anything saved up, you'll need to work towards that before you can implement your strategic banking plan.

"This is great," Jessica said. "I'm stoked to try it out."

When I checked in with her three months later, she was pleased with her strategic banking plan.

"So, how's everything going?" I asked. "Is the plan helping you make a dent in your debt?"

"Yes! I've never had such clarity before," she said, her excitement contagious. "I still use my credit card for some spending from time to time, but I log in every day and move the money over, so I haven't overspent once."

I laughed. "That's okay with me, as long as you don't add new amounts owing."

"I'm not. I've never felt so in control before and I've never felt less afraid. I got my nails done the other day and I felt no guilt. No-guilt Shannon."

I smiled. "Hey, that's what I'm here for."

"But for real, it was the day before payday and I still had $50 in my Spending Account. It was so liberating to know that I didn't have to feel bad about pampering myself a bit." She beamed. "What a relief."

"And the debt?"

"Going down. I've put the extra $300 each month towards my debt, and not once has the amount I owe grown. It's working. I can feel the momentum."

"I'm so excited for you! You've still got about two years to go until you're entirely debt-free, but with this spending plan in place, you'll get there, I know it."

"Oh, totally! I've never believed that until now. This is so manageable. It just makes everything feel so doable and not restrictive. I can absolutely live like this for three years—no problem. I'm even putting money aside for vacations."

I was so happy for her. She had found a way to pay down her debt and have a life. That is the key to actually making your Debt Game Plan last. You have to love your Debt Game Plan if you want to stick with it. Using a strategic banking plan allows you to spend your money safely and without guilt or fear while you're repaying debt. It's the key to taking control of your cash flow forever, so you don't drop back into the Debt Loop.

Part Three

Debt-Slammers

One of the most amazing moments for me as a financial planner is when I get to show someone how much sooner they will be debt-free if they stick to the Debt Game Plan we've just made.

"Oh my god, no way!"

"Are you serious? I never even dared to think that was possible."

"Squeeeeee!!"

It's the best part of my job. After all these years, I still get a high from those moments because that excitement is exactly what's needed to survive a long-ass Debt Game Plan. The promise of living debt-free sooner rather than later is so, so motivating.

Because I know that the Magic Amount and the Debt-Stacking Plan I've worked out for someone are completely realistic, when I show them to people, I have total confidence that the promise of their debt-free timeline is perfectly reasonable. Of course, there are some other levers people can pull to speed things up even more—things like cashing in certain types of savings, consolidating debt, and finding extra earned money where you can. I call these Debt-Slammers. Debt-Slammers are acceleration levers that will help you slam through your debt as fast as you can in a realistic way.

I usually like to show someone their Debt Game Plan first, with no Debt-Slammers added. Just their original Magic Amount and their Debt-Stacking Plan. That way I get to gauge their excitement over the proposed timeline. I do this because I want them to know there's a really good Debt Game Plan in place that will rock their financial world no matter what—even if they don't use any Debt-Slammers. Some people can't, and that's okay.

You'll note that I've done the same for you. Up to this point you have an original Magic Amount and a Debt-Stacking Plan. No tricks. You know your proposed timeline regardless of your savings, income or ability to consolidate your debt. You are empowered by the plan as is. Huzzah! But if you want it all to happen faster, you need one of the two Debt-Slammers (or both!): (1) lower the interest rate on your debt, or (2) put lump-sum payments towards your debt whenever you can.

Lower the interest and put more money towards it. Duh. Sounds obvious, but I can tell you from experience that people are often not sure how to actually do this. The logistics are where they get caught up: *Should I apply for a consolidation loan or a line of credit? Should I pull money from my investments to pay back debt? Should I stop my RRSP contributions?* The list of questions goes on. In addition, plenty of people believe that none of those actions will have a big enough effect on their debt to make it worth the administrative annoyance.

Let's face it, going to your bank, applying for a line of credit or waiting can be administratively annoying. Everyone is beyond busy these days, and sometimes making these appointments requires you to take time off work. If you don't truly know or believe in the financial benefit of your actions, why bother? Well, that's why I want to show you that small changes can go a long way. These Debt-Slammers will shrink the timeline and have you living debt-free even sooner!

CHAPTER 10

Debt-Slammer #1:
Lower the Rate and Consolidate

Most people know that having a high interest rate on any debt is not a great thing. But I want to explain why. Let's take credit cards, for example. Credit cards are the most common high-interest-rate debt that I see, more so than payday loans or overdraft. Credit cards are everywhere, and they typically come with a doozy of an interest rate.

Sometimes I say that credit cards are like your best friend and your worst enemy. On the friendly side of things, credit cards are convenient, often have rewards programs associated with them, and if you pay them in full each month, are interest-free. But if you can't pay them back within the grace period (usually 21 to 25 days), you are charged interest, and usually at a high rate. That's when a credit card becomes your enemy.

The kicker is that any payments you make will go towards interest first and then actually hit the principal. Let's say that at the end of the grace period you owe $10,157.35, which represents $10,000 that you actually borrowed and $157.35 in interest. If your minimum payment was $305, you'd be paying $157.35 in interest and only $147.65 towards the balance owing (the principal). The balance left to repay would then be $9,852.35 ($10,000 − $147.65).

Suffice to say, high interest rates are not fun. That's why people hate credit card debt so much. You and your money have to work so hard to repay even some of the principal. That's why lowering your interest rate is so helpful, if you're able to.

Lower That Rate and Consolidate (I love that it rhymes)
Step 1: Call your lender and try to negotiate a better rate.

So many people don't take the time to do this. Yes, I know the hold music is the worst, but that Muzak version of "The Girl from Ipanema" could become the anthem for your financial freedom. Don't forget, you are a customer of your financial institution. You can call and ask for a better rate. If you have a good credit rating you may be able to catch a break. The worst-case scenario is that they'll say no, and you're no worse off than before. But at least you tried, right?

My client Anthony couldn't manage to pay more than the monthly minimum $150 payment on his $5,000 credit card, which was charging 19.99 percent. But he called his bank and managed to negotiate the interest rate down from 19 percent to 16 percent. Yay, Anthony!

Using the Debt-Payoff Calculator and the $150 monthly minimum payment, we were able to compare the difference for Anthony.

Rate	Interest Paid	Time to Pay Down
19.99%	$2,357	4.2 years (50 months)
16%	$1,656	3.75 years (45 months)

See? The same $150 monthly payment had a bigger impact on the principal, decreased the interest paid by $701 and decreased the time until debt-free by five months! This is with no additional money going towards his Debt Game Plan. All this financially good stuff just from reaching out to his bank and sitting on hold for 20 minutes. Not too shabby.

Step 2: Consolidate your high-interest debt with a line of credit or consolidation loan.

The next step is to try to consolidate your debt. I say "try" because some of the methods I'm about to explain are things you need to qualify for. No matter what your credit score or debt-to-income ratio, I think it's worth a conversation with a lender to see if you qualify. At least you can say you tried.

So, what do I mean by consolidating your debt? Basically you wipe out an existing higher-interest debt like a credit card and replace it with another debt that has a lower interest rate, such as a line of credit or consolidation loan. You still have the same amount to pay back, but at a much lower interest rate, which means more of your payment goes to the principal, even if you don't have additional cash flow to put towards your Magic Amount. Lowering the interest rate will do a lot of the heavy lifting for you.

Meet Janis

Age: 26
Relationship status: it's complicated :)
Kids: my dog? (#furbaby)
Annual gross household income: $40,000
Assets: $800 in emergency account
Liabilities: $14,100 credit card debt; $6,500 student loan

Janis's Debt Map			
Debt	Amount Owing	Interest Rate	Minimum Payment
Credit card A	$7,700	20.2%	$230
Credit card B	$3,000	19.99%	$90
Credit card C	$3,400	19.0%	$100
Government student loan	$6,500	5.6%	$80
Total	**$20,600**		**$500**

"These minimum payments are killing me," Janis said. "Totally cramping my style."

I laughed. "Yeah, they will do that. Question: Is your debt going up? Going down? Staying the same?"

"The same. I can't seem to make more than the minimum payments, which add up to $500 a month!"

"At least you're able to make the minimum payments on time."

"Well, that's not entirely true. I've missed a few payments on my credit cards."

"Was that because you didn't have enough income to make the payments?"

"No. Since I got my new job, from a financial perspective I've been able to make the minimums. It's because they come out at different times from different accounts, and sometimes I forget how much is due when. On the plus side, I brought cookies for this meeting." She pulled out a tin of homemade chocolate chip cookies and smiled. "It's not whisky, which is probably what I should have brought."

I laughed. She handed me a cookie and we ate them while we talked about things that had nothing to do with debt. Then I leaned in. "Okay, ready? Let's have a look," I said and opened up her file.

Janis's Financial Snapshot	
Monthly After-Tax Income	$2,726
FIXED EXPENSES	
Rent	$1,200
Renters' insurance	$25
Cellphone	$70
Cable/Internet/subscriptions	$50
Minimum debt payments:	
Credit card A	$230
Credit card B	$90
Credit card C	$100

(continued on next page)

Student loan	$80
Total Fixed Expenses	**$1,845**
SHORT-TERM SAVINGS	
Big purchases	0
Emergencies	$50
Total Short-Term Savings	**$50**
SPENDING MONEY	$831
TOTAL COST OF LIFE	**$2,726**
Meaningful Savings (Magic Amount)	**$0**

"I promise, I don't live extravagantly," she said. "Just life, and these minimum payments are driving me bananas."

She wasn't exaggerating. When I looked over her spending history, each month was coming in at between $800 and $850. She was right on the money. That's what it cost her to live.

"It's depressing to see it laid out on paper like this," she said.

"What do you mean?" I asked.

"There's literally nothing going to savings or debt, and I try so hard not to overspend. I feel like there's nothing I can do. I've already cancelled the cable, lowered my phone bill and got rid of my gym membership, and I have free banking. I don't go on vacations. I don't buy fancy clothes. Like, I've done all the things. I can't reduce any more. I've tried and tried."

"Well, I agree. We can't realistically reduce expenses any lower. I mean, I could tell you to, but looking at your past spending, I don't think it would work in the long run." I knew I needed to give her some hope right away. "Things feel tight right now because they are. Your Fixed Expenses are 68 percent of your take-home income. You've done an amazing job getting yourself to a place where you're not going into more debt. That's a huge first step."

She sighed. "It's just frustrating. Sometimes I feel like life is financially built for two incomes. Single people like me have to work so much harder just to stay afloat, unless they make megabucks."

"You're absolutely right," I said. "It is much harder. You're shouldering the entire cost of housing and transportation."

"I've lived in the same crappy apartment since I was 21 years old, and I'm afraid to move because my rent is so cheap. It makes me want to move in with someone just to save on rent and get a nicer place," she joked.

I laughed. "Well, let's make sure you have your own financial house in order, regardless of someone else's finances."

"Oh, totally. I'm just kidding . . . sort of."

We laughed again.

"Okay, look at this." I deleted the minimum debt payments from her spreadsheet. "If I remove the $500 you have going towards your total debt each month, you are actually living within your means. Your Fixed Expenses are only 50 percent without the debt payments. So that's great. Imagine what you can do when that $500 frees up!"

She let out a sigh. "Yes, but how long is that going to take?"

As it stood, Janis had a Magic Amount of zero. She'd be paying back her debts with minimum payments only. So I knew that lowering her interest rates by consolidating her debt would have a wonderfully positive impact on her Debt Game Plan, and it might be the only Debt-Slammer she could take advantage of right then.

On her current trajectory, here's how her Debt-Stacking Plan would play out:

Debt	Paid Up By	Interest Paid	Money Freed Up
Credit card A	Month 50	$3,723	$230
Credit card B	Month 50	$1,414	$90
Credit card C	Month 50	$1,520	$80
Student loan	Month 58	$1,284	$100
Total interest		**$7,941**	
Total time		**58 months (4 years, 10 months)**	

"Worst case, you're looking at just under five years and about $8,000 in interest," I said.

She did not look happy.

"Not okay?" I asked.

"No, not okay. Five years? I can't live like this for five years."

"Let me ask you something. Answer this: 'If I don't have this entire debt gone by (blank), I will be so unhappy.'"

She thought about it. "Four years. By the time I'm 30."

"Why 30?" I asked.

"I don't know. I just feel like student debt put me behind the eight ball when I graduated and I've never really recovered. I need to pay off this debt and get my life together. I can't have this carry forward into my future."

"Okay, but keep in mind that this is your worst-case scenario. Nothing extra towards your debt but minimum payments, no raises, no windfalls, nothing. But this is also what we know we can control. I like to make plans based on what you can control."

She sat there for a minute. "So if this is the worst-case scenario, what's the best-case scenario? Besides taking a lover who also shares the rent."

I smiled. "We get the interest rate down as low as humanly possible and knock the sh*t out of it."

"I like that. How do I do it?"

"We need to consolidate your debt."

"But I only have $10,000 available on my line of credit and, like, $20,000 in debt."

"Hold the phone," I said. "You have a $10,000 line of credit with nothing owing?"

"Yes, but I don't want to use it," she said, a bit sheepishly. "That's why I didn't mention it before."

"This is a game-changing piece of information," I said excitedly. "Why don't you want to use it?"

"I feel scared to. My line of credit is my emergency fund. I only have $50 a month going to emergency savings, and what if I lose my job? I don't know. It makes me feel safe leaving it untouched."

I understood how having an unused line of credit could make her feel safe, but I had a hunch that seeing how much faster she could be debt-free would make her feel even safer. "What's the interest rate on your line of credit?" I asked.

"Five percent."

"Can I show you something?"

"Sure."

"Let's take the $7,700 credit card at 20 percent. We know it will take you over four years to pay down and will charge you $3,723 in interest if you keep making the $230 monthly minimum payment. If we consolidate that card with your line of credit at 5 percent, the $230 that you put towards it will ensure that you'll be done with this debt entirely in three years. Plus you'd save $3,113 in interest."

She looked at the screen. "Wow! That's a big difference." She was impressed.

"And here's the thing. Since you're paying down a line of credit, you can always borrow back the money if there's an emergency. So if in Year 2 you've paid back $6,000 but an emergency happens and you need to borrow back $2,000, you can. Sure, it will slow down your Debt Game Plan, but you won't lose access to that money, unlike when you're paying back a student loan or a consolidation loan. Once you've paid those off, you can't borrow back the money. Which is great from a debt-repayment point of view but not from an emergency *oh crap* point of view."

"Huh, I never thought about that. So even though I'd used the entire line of credit, I wouldn't be in trouble with no access to cash once I started to pay it back down."

"No, because anything you put towards it can be borrowed back in the case of an emergency. So please, please, please pay off that card and $2,300 of the 19.99% card—tonight."

She laughed. "I will!"

I was pleased. "So let's see what else we can do to speed this up for you. You may need to up the limit on your line of credit or apply for a consolidation loan to lower the rates on the other debts."

"I've thought about that before. But won't borrowing more affect my credit score negatively? It's already taken a beating from my missed payments and being constantly maxed out."

"It depends on what happens to the debts you're paying off. If you close your other credit cards, your credit score may take a small ding in the short run because you'll be maxed out on your line of credit, and the average age of your credit could also ding your score. However, after 12 to 18 months, consolidating your debt will likely raise your credit score again."

"How?"

"Since you are maxed out now, your debt utilization is high, which isn't great for your credit score. But once you consolidate you'll be able to make a dent in the amount owing much faster than before. And you are way less likely to miss payments if all your debt is simplified into two monthly payments. Overall, consolidating should have a positive impact on your credit score, regardless of short-term dings. My tip would be to pay off but not close your oldest credit card."

"Okay. So let's do this," Janis said.

I gave her some homework and told her to check in with me once she was done.

Janis's Homework

- Pay off your highest-interest cards with the $10,000 you have available on your line of credit—tonight—and keep paying the $230 to the line of credit.
- Keep making minimum payments on all other debts.
- Stay on your steady budget and don't take on more debt.
- Call your bank to see if you can get the credit card interest rates lowered.

- Apply for another consolidation tool, such as a higher limit on your line of credit or a consolidation loan, so that you can consolidate the other high-interest debt.

Janis and I met up a couple of weeks later to check on her progress. "How'd it go?" I asked.

"Okay," she said. "A few things: I couldn't get my rates lowered, but the bank said I would qualify for an additional $6,000 on my line of credit."

"That's amazing! It will make such a huge difference."

You may be wondering why I was so excited about Janis borrowing even more money. It's a fair question, especially because I have mixed feelings about lines of credit. For starters, they can be an amazing way to consolidate high-interest debt like Janis's. And the flexibility means that if you do have an emergency while you're paying back debt, you can borrow on it again.

But that's exactly the problem too. Lines of credit are revolving, which means you can borrow back at any time. Many people who are in debt may find themselves with a never-ending, ever-increasing line of credit if they don't make the other changes in their life that are necessary to stop taking on more debt. If you are in a situation where your debt is already ever increasing, a line of credit may not be the best solution for you. If you qualify, a consolidation loan might be better.

A consolidation loan is a personal loan that has an impact similar to that of a line of credit on your debt. You use it to pay off your higher-interest debts and replace them with one monthly payment at a lower interest rate. The difference is that you can't borrow back on a consolidation loan the way you can with a line of credit. You can't use it for emergencies and you can't increase or decrease the monthly payments. From a debt-repayment perspective, of course, this is wonderful. You can't take on more debt and you're forced to make fairly substantial monthly payments to pay back not only interest but principal too.

For Janis, I knew that a line of credit would be okay because she had her spending under control and wouldn't risk overspending anymore. Recall Janis's Debt Map:

Janis's Debt Map			
Debt	Amount Owing	Interest Rate	Minimum Payment
Credit card A	$7,700	20.2%	$230
Credit card B	$3,000	19.99%	$90
Credit card C	$3,400	19.0%	$100
Government student loan	$6,500	5.6%	$80
Total	**$20,600**		**$500**

"I want you to fully pay off the other two credit cards," I said. "This will free up another $190 in minimum payments. Your total payment to the line of credit will then be $420 ($230 from credit card A + $90 from credit card B + $100 from credit card C)." This would bring her line of credit to $14,100 (her total credit card debt), leaving $1,900 unspent on the $16,000 line of credit.

She paused to think. "Should I pay down my student loan with the $1,900? Or pay that down first? The interest rate is lower on the line of credit," she said.

That was a great question, one that I get asked often. Sometimes it makes sense to prioritize paying off a government student loan with a line of credit and sometimes it doesn't. In Janis's case, I wanted to prioritize the line of credit, even though it had a lower interest rate.

"It's not necessarily a lower interest rate. In Canada, the interest you pay on your national student loan qualifies for a 15 percent tax credit, so if your interest rate is 5.6 percent, you're paying only 85 percent of it, which is 4.76 percent."

"Good to know the old student loan is workin' for me," she joked.

"It is. Also, one of your fears is job loss. With government student loans, you can ask for repayment assistance. If you lose your job, you may qualify to stop payments while you're out of work. You can't do that with a line of credit. Whatever the payment is, it's likely due, regardless of your employment or income situation."

"That's a good point. And work is so sketchy these days. It doesn't seem to matter if you're self-employed or an employee—everyone has risk."

I totally agreed. "And one last thing," I said. "You'll still have $1,900 available on your line of credit in case you have an emergency before you build up your savings or start making a larger dent in the line of credit."

"That all makes a lot of sense," she said. "So now when will I be finished paying off everything?"

I busted out the Debt-Payoff Calculator again and got to crunching her new plan.

Janis's Debt-Stacking Plan					
Debt	Amount Owing	Interest Rate	Minimum Payment	Magic Amount	Payments Made
Line of credit	$14,100	5%	$420	0	$420
Government student loan	$6,500	5.6%	$80		$80
Total	**$20,600**		**$500**		**$500**

Janis's Predicted Results			
Debt	Paid Off By	Interest Paid	Amount Freed Up
Line of credit	Month 37	$1,120	$420
Student loan	Month 47	$1,067	$500 ($80 + $420)
Total	**Month 47**	**$2,187**	**$500**

"Okay," I said. "Ready?"

"Ready," she said.

I turned my screen around dramatically. "You'll be done in three years and eleven months and you'll save about $5,800 in interest."

"Wow!" she said. "That's good, right?"

"Yes, I think so. But how do you feel about the timeline?"

She laughed. "I'll still be 30 when I'm done. So even though it won't be in time for my birthday, I won't have turned 31 yet—not for another four months."

"How will you celebrate being debt-free?" I asked.

"Oh, wow. I haven't dared to dream about celebrating that in so long." She let out a really happy sigh. "I think I'd like to go on a trip. Nothing huge. Maybe just go lie on a beach for a week and read a million books."

"That sounds dreamy. Once you're living debt-free, you'll have an extra $500 a month. So if you put aside that $500 every month, you'll be able to save up $2,000 in four months. And then you can go on that trip in time for your 31st birthday!"

"That's rad."

"Totally," I said.

I'm happy to report that Janis finished her Debt Game Plan, never missed another payment and was able to blow $2,000 on her celebration trip. Consolidating her debt was the game-changing Debt-Slammer that took her from juggling three credit cards and making only minimum payments to a simplified, effective plan that was full of hope, without unrealistically eating into her Spending Money.

Janis was lucky to qualify for the line of credit. Approval criteria vary from lender to lender, so it's worth talking to a few potential lenders to see if you have a chance at qualifying. They should be able to run a preliminary test that isn't an actual application for credit to see if it's likely you'll qualify. That way it doesn't ding your credit, because you're not making a formal application.[*]

---

[*] See "Consolidation Methods" in the Resource Library (page 308).

If you don't qualify for a consolidation loan, line of credit or secured line of credit, don't lose hope. There could be other ways to hammer your debt down. Read on, my friend, read on!

Balance Transfers: A Like/Hate Relationship

I have a like/hate relationship with credit card balance transfers. If I had to pick a relationship status with balance transfers on social media, it would have to be "It's complicated." There's nothing simple about the decision to use or avoid a credit card balance transfer.

What is a credit card balance transfer? It's when a financial institution offers you a promotional interest rate such as zero, 1 percent or 2 percent for a certain length of time (usually six months to a year) to get you to transfer your existing, higher-interest credit card debt from another financial institution to the lower card. For example, if you had a credit card with a $4,000 balance that charged 19 percent interest, you might transfer the balance to another credit card charging no interest for a year.

The financial planning idea behind balance transfers is that you lower the interest rate on your debt and, if you can pay back the entire amount within the year, you save a ton of interest. Essentially this is a short-term debt-consolidation method. Ideally you save on interest and simplify multiple payments, and as a result you are able to pay down debt faster. This is the like part of my relationship with balance transfers.

The hate part of my complicated relationship with balance transfers stems from what happens if you don't manage to pay off the entire card—which happens, a lot. If you don't pay off the balance by the time the promotional rate is over, your interest rate is likely to skyrocket. I've seen it go as high as 24 percent! That's no good.

Let's use my client Lee as an example. Lee had $3,000 outstanding on a credit card that charged 18 percent interest, with a minimum payment of $90. He was tired of having the $90 pay mostly interest. We had a look at his income and expenses. There were no places to reduce his Fixed Expenses, and he and I agreed that a reduction in Spending Money would be unrealistic; he'd just keep taking on debt.

Unable to qualify for a line of credit or consolidation loan, Lee was considering a credit card balance transfer. Here's what the promotion offered: zero interest for 12 months (great), a 1 percent balance transfer fee (normal), no annual fee (great), and a 23 percent interest rate after the promotion ended (boo-urns). He qualified. Let's move Lee through two potential possibilities.

Possibility 1: Lee Succeeds

Lee transferred the $3,000 from the higher-interest card at 18 percent to the zero percent card. He now owed $3,030 (because of the 1 percent balance transfer fee). With no interest being charged, the $90 he paid each month was all going towards principal. When we sat down, I explained to him that if he didn't pay off the entire amount within the 12-month promotional period, his interest rate would shoot up to a whopping 23%.

Lee's Financial Snapshot	
Monthly After-Tax Income	**$2,195**
FIXED EXPENSES	
Rent (his share)	$900
Cellphone	$80
Cable/Internet/subscriptions	$60
Minimum debt payments:	
Credit card	$90
Student loan	$200
Total Fixed Expenses	**$1,330**
SHORT-TERM SAVINGS	
Big purchases	$90
Emergencies	$200
Total Short-Term Savings	**$200**

SPENDING MONEY	$665
Meaningful Savings (Magic Amount)	**$0**

"I could stop putting $200 into my emergency savings," he said.

I didn't want that for him. Lee had just landed a job after a stint of unemployment that led to the credit card debt in the first place. I wanted him to rebuild his emergency funds as well. However, there weren't really a lot of other options to lower his interest rate. I waffled. "How's your job security?" I asked.

"Good. Things are going okay. Why?"

"Well, if you redirected the $200 going into emergency savings to your debt, then you could pay off the transferred balance within 12 months. But that makes me really nervous—we'd be leaving you with no safety net. I mean, if anything goes wrong, there's no other way to pay than with more credit card debt. I just don't know."

"It will be fine. It's only a year. I'm pretty sure everything will be okay."

In the end, that's what he did. Lee proceeded with the balance transfer and redirected the $200 per month from his emergency savings to the credit card so that he was putting $290 per month towards the debt. He continued to live within his $665 Spending Money so he didn't take on more debt. A year later, Lee was living debt-free and had freed up that $290 per month. I had him restart putting $200 per month into his emergency account and $90 into his big purchases account, to handle future spikes in spending without going into debt.

"Do I ever start saving for a down payment or retirement?" he asked.

"Once you've got enough money in your emergency account to survive for three months without income, you can start putting the $200 per month to your nest-egg savings." It was our best-case scenario. Phew!

Possibility 2: Lee Does Not Succeed

"It will be fine. It's only a year. I'm pretty sure everything will be okay." Famous last words. The financial industry equivalent to the horror movie trope "I'll be right back."

Lee proceeded with the balance transfer and redirected the money from his emergency savings to the debt so that he was putting $290 per month towards the credit card. He continued to live within his $665 Spending Money—for about four months. Then he received a letter from the Canada Revenue Agency (CRA) saying that he owed them $325. The previous year, Lee had worked at several jobs. One of the jobs hadn't sent him a copy of his T4, so his accountant never got it. Lee received a refund of $500 that should have been only $125. He had no idea, and the money had been spent months ago.

That was Financial Tripwire Number 1. From his next paycheque he paid the CRA the $325 he owed, which reduced his Spending Money that month from $665 to $340. Which was not realistic at all for him. He ended up using his credit card to buy groceries the following week because his chequing account was all but empty. By the end of Month 4, the balance of his balance-transfer credit card had risen from $1,870 to $2,195.

Two months later, Lee overspent during the holidays and ended up with an additional $400 on his credit card. That was Tripwire Number 2, taking the balance in Month 6 from $1,615 to $2,015. Finally, in Month 10, he hurt his knee playing soccer and had to go to four physiotherapy sessions, which cost $120 a pop because he didn't have benefits at his job. Tripwire Number 3 = $480, which took his balance from $855 to $1,335.

As a result, Lee ended up with $755 left owing on his credit card when the promotional rate ended after Month 12. The interest rate shot up, and now he had to pay back $755 at 23 percent. Bummer. It was clear to me—and to him—that he needed to put money towards his Short-Term Savings for emergencies and big purchases. But if he continued to put $200 per month towards Short-Term Savings, he'd have only $90 to put towards his debt. At 23 percent interest, it would take him another nine months to pay it off.

Either way, the balance transfer was a gamble. There's a lot to be said for a promotional zero percent interest rate. Balance transfers are tempting and they can lower your interest rate so you can pay down debt fast. However, in order to meet the timeline given for the promotion, you may have to make unrealistic sacrifices in your spending and emergency savings. If you don't manage to pay it all back by the time it's over, your rate skyrockets to a level that's likely above the one you started with. Sure, you'll potentially owe less, but oftentimes I see people end up owing the same amount of debt, if not more.

Remember that the reason lenders offer these promotions is they want to make money. They are betting that you will move your money over to their credit card, then continue to use the card after the promotional period, at the much higher rate. Balance transfers are not aimed at helping you out of debt.

When Lee met me again after not being able to pay the balance transfer in full, he asked me something that usually makes me say *eep!!* "Should I do another balance transfer?"

"Eep!! No!"

Do not get stuck in a balance-transfer loop if you can help it. A balance-transfer loop is like a Debt Loop on steroids. Every time you apply for a transfer, it dings your credit rating because you're opening a new credit account while still maintaining a high debt level. The more balance transfers you do, the worse your credit score becomes. Then, when your promotional interest rate runs out, you have a balance on your card at a ridiculously high interest rate and you may not qualify for more transfers or other consolidation methods because your credit score is so low.

Here, then, is my advice when it comes to consolidating high-interest debt with a balance transfer. User beware, and err on the side of *do not use*.

- If you are determined to use a balance transfer, have a plan in place that has you *realistically* paying back the amount owing within the promotional rate period. No ifs, ands or buts. It must work.
- Watch the fees. If the balance-transfer fee adds more than 1 percent to the amount owing, avoid it.
- Pay attention to the terms. Are you allowed to use the card for new purchases? What happens if you miss a payment?
- Avoid the temptation to move from transfer to transfer. This creates a treacherous Debt Loop!

▶

Overall, lowering your interest rate and consolidating is a great way to ensure that the payments you make towards your debt hit more principal so you pay it back faster. Consolidating debt can also help you stay organized, because you may be swapping multiple payments to various cards and debts for one efficient monthly payment. It will feel so good to be able to focus on paying that back.

CHAPTER 11

Debt-Slammer #2: Lump Sums

Having savings in your bank accounts feels so good—it's like a warm blanket of calm. If you have a bad day or your boss is acting weird, you don't need to freak out because you know you've got a cushion. Or if you look at your credit card statement and it makes your stomach drop, you think, *It's okay. I still have my RRSP*. Aahhhhh. Calm. It's okay.

Imagine seeing $1,000 sitting in a savings account waiting for you. The possibilities for that $1,000 are endless. Maybe it's a trip or a bail-out; maybe it's part of a future down payment. Whatever it is, seeing your savings grow is powerful. It makes you feel financially responsible and capable. That $1,000 in savings increased your net worth by $1,000. Remember: your net worth is calculated by adding up your assets (everything you own) and subtracting your liabilities (everything you owe.)

Unfortunately, paying down debt doesn't give a lot of us the same warm-and-fuzzies as building savings. If your overall debt load decreases from $34,000 to $33,000, you've improved your net worth by $1,000, but it doesn't feel as exciting as seeing $1,000 in your savings account. Debt Game Plans give that same level of excitement only once you start to see change and believe, finally, that there is a light at the end of the tunnel. That's the key. It has to feel real to you, not me. I'd be stoked about a $1,000 decrease in your debt. But if that doesn't feel exciting to you, you may resent the money going towards debt instead of savings, which can rob you of your motivation.

I think the most common question I hear regarding debt is "How do I balance saving versus paying down debt?" It doesn't matter if you have oodles of money in your savings account or only $80 to your name, the drive to save money is strong and the irritation at seeing your hard-earned money go to pay back the past is often stronger. I also think that people feel guilty about taking their money out of savings to put it on debt, like it's a waste. They worked so hard to save, and *poof!* It's gone.

Savings let us dream about the future, and paying back debt feels like it has us stuck in the past. Here's the thing, though. Most times it makes more financial sense for you to stop putting money towards your savings and to redirect it towards your Magic Amount so you can hammer that debt. So my job is to get you to see that paying back the past is the best way to build your future.

Remember, by paying down debt above the minimum, your Magic Amount is actually a form of savings. It may not feel like it, but you are increasing your net worth, and that means you're making yourself better off financially. That's savings! There are times when you should save and times when you shouldn't.

Big Chunks of Change: How to Safely Pull Money from Savings

Meet Rod

Age: 35

Relationship status: just moved in with partner, Todd, but too soon to combine finances

Kids: 0

Annual gross household income: $58,000 (sole proprietorship)

Assets: $20,000 savings; $8,000 Tax-Free Savings Account (TFSA); $10,000 RRSP

Liabilities: $17,400 credit card debt

Rod's Debt Map			
Debt	**Amount Owing**	**Interest Rate**	**Minimum Payment**
Department store card	$2,000	21%	$60
Credit card A	$8,000	20%	$200
Credit card B (business)	$7,400	18%	$220
Total	**$17,400**		**$480**

Rod was a freelance web developer who lived in Toronto. He came to see me just over a year ago to make a savings plan.

"My partner, Todd, and I've just moved in together." He smiled. "Yes, we are Rod and Todd." He laughed and I giggled, because I'm a *Simpsons* fan and I also like things that rhyme.

"Todd is going back to school in 11 months, so I'm going to have to take on almost $1,000 more a month for our bills."

"Eep!!" I said.

He smiled. "Totally, but it's got to happen. We're playing the long game."

"Aw, that's great. I love how supportive you are of his career. So how long will he actually be in school?" I asked.

"It's a full-year program, 12 months straight."

I thought about that for a moment. "And how long until he gets a job or brings in income after school? If you had to guess . . ."

"He's pretty awesome and a really hard worker. To be conservative, let's say six months until he'll likely be able to land a new gig."

"Awesome. So that's 12 months in school and 6 months afterwards. Basically we need to ensure that you're okay for 18 months in total."

Rod needed to cover $1,000 extra each month for the next 18 months, once Todd starts school. "You'll need about $18,000 to make it all work," I said.

"You're right. I didn't think about the time after school ended. Are we in trouble?"

"Let's have a look."

Rod's Financial Snapshot	
Monthly After-Tax Income	**$3,500**
FIXED EXPENSES	
Rent (his share)	$850
Renters' insurance	$20
Cellphone	$100
Parking spot	$50
Car insurance	$120
Cable/Internet/subscriptions	$80
Gym membership	$65
Minimum debt payments:	
Department store card	$60
Credit card A	$200
Credit card B	$220
Total Fixed Expenses	**$1,765**
SHORT-TERM SAVINGS	
Vacation fund	$150
Emergencies	$50
Total Short-Term Savings	**$200**
SPENDING MONEY	$990
TOTAL COST OF LIFE	**$2,955**
MEANINGFUL SAVINGS	
TFSA (down payment fund)	$100
RRSP (down payment fund/retirement)	$100
Magic Amount	$345
Total Meaningful Savings	**$545**

"Tell me about the debt," I said.

"I've had debt in some form or another since graduating. The balances go up and down. The department store card is from when we bought a bunch of furniture, when we moved in together."

"Well, I think it's great that you're managing to put so much towards your debt in addition to the minimums," I said. "Your Magic Amount is $345. That's big!"

"Yes, well, without that I think it was going to take me years to pay back the debt, and I'd like to be done with it at some point."

I checked the Debt-Payoff Calculator. If Rod put nothing extra towards his debt and paid only the minimums, his Debt-Stacking Plan would take him approximately five years and he would pay approximately $10,000 in interest. With the Magic Amount of $345, his plan would play out like this:

Rod's Debt-Stacking Plan ($445 Magic Amount)					
Debt	Amount Owing	Interest Rate	Minimum Payment	Magic Amount	Payments Made
Store card	$2,000	21%	$60	$345	$505
Credit card A	$8,000	20%	$200		$200
Credit card B (business)	$7,400	18%	$220		$220
Total	**$17,400**		**$480**	**$345**	**$825**

Rod's Predicted Results			
Debt	**Paid Off By**	**Interest Paid**	**Amount Freed Up**
Store card	Month 6	$110	$505
Credit card A	Month 21	$1,776	$605 ($200 + $405)
Credit card B	Month 31	$2,314	$915 ($220 + $605)

Rod would have his debt paid off in two years and seven months, saving him just under $6,000 in interest. That was a great plan!

"Question," I said.

"Shoot."

"You've got loads of money in your savings account and you've also got money going to a TFSA and an RRSP. Why isn't all your extra money going towards your debt?"

"The $20,000 is already spent," he said.

"Lay it on me."

"Our vacation will cost me $2,500 in 10 months; about $7,500 is ear-marked for my income taxes, since I'm self-employed; and the rest is for emergencies."

"And the monthly savings to the TFSA and RRSP?"

"I've been saving up for a down payment in my TFSA. I started saving $100 to my RRSP every month when I was 25. My dad drilled that into my head."

I thought about it for a moment. "Rod, why do you think you haven't put any of your savings towards the debt?"

He put on a horrified expression. "It's scary!"

"What do you mean?"

"One time I did take a chunk of savings and put it towards my credit card, but it made me so nervous afterwards. I can't just empty my accounts. I feel safer with money in the bank."

I totally understood. That's why it's so important not to drain your accounts to the point where you have no emergency savings. Rod's worries were totally valid.

"Now tell me about the $100 per month to the RRSP. You can't use that money in a pinch, so why not shuffle that $100 to debt instead of your RRSP?"

"I guess I don't want this debt to hold me back forever. I want to buy a house one day. It makes me feel good to save it there. I've thought about it so many times, but it feels like it would take so long to become debt-free. And I'm worried that I'll never be able to bring my savings back up again." He sat back in his chair and let out a long sigh. "I just want to ensure that I'm getting the biggest bang for my buck."

Rod had made some great points. But right now he wasn't getting the best bang for his buck, emotionally or financially, with his current strategy.

"How do you feel about my toying with the idea that we use your savings to pay off debt?"

"I don't know. I'm getting a 6 percent return on my investments in the TFSA. My plan is to withdraw from it only if I need to."

At his current savings rate, he didn't have enough capacity to save up the $18,000 in the next 11 months. He would need to save $1,636 per month in order to do that, so he would definitely need to withdraw from his TFSA. This is a classic example of how people create guilt around using their savings, when there's no need. Rod wasn't prepared to use the money in the TFSA, even though he would have to, without a doubt.

I knew when he said "if I need to" that Rod would feel tremendous guilt every time he was forced to withdraw from his TFSA. He was (unrealistically) hoping that he wouldn't end up needing to do it. That would set him up for failure: he would resent his debt even more and potentially resent that his partner had gone back to school.

"I think we can put that money to better use," I told him. "Let's see what happens if we use a large chunk of it to pay back debt." I busted out the calculator.

Rod needed to have $18,000 available in 11 months, when Todd went back to school, so he could access $1,000 per month for 18 months. His available savings were as follows:

Rod's Available Savings	
Savings account	$20,000
TFSA	$8,000
Total	**$28,000**

I didn't include Rod's $10,000 RRSP in his available savings, since I did not want him to withdraw from his RRSP to pay down debt. Since Rod had a high income, he would have to pay taxes on the withdrawal at his marginal tax rate of 30 percent. Losing 30 percent to taxes would be expensive—more expensive than the interest rate he was paying on his debt. Between his non-invested savings and the invested $8,000 in his TFSA, his total Available Money was therefore $28,000.

But a lot of that money was something I call Earmarked Short-Term Savings. That means it's there in your savings account but you can't use it to pay down debt, because it's already promised for something else. Earmarked Short-Term Savings usually include things like

- Trips already half paid for. They are happening for sure.
- Big events like weddings that you've RSVP'd to already. You're definitely going.
- Emergencies:
  - house repairs that must happen
  - car repairs that must happen
  - medical spending that's likely to happen
  - job loss
  - unexpected tax bills

For Rod, his Earmarked Short-Term Savings included his taxes, a vacation and his emergency savings. I wanted to double-check the numbers.

Rod put aside 25 percent of his business revenue for income taxes. So far that year he had made $30,000 after deducting business expenses (excluding sales tax) and expected to earn $58,000 in total for the calendar year. To date he knew that he needed to have $7,500 ($30,000 × 25 percent) in his savings account for income taxes,[*] so we couldn't touch any of that. Dang.

---

[*] Rod and I used the online tax calculator in the Resource Library (see "Tax Estimator," page 301).

He was also putting $150 per month towards his vacation and needed to have $2,500 available in 10 months. At $150 per month, he was going to be able to save another $1,500 over that time. So $1,000 ($2,500 – $1,500) of his current savings was earmarked for the trip. Also non-negotiable. Dang again.

Last, I wanted to look at his emergency savings. His Fixed Expenses were $765 and he figured he would need about $640 per month for food, gas and basic life if he didn't have any money coming in. This came to $2,405 per month. Since he was self-employed, I suggested that he have four months minimum saved up. Therefore he needed $9,620 ($2,405 × 4). Dang, dang, dang.

Rod's total Earmarked Short-Term Savings were $18,120 ($7,500 + $1,000 + $9,620). Therefore only $1,880 of the $20,000 in his non-invested savings account was up for grabs. If he needed $18,000 to help cover Todd's half of expenses for the next 18 months, he would be short $16,120 ($18,000 – $1,880), proving that at some point money was going to have to come out of the TFSA, one way or another.

The next thing to consider was the fact that Rod was earning 6 percent on the investments in his TFSA. Which is great, but it's not 18 percent, 20 percent or 21 percent—the interest rates he was paying on his credit card debt.

Let's break it down for a second. The math usually works in favour of paying down debt. It's the rare situation where you'd be looking at an interest rate on debt that is lower than the return you're getting on your investments. I get asked about this often when the stock markets are good and debt is cheap. The classic example is not paying down a line of credit and keeping the assets invested. If you're earning 6 percent on investments but being charged only 3.5 percent on your line of credit, on paper at least, it makes more sense to invest.

But think about this for a moment. Stock markets, bond markets, cryptocurrency markets, gold coins—all of them have risk. They are naturally volatile. They go up and they also go down. And some are more volatile than others. That doesn't mean you should be scared of investing, far from it. My point is that it's normal for investment markets to rise and fall; that's a normal part of investing. Investment market returns are *not guaranteed*. Whatever you got last year, last quarter or even since you started investing is not guaranteed going forward. No one has a crystal ball—no one.

If you've got investments, check the amount they are worth today. Tomorrow they could be worth more—or less. That's the nature of investing. Here's the thing: the 19 percent you are being charged on your credit card and the 3.5 percent on your line of credit *are* guaranteed. You're going to pay that interest whether you like it or not.

So comparing the returns from money going towards your debt to the returns you get in the stock market is like comparing apples to oranges. They are different. What you really should be comparing your debt to is a financial product called a guaranteed investment certificate (GIC). GICs pay a guaranteed amount of interest on the amount you invest. If you have a GIC with an annual interest rate of 2 percent and you invest $100, at the end of the term you'll get 2 percent in interest plus your $100 back—guaranteed. In this case, that would come to $102.

To me this is much more comparable to the interest you're paying on your debt. So if you're debating whether paying down debt will get you the best bang for your buck financially, don't compare it to returns from your investment account or the ones the person at the watercooler was bragging about (can you tell I have a 1990s vision of an office workplace?). Compare the interest rate you're being charged on your debt to the interest you'd make on a GIC. You'll see that the best bang for your buck is almost always to pay back debt— financially *and* emotionally.

For Rod, I wanted to see if it was possible for him to be debt-free by the time Todd stopped working. This would free up $825—his $480 minimum debt payments plus the $345 Magic Amount—almost the

$1,000 he would be short each month. It would be a two-step process. First he would use his available savings to pay down as much debt as possible. Second, he would redirect his monthly contributions from the TFSA and RRSP to the debt.

Recall that Rod had $1,880 in his non-invested savings account that I could put towards his debt, plus a withdrawal of $8,000 from his TFSA. That would give him $9,880 that he could pay as a lump sum towards his Debt-Stacking Plan. He also had $10,000 in an RRSP, but I didn't want to use those funds; he would have to pay too much tax on the withdrawal.*

Of the $9,880 lump-sum payment, Rod would use the first $2,000 to pay off the department store card, freeing up $60 per month, which he would add to the Magic Amount, bringing it up to $405. Then the $6,880 left over would go to credit card A, leaving only $1,120 to be repaid. In addition, I would redirect the $100 per month that was going to the TFSA and the $100 a month going to his RRSP to his Magic Amount, making the amount above minimum payments that he put towards debt $605 ($405 + $100 + $100).

With the department store card paid off, his new Debt-Stacking Plan would look like this:

Rod's New Debt-Stacking Plan					
Debt	Amount Owing	Interest Rate	Minimum Payment	Magic Amount	Payments Made
Credit card A	$1,120	20%	$200	$605	$805
Credit card B (business)	$7,400	18%	$220		$220
Total	**$8,520**		**$420**	**$605**	**$1,125**

---

* Check out the Available Money section on pages 188–190 to learn about the tax and investment implications of doing this.

Rod's Predicted Results			
Debt	Paid Off By	Interest Paid	Amount Freed Up
Credit card A	Month 2	$24.23	$805
Credit card B	Month 9	$645	$1,025

Then, save $1,025 for the last two months before Todd goes back to school.

Oh yes, he would be debt-free in 12 months!

"Check it out!" I exclaimed excitedly. "By using your savings now to pay off your debt in a big chunk, you can be living debt-free in only nine months from now with $2,050 in the bank. Just in time for Todd to go back to school! Paying back your debt frees up enough money each month that you will be able to handle the $1,000 increase in bills and still save $75 to your RRSP. Plus, you'll still be putting $150 into Short-Term Savings!"

"Are you serious?" Rod said. "No, that's not possible."

"Take a look," I said, and pointed to the screen. "The numbers don't lie!"

"But what about retirement? Shouldn't I at least keep putting money towards my RRSP?"

"You're 32 years old, Rod. You have at least 33 years until you retire! That's a lot of time to do a lot of saving. Taking 12 months off to repay debt is not going to make or break your retirement plan, but it will make or break your debt-repayment plan."

"Everyone always says, 'Start young, start young.' It makes me nervous not having anything going towards retirement."

"Paying down debt *is* a form of retirement savings. The money going towards your debt right now in minimum payments and interest is money that could be going into your RRSP and TFSA in the future. Freeing up cash flow by paying off these debts will allow you to save more in the future. Let me show you," I said.

Rod's New Financial Snapshot		
	New Plan	**18-Month School Plan**
Monthly After-Tax Income	**$3,500**	**$3,500**
FIXED EXPENSES		
Rent (shared)	$850	$1,700
Renters' insurance (shared)	$20	$40
Cellphone	$100	$100
Parking spot (shared)	$50	$100
Car insurance	$120	$120
Cable/Internet/subscriptions (shared)	$80	$160
Gym membership	$65	$65
Minimum debt payments:		
Department store card (paid with lump sum)	0	0
Credit card A	$200	0
Credit card B	$220	0
Total Fixed Expenses	**$1,705**	**$2,285**
SHORT-TERM SAVINGS		
Vacation fund	$150	$50
Emergencies	$50	$100
Total Short-Term Savings	**$200**	**$150**
SPENDING MONEY	$990	$990
MEANINGFUL SAVINGS		
TFSA (down payment fund)	0	0
RRSP (down payment fund/retirement)	0	$75
Magic Amount	$605	0
Total Meaningful Savings	**$605**	**$125**

"You're about to free up $1,025 per month, once you are debt-free. Then you'll be able to use $1,000 to survive life while Todd is in school.

Once Todd is out of school and has a job, you can save that $1,000 per month for retirement, because you won't have debt anymore! That's 29 months from today and you will be 35 by then. Assuming that you'll have $2,210 in your TFSA and $10,000 in your RRSP 29 months from now—the existing $8,000 plus the $75 per month you'll put in for 18 months, with a net rate of return of 5 percent—once you're 35 you can save an additional $1,000 per month towards retirement. Which is a ton of money to save! If you sustained that, with a 5 percent rate of return you would have $889,900* in retirement savings by the time you're 65 years old—simply by redirecting the money that used to go towards debt into your retirement savings."

"Oh. Wow. Okay," he said.

"So, long story short, you're fine," I said with a smile.

He ran his hands through his hair and sat back. "I can't even comprehend being debt-free in a year. I don't know what life is like without debt."

"Who will debt-free Rod be?" I said. "I'm so excited for you to find out!"

"I'm so in. I can't wait to tell Todd. This is such a wild turn of events."

"Why do you think it feels so surprising?" I asked.

"I guess my debt has made me feel so broke for so long that I just got used to it being there. Having debt scared me less than emptying savings accounts. It's weird."

"Like an old friend."

He laughed. "Kind of, actually. I just expected to have it for a long time."

Now that I had Rod's buy-in, it was just a matter of logistics. "The only thing we need to be careful of is how you sell the investments in your TFSA."

"What do you mean?"

"Since you invested, it's possible that your investments have moved to a gain or loss position. If you've made money, it's likely that they're in a gain position; that means you bought for less than they are worth

---

* See "Long-Term Savings Calculator" in the Resource Library (page 308).

today. If you've lost money, your investments will be worth less than you bought them for, which is a loss position. Since you're withdrawing money from a TFSA, when you sell them, you won't have to pay tax on any money you've made. So let's hope your investments have made money."

"Buy low, sell high, right?" he said.

"Exactly. Ideally, you don't want to sell when you're in a loss position. That's called 'locking in a loss.' Because essentially you're buying high and selling low."

We logged in to his financial institution. The market value of his index fund was higher than the book value (the price he paid). So Rod was in a gain position and therefore could sell $8,000 in investments and withdraw the money from the TFSA without worrying about locking in a loss or paying tax. It was ideal.

I checked in with Rod in Month 11 to see if he had made it. "So, how did it go?" I asked.

"We did it!" he exclaimed. "I'm debt-free and have $2,050 back in my TFSA."

"And how do you feel?" I asked.

"It doesn't feel real. I keep logging in to my bank just to look at it. No debt—I can't believe it."

"Congratulations!"

"Thank you so much for everything."

"Don't thank me. You're the one who saved up the money and executed the plan. All I did was show you how to make your money work better for you."

"Totally. I never would have had the guts to use my savings to pay down debt. It's like I knew I should but I just couldn't pull the trigger."

I was so proud of him. Pulling money out of savings or redirecting savings towards debt can feel scary, and for good reason. Saving money takes time and it can feel like you worked so hard to build it up. But I promise you, paying down your debt *is* savings. You're making your future better and you're getting the biggest bang for your buck—financially and emotionally.

Trust me. Prioritizing paying debt over building savings can shave years and years off your Debt Game Plan and save you thousands in interest. Don't be afraid to empty out those bank accounts to put lump sums towards your debt. As long as you've covered your butt for any Earmarked Short-Term Savings and you're not paying tax penalties on your withdrawals, you're likely getting the very best bang for your buck.

How to Efficiently Withdraw Money from Savings to Pay Down Debt

Step 1: Separate your savings.

Separate savings accounts that are invested from accounts that are not invested. You'll want to prioritize withdrawing money from accounts that are not invested over accounts that are, so you won't have to worry about investment markets and whether you are in a loss or gain position.

Step 2: Calculate your Available Money.

Available Money is money that you can *potentially* withdraw safely to pay down debt.

Non-invested money should be considered first. You'll note that I have not included RRSP accounts in the list below. Yes, I know I did that very thing, but—depending on your situation, age, goals and income—it may not be worth it to use your RRSP to pay down debt. There is no black-and-white answer here. I know it seems like a cop-out, but I can't give you a definite answer. What I can tell you is that you need to get some customized, unbiased financial advice. Until then, assume that you will not be pulling money from an RRSP to pay down your debt.

In order of priority, non-invested money includes money in

- chequing accounts
- savings accounts
- Tax-Free Savings Accounts

Invested money comes next. There are potentially complex investment and tax consequences of withdrawing money from invested non-registered or TFSA accounts. I am also flagging this as something you should get some unbiased financial advice on before proceeding with any of the transactions below. In order of priority, invested money includes money in

- **Non-registered accounts**

  If the account is in a gain position, you will have to pay tax on the amount of capital gains. Be sure to get customized advice on the tax consequences of this so you put aside enough for taxes.

  If the account is in a loss position, you do not need to pay tax on any part of the withdrawal. Note that you are locking in a loss by doing this (buying high and selling low). However, because this happened in a non-registered account, it likely qualifies as an allowable capital loss, which you can apply against any taxable capital gains you made for the three preceding years or in any future year. That's great! Even though you're taking a loss, at least it can help lower your previous year's or future taxes. That doesn't happen when you lock in a loss with a TFSA or RRSP. Even so, I still suggest that you get custom advice from your financial planner or accountant.

- **TFSAs in a gain position**

  Because you can't use a capital loss in a TFSA against taxable capital gains (because it's a tax-sheltered account), it's not ideal to withdraw money from a TFSA that's in a significant loss position. If the market value (what it's worth today) of your TFSA investments is lower than the book value or adjusted cost (what you paid for them), then you have a tough choice to make. This is unique to your situation, so it's impossible for me to give advice that will be right for you. I suggest that you get custom advice from your financial planner or accountant.

189

Add up all the money that is available to withdraw. This is your total Available Money.

Non-invested money in a chequing account	$ _____
Non-invested money in a savings account	$ _____
Non-invested money in a TFSA account	$ _____
Approved invested money in a non-registered account	$ _____
Approved invested money in a TFSA account	$ _____
Total Available Money	$ _____

Step 3: Tally up Earmarked Short-Term Savings.

If you have money in savings, there may be some that you need to leave there because you have a short-term use for it. Such savings typically include

- Taxes, especially if you're self-employed.
- Trips already half paid for—they are definitely happening and can't be cancelled.
- Big events like weddings that you've already RSVP'd to—you're definitely going.
- Your own wedding fund—it's happening in a few months and there's money saved up.
- Emergencies:
  - house repairs that must happen
  - car repairs that must happen
  - medical spending that's likely to happen
  - job loss

Think about expenses that you must pay for in the next six months to a year that you absolutely cannot get out of. Tally them up.

Step 4: Calculate your Safe Money.

Subtract your Earmarked Short-Term Savings from your Available Money. That's the amount you can safely withdraw in order to pay down debt.

Step 5: Pull the trigger.

Withdraw your Safe Money and pay down that debt! Then do a happy dance, because you've just shaved years off your timeline and tons in interest!

Little Chunks of Change

If you don't have any money in savings right now, that's okay! There are other ways to come up with some money to pay off your debt. My client Grace lived in Winnipeg. She had $125 to her name and was $6,000 in debt. "It feels hopeless," she said.

Meet Grace

Age: 30
Relationship status: newly dating but not living together
Kids: Do nieces that I'm obsessed with count?
Annual gross household income: $40,000
Assets: 0
Liabilities: $6,000 credit card debt

Grace owed $6,000 on a department store credit card that charged 19 percent interest; the minimum monthly payment was $180, but she didn't have any wiggle room in her monthly expenses to put more than $110 towards the card. She had already called her lender, and they wouldn't reduce her interest rate. She didn't qualify for a line of credit or a consolidation loan and could not realistically pay back a transferred balance within a 12-month promotional period.

"It's never hopeless," I assured her. "We just need to think creatively."

Grace's Financial Snapshot	
Monthly After-Tax Income	**$2,500**
FIXED EXPENSES	
Rent	$1,400
Renters' insurance	$25
Cellphone	$80
Life insurance	$45
Disability insurance	$70
Cable/Internet/subscriptions	$70
Minimum debt payment: credit card	$110
Total Fixed Expenses	**$1,800**
SHORT-TERM SAVINGS	
Vacation fund	0
Emergencies	0
Total Short-Term Savings	**0**
SPENDING MONEY	$700
TOTAL COST OF LIFE	**$2,500**
Meaningful Savings (Magic Amount)	**0**

If you're in a situation where you can't lower the interest rate on your debt, qualify for consolidation or afford to put much towards it per month except the minimum payment, that's okay. The big lever you need is to find a way to lower the *amount* of debt you owe right away, even if it's by only a small amount, so that your monthly minimum payment has a chance of hitting the principal. Basically, haul ass to see if you can find chunks of change.

"We need to find a way to put a chunk of money into your credit card right away," I said.

"Obviously I'd love that too," Grace said. "But I'm not in the will of a rich great-uncle or anything."

"Is there any chance you could have a sort of online garage sale?" I asked. "I've had clients in similar situations do that, and it was very successful."

"I guess so." She paused. "I mean, I've got clothes and stuff that I never wear and loads of books, but I don't think I could make more than $150. Maybe $200 max," she said and shrugged her shoulders.

"That's great!" I said excitedly.

"Is it? I mean, what can $200 do?"

"Since you only have the $110 each month to put towards the credit card, only a small portion is actually hitting the principal. Most of it is just going to interest. We need to figure out a way to lower the balance by any amount we can, since we can't lower the interest rate. Right now, if you keep paying only the $110, it will take ten years and five months to pay it back, with $7,951 in interest, and will hurt your credit."

"That's totally depressing," she said.

"But wait." I pulled out the Debt-Payoff Calculator. "If you put $200 on your credit card this month from your garage sale, you'll bring the balance outstanding to $5,800. That would reduce your overall timeline to nine years and five months. Basically, $200 would save you an entire year of your repayment plan. That's nothing to scoff at!"

"Two hundred dollars would shave off an entire year?" she said.

"Yes, look!" I showed her.

"Wow. Okay, that's actually super-motivating. I didn't think such a small amount could do anything."

"It's because you're using it as a lump-sum payment right away. Every payment after that will hit more and more principal."

"That's amazing! I'm definitely going to do that."

"Awesome. Yes, little chunks of change have a big impact, so if there are any other ways you can bring in a larger sum of money right away, I'm all for it."

She thought for a moment. "Well, I could do the garage sale thing, but I could also use an online B&B site to rent out my apartment. I'm gone for two weeks next month, so I could probably make $500, and I know my landlady is cool with it."

"That would be amazing. It will translate into approximately $400 after tax.[*] Don't forget to put aside 20 percent for income taxes."

"Right," she said. "Speaking of taxes, I usually get a refund. The past two years it's been about $300. Oh, oh! And I get those government cheques—$106 every three months."

"Wonderful. Yes, the GST credit.[†] See? There *is* extra money!"

"Yeah, you're right. I think I'm so used to feeling desperate that when those chunks of money come in, I don't want to put them towards debt. I want to keep them. But I think it's also because I didn't believe they would have an impact."

"Well, they do. Let's brainstorm and tally up all the potential money you could bring in, either in lump sums or in extra income."

Lump-Sum Sources	
Online garage sale	$200
Short-stay apartment rental	$400 (after tax)
Total lump sums to debt	**$600**
New timeline	8 years
Interest saved	$2,835.36

"Okay, so if you did only the online garage sale and the online rental once," I said, "you would shave two and a half years from your plan and save $2,835 in interest."

She laughed. "Holy sh*t, that's amazing! And what about the GST credit cheques and tax refunds?" she asked. "And what if I took up my neighbour on her offer of $20 to shovel her driveway in the winter?"

"Well, let's see."

[*] See "Tax Estimator" in the Resource Library (page 301).

[†] See "GST/HST Credit" in Additional Reading (page 311).

Extra Income Sources	
GST/HST credit cheques	$424 ($106 every quarter)
Tax refund	$150 in April (Grace's tax refund was usually $300, but I suggested she put half towards her debt and keep half to help pay for daily life.)
Snow shovelling	$120 in January–February
Total per year	$704

"I'm going to assume that the numbers remain the same over your entire Debt Game Plan, but it's possible they may change. If your income goes up you may not qualify for the GST credit anymore. If your tax situation changes, you may not get a refund. See what I mean?" I said.

"Yes, for sure."

"So the assumption is that if these things do change somehow, it's likely because your income has gone up. Hopefully, with that higher income you would manage to find other creative ways to still put $704 per year into your debt in addition to the $110 payment."

"If my income goes up, I'll be able to save. Or I might still be able to rent out my place or hustle up something else."

"Okay, so here we go." We crunched the numbers. The impact on Grace's Debt Game Plan was significant: a six-year timeline and $4,517 in interest saved.

I showed her the Debt-Payoff Calculator. "See? This shaved four and a half years off your timeline and saved over $4,500 in interest, just by paying a small lump sum at the beginning and then getting creative with small boosts in income through the year. You can do this all without reducing your spending to an unrealistic level."

She was stoked. "This is amazing! I still can't get over the fact that the garage sale and the one-time rental income reduce the timeline by two and a half years. That's bananas!"

"The more lump sums or additional windfalls you can throw at the debt, the better. Everything helps, and a little goes a very long way—and, of course, not taking on more debt."

She laughed. "Obviously."

"How does this feel?" I asked.

"Good. I feel empowered that I can actually do something. I felt like I didn't have any options, and when you have lots of debt, $200 from a garage sale feels like a drop in the bucket. I didn't realize that it could make such a difference overall."

"The sooner you can put any lump-sum amount towards your debt, the better the entire plan works."

Just as Grace realized, don't ever lose faith. Small amounts of money can do a lot of heavy lifting. Have a look for yourself, using the Debt-Payoff Calculator. See how long it will take to pay back your debt and how much interest you'll pay without making any additional payments. Then reduce the balance owing by $100 and see the change—$100 goes a long way! Lump sums are very powerful because they reduce the amount owing from the get-go, so the minimum payments you're making will hit more principal from the start. This will set your Debt Game Plan on an entirely new trajectory.

Selling things, earning side-hustle money, using tax credits or refunds, extra paycheque money once CPP and EI are maxed out, bonuses—these are all examples of powerful Debt-Slammers. They can be used to seriously improve your finances and accelerate your Debt Game Plan. You don't have to put an epic amount of money onto your debt to get an epic outcome.

Part Four

Paying Down Debt When Real Life Happens

By this point you've done a deep dive into yourself and your monthly cash flow and you've made a sustainable, motivating Debt Game Plan—*your* Debt Game Plan. Well done!

You now recognize your Financial Tripwires and know how to avoid them. You've got your Financial Touchstone to remind you in your weak moments why you're doing this. And you know your Magic Amount—how much you can realistically put towards debt without setting yourself up for failure—and how to speed up the process with Debt-Slammers.

Then why isn't the book over? I mean, you've got everything you need, right? Wrong. Debt is complex and so is life, and some complicated life stuff is bound to happen to you during your Debt Game Plan. Things like borrowing money from people who want it back too soon; how your debt affects your relationships with others; and being too broke to put any money towards your debt. Also, what happens if you actually need to talk to a bankruptcy trustee? You know, real-life stuff.

This part of the book will help you survive real life with debt. Because that's the point. You need to be able to live your life and still pay down debt.

CHAPTER 12

The Emotional Cost of Debt

Debt is complex, and how you feel about your debt is even more complex. When you've got multiple debts—credit cards, line of credit, income taxes due, overdraft, student loan—it may take you a few years to pay everything down and you may have entirely different feelings about each one. Maybe you don't mind living with your student loan for the next 20 years, but if you have to look at that negative chequing account balance one more time, you're going to freak out.

As I mentioned in Chapter 8, usually your Debt-Stacking Plan should prioritize paying down debt according to interest rate. This is definitely the mathematical best bang for your buck, hands down. But is prioritizing debt by interest rate the most motivating? Not always. Sure it is for the first three to six months, when everyone is all amped up, but then life sets in.

The daily grind requires you to constantly choose between supporting your Debt Game Plan and doing what probably seems more fun, more exciting and much easier. It's hard, especially if your Debt Game Plan will take years. With a Debt-Stacking Plan, your debts with lower interest rates might hang in there for years, simply getting the minimum payment while you focus on paying down the higher-interest debts. That doesn't always sit well with people.

The idea of a certain debt just sitting there for years getting only the minimum can give people anxiety. Then, in a fit of panic (*I can't take it anymore!*), they'll ramp up their Magic Amount to an unrealistic level to start hammering debt down faster, setting themselves up for failure and then giving up entirely. Or perhaps they'll empty their emergency fund and then get stuck having to bail themselves out of debt again. Either way, they end up stuck in the Debt Loop over and over.

Why does this happen? Why would you freak out halfway through your Debt Game Plan and go back to yo-yo budgets, overly aggressive timelines and failure? Because you probably didn't take the emotional cost of your debt into account.

The Emotional Cost of Debt

Some debts can be more emotionally painful than others, even if the interest rate is lower. It's the debt you hate the most that has the highest emotional cost for you. If you have a debt that has a high emotional cost but a low interest rate, stacking your debt and prioritizing by highest interest rate is going to make you miserable the entire time you're paying down the debt. You're prolonging your aggravation, frustration, lows.

My client Bob had a $5,000 interest-free loan from his parents. Obviously this was the lowest financial priority in his Debt-Stacking Plan. His overall Debt Game Plan was going to take 37 months, or just over three years. Since the family loan was interest-free, it would be paid last because he'd be focusing on paying off higher-interest debts for the first two years. But he felt incredibly guilty about the fact that he wouldn't be making any additional payments to his family for two years, and the loan had created awkwardness between him and his dad—Thanksgiving had been uncomfortable. He felt guilty about paying off other debts first, even though mathematically it was the smarter thing to do. In addition, having the family loan outstanding while making only minimum payments to his dad made him feel as if he wasn't allowed to spend anything at all on vacations or clothes—nothing beyond the necessities—until the balance was paid off.

I didn't know if Bob's dad was doing anything to make him feel that way, but it didn't really matter. That was how Bob felt. Had I forced him into paying the highest-interest-rate debt first, two things would have happened. First, his entire three-year Debt Game Plan would be so much more stressful for him, because the family loan would always be lurking, constantly making him feel guilty. Second, he would likely give up and do it his way, paying money towards the family loan first but feeling sheepish and financially irresponsible the entire time.

So I gave Bob permission to pay off the family loan first, even though it wasn't the biggest financial win to do so. Getting that loan off his plate freed him from the Shame-and-Blame Mentality that kept him feeling like a failure. Knowing he would soon be free of family debt meant he could coexist with the rest of his debts, keep calm and carry on. An emotional win is just as exciting (if not more so) than a financial win.

Not a lot of financial planners acknowledge this very important point, but it's imperative for your motivation and ability to stick to your Debt Game Plan. Acknowledging the emotional cost of debt can make it so your Debt Game Plan doesn't feel like punishment. Paying debt can feel as good as saving if it's not hellish for you.

It's not like you pay off the most emotionally exhausting debt first and then just chill. You probably picked up this book because you're in a place where you want to be living debt-free again. I'm just saying, if there's a particular debt that's taking an emotional toll on your overall well-being, it's okay to pay that down first, even if it's at a lower interest rate, so you can keep motivated and on track with your overall Debt Game Plan.

My client Tammy is a great example of how to prioritize your debt by emotional cost so that your life isn't hell the entire time you're paying back other debts.

The Breakup-Debt Debate

Meet Tammy

Age: 37

Relationship status: single (recent *terrible* breakup)

Kids: not yet

Annual gross household income: $60,000

Assets: condo valued at $450,000; $3,000 in emergency account

Liabilities: $220,000 mortgage; $4,000 credit card debt; $5,000 line of credit

Tammy's Debt Map			
Debt	Amount Owing	Interest Rate	Minimum Payment
Credit card	$4,000	19.99%	$200
Line of credit	$5,000	5.00%	$60
Total	**$9,000**		**$180**

When Tammy booked her appointment, she left a specific note to me on her intake form: *Need to get in as soon as possible. Debt emergency.* When I looked at her finances, I was kind of shocked. Debt emergency? Maybe I've seen too much, but I didn't really sense the same need for urgency as she did. She had a great income, could afford her home and was carrying $9,000 in debt, $5,000 of which was on a lower-interest-rate line of credit. Was I missing something? Was there a secret payday loan lurking?

"Tammy, what is the debt emergency?" I asked.

"This." She pointed to the colour-coded financial binder she had brought along (a Virgo!). "I need to be debt-free as soon as possible and I can't seem to make headway. I need help." She was talking really fast (I'm a fast talker, so that's saying something). Her anxiety was palpable.

"Tell me about your debt," I said. "Has it been building over a long period of time? Or did it come all at once?"

"All recent. The credit card is a trip I went on and some new furniture after a move." She paused for a moment and took a deep breath. "I was engaged."

"Okay," I said.

"He called it off four months before the wedding. It's been—" Her voice cracked and I reached out to put my hand on hers. She took another deep breath. "It's been a f*cked-up year."

"I can only imagine. I'm so sorry you're hurting."

"Thanks," she said, and I passed her some tissues.

"I hate that I'm still crying over this." She shook her head as if to snap herself out of it. "Anyway, the f*cking line of credit is the $5,000 I got left with after putting down deposits for the wedding that he totally let me pay even though he was seeing someone else. That jerk. Ten years—so much time, so much money. All wasted."

And there it was, the reason that $9,000 of debt felt like an absolute emergency. To Tammy it was—an emotional emergency.

"That must have been really difficult."

"Yeah, well." She brushed away the tears, took a big settling breath and forced a smile. "Can you help?"

"Absolutely," I said.

Here's a snapshot of Tammy's finances after we calculated her original Magic Amount:

Tammy's Financial Snapshot	
Monthly After-Tax Income	**$3,550**
FIXED EXPENSES	
Mortgage	$1,085
Condo fees	$500
Property tax	$200
Home insurance	$75

Cellphone	$100
Life insurance premiums	$70
Cable/Internet/subscriptions	$40
Minimum debt payments:	
Credit card	$120
Line of credit	$60
Total Fixed Expenses	**$2,250**
SHORT-TERM SAVINGS	
Psychotherapy	$200
Vacation/big purchases	$100
Emergencies	0
Total Short-Term Savings	**$3,000**
SPENDING MONEY	$900
TOTAL COST OF LIFE	**$3,450**
Magic Amount	**$100**

Tammy's Debt Stack, Prioritized by Interest Rate					
Debt	Amount Owing	Interest Rate	Minimum Payment	Magic Amount	Payments Made
Credit card	$4,000	19.99%	$120	$100	$220
Line of credit	$5,000	5.00%	$60	0	$60
Total	**$9,000**		**$180**	**$100**	**$280**

If Tammy stuck to the traditional Debt-Stacking Plan, prioritizing the highest interest rate first, her Debt Game Plan would play out like this:

Tammy's Predicted Results			
Debt	**Paid Off By**	**Interest Paid**	**Amount Freed Up**
Credit card	Month 22	$804	$220
Line of credit	Month 38	$558	$280 ($60 + $220)

"Okay, Tammy, on your current trajectory it will take just over three years to pay all this down, plus $1,391.39 in interest," I said, and showed her the screen.

"Wait. Am I not touching the line of credit until the end of Year 2?" she said as she studied the numbers.

"Correct. You'll focus your additional monthly savings—your $100 Magic Amount—on the credit card first, because it has the higher interest rate. Once that's paid down to zero, you'll scoop up the additional minimum monthly payment and pop that onto the line of credit." I smiled. "It's called debt stacking—"

"No, no, that's not going to work," she said, almost panicking. "It has to happen faster than that. I can put more on. I used to save $450 a month before the breakup."

"When we calculated your Magic Amount, it was based on some pretty realistic numbers," I said. "But the Magic Amount came to only $100. Have you been able to sustainably put $450 towards your debt?"

She sighed. "No. My expenses have gone up since the breakup. I've got full housing costs and have been going out more with friends and seeing my therapist twice a month."

"It doesn't seem like you're living extravagantly, but you may not be used to the higher cost of housing now that you're on your own. I'm happy to go through the list with you and look for ways to reduce spending, but do you honestly feel that's realistic? I don't want you to leave here with a plan that you can't follow through on because it doesn't reflect what you need in your life right now, while you're healing."

"No, you're right." She groaned. "I'm just so frustrated that I can't do more. This can't take three years. It just can't."

"Tell me why."

"Because I can't even log in to my online banking without wanting to throw up. Every time I see that line of credit there, it represents $5,000 spent on a wedding that will never happen, $5,000 from a life that I don't lead anymore. I feel like I can't move forward until it's gone, because it's a constant reminder of my failed relationship. Having it sit there for two years before I manage to put more money towards it makes me feel so stuck." Tears rolled down her face again. Man, this was tough.

"I hear you," I said gently. "What if you paid down the line of credit first?"

"What do you mean? Isn't the credit card's interest rate ridiculously high?"

"It is, but it's not always only about the numbers on paper," I said. "My job is to find the sweet spot between financial responsibility and happiness. That's where you'll have the most success with any financial plan. Would putting your extra $100 a month towards the line of credit make you feel as if your life is moving forward again?"

She thought about it. "Yes. If I could just see that amount dropping, I'd feel as if I was moving towards getting it done, like I'm not stuck in a rut. I need that $5,000 gone."

"Then that's what we'll do. Obviously the emotional cost of your line of credit is much higher than the emotional cost of your credit card. So why don't we give you some relief and start there."

"Won't I be wasting a ton of money?" she asked.

"Let's find out." We used the Debt-Payoff Calculator to work out both solutions.

Tammy's Debt Stack, Prioritized by Emotional Cost					
Debt	Amount Owing	Interest Rate	Minimum Payment	Magic Amount	Payments Made
Line of credit	$5,000	5.00%	$60	$100	$160
Credit card	$4,000	19.99%	$120	0	$120
Total	**$9,000**		**$180**	0	**$280**

Predicted Results			
Debt	**Paid Off By**	**Interest Paid**	**Amount Freed Up**
Line of credit	Month 34	$368	$160
Credit card	Month 40	$1,758	$280

The Comparison		
	Traditional Debt Stack	Emotional Cost Debt Stack
Time to pay off	38 months	40 months
Interest paid	$1,362	$2,126

"Tammy, if you prioritize your debt by highest emotional cost, your Debt Game Plan will take you an extra two months and you'll pay an additional $764 in interest. Does that feel worth it to you?"

"Yes. One hundred percent yes," she said immediately. "I would literally pay someone $764 right now to feel as if I can start my life again. And two months is nothing in the grand scheme of life."

I agreed. You cannot put a price tag on your emotions. Maybe for you paying an extra $764 wouldn't feel worth it. Maybe you think Tammy was making a huge mistake. Or maybe you would pay even more interest for some emotional relief. The only way you can put a dollar value on the emotional cost of debt is to compare it with how your traditional Debt Stack would play out and see how it feels to you. If it does not make sense, then you know your emotional cost of debt has a lower dollar value.

"Let's attack the breakup debt first," I said. "As long as you know what you're giving up in terms of time and money, it's a mindful decision."

Tammy left my office pleased. She was starting her new life, feeling good about having "permission" to pay down the wedding hangover on her line of credit, even if it didn't make the most financial sense.

When Tammy and I checked in again, she was 28 months into her plan. The line of credit was almost paid off, with only six more months to go.

"How's it going?" I asked.

"Great. I have no regrets. Every month I'm actually excited to check my banking because I know I'm putting money into the line of credit. Sure, the credit card debt bugs me, but only on a financial level. It doesn't bug me on both a financial *and* an emotional level." She laughed. "I didn't realize that paying my debt the other way—the 'smart way'—was putting me in a bad mood every day. It was perpetuating my feelings of hopelessness and resentment."

"Sounds like choosing to prioritize your debt by emotional cost was the right call."

"No question. It gave me back a sense of control. It's helped me feel like I'm doing something to heal my past," she said.

"I'm so glad," I said.

"Me too," she replied.

It's not always about the math. Money makes us feel a whole whack of things, some good, some bad and—if you've got debt—some ugly. If your Debt Game Plan is going to take years and one of the debts that will be hanging out for some time perpetuates a sense of fear, hopelessness or resentment, I hereby grant you permission to attack it first, as long as you calculate the extra time and money it will take and still feel that it's worth it.

But what happens if you prioritize your debt by emotional cost and realize it's not worth it? Do you simply have to feel like sh*t for the entire time you're paying down debt? The answer is no. You just need a Debt Rejig.

The Debt Rejig

Meet Clayton and Karusia

Ages: 51 and 47

Relationship status: married

Kids: 2, ages 19 and 16

Annual gross household income: $60,000 (Clay) + $70,000 (Karusia) = $130,000

Assets: house valued at $750,000; $160,000 in RRSPs; $800 savings account

Liabilities: $585,000 mortgage; $28,000 credit card debt; $20,000 line of credit; $5,000 income taxes owing (Clayton)

Clayton and Karusia's Debt Map			
Debt	Amount Owing	Interest Rate	Minimum Payment
Credit card A	$13,000	24.99%	$390
Credit card B	$15,000	19.99%	$450
Taxes owing (Clayton)	$5,000	5.00%	$450 (government structured plan)
Line of credit	$20,000	3.39%	$250
Total	**$52,000**		**$1,540**

I hadn't met Clayton and Karusia before, but when they came in to make a Debt Game Plan, things felt tense between them from the get-go.

"What do you want to get out of today's session so you'll feel it was totally worth it?" I asked, as I ask every client.

They both just sat there. Karusia had her arms crossed. "Well?" she said to Clay. "What are you hoping for?"

"I don't know. You're the one who wanted this meeting." He sounded slightly exasperated. Neither of them looked at me, or at each other.

Oh boy. This definitely wasn't my first rodeo when it came to tense, emotionally charged meetings, but I could tell this one might be a doozy.

I started with Karusia because it was true, she had booked the meeting. "Karusia, tell me why you wanted this session."

"We need a plan to get out of debt and never get back into it," she said.

"Clay, do you agree with that?" I asked.

He nodded.

"Well, that's a great starting-off point. The first thing we need to do is go over your Debt Map. As we go through the different amounts you owe, if you could let me know whether it's something that happened all at once or has been building for some time, that would be great."

"Why do you need to know that?" Karusia asked, sounding defensive.

"Because if I know the story behind it, I can better help with a solution. For example, if it's been building over time regardless of your efforts to pay it down, it may be a symptom of spending and unrealistic debt-repayment strategies. But if it's all happened recently, there are different motivation tactics we can use. Basically the more I know, the better the solution. Make sense?"

They both nodded but said nothing.

"Tell me about the credit cards," I said.

Silence.

"Clay?" I felt like a teacher who has to randomly select students to answer when no one makes eye contact.

He cleared his throat. "I think it's been building over time, because of normal life stuff. We have two teenage boys and they've been in sports for a while, plus they eat a lot, so groceries are expensive. I also feel like I spend at least $100 a week on random home-repair stuff." He shrugged. "Just life."

"Karusia, what would you add to that?" I asked.

"I wouldn't. It's fairly accurate, except that we could pay it down faster if we didn't now have this massive tax bill."

Oof. It was Clay's tax bill, and clearly she regarded it as *his* problem. I waited to see his response.

He looked directly at me. "I told her I couldn't put away enough money for taxes this year the way I normally do, because our expenses are too high."

For the record, Clay was self-employed and therefore responsible for paying his own income taxes. He had already managed to cover $10,500 of his total tax bill, which was $15,500, but didn't have enough saved to pay the whole thing. Now his income taxes were officially late and he was being charged interest. He was on a repayment plan of $450 per month, but no one likes owing money to the government.

Karusia finally looked at him. "I thought you made enough money to help with our household finances and also pay your bills."

That was enough for me. Shaming and blaming are not okay at the New School of Finance. "Okay, I'm stopping this right here. Obviously you're both really frustrated with each other—money issues have a way of doing that. But you're here for a reason, right? No one shows up for a financial session unless they are serious about making changes, especially when it comes to debt-repayment plans. So can I assume you're both aligned on that at least?"

"Yes," they said in unison, which broke the tension.

"Good. See? That's teamwork," I said and they dared to crack smiles.

Okay, problem not solved but at least we were making progress past the insults. "These debts seem to be a bit emotionally charged for both of you," I said. "Am I right?"

They chuckled a bit. "You could say that," Karusia said.

"Well, regardless of the cause of the debt, the solution does require teamwork. So you're going to have to work together to come up with a plan, or this is all a big waste of your time."

"No, you're right," Clay said. "That's actually why we thought it would be best to come to see someone. Every time we try to make a plan ourselves, we end up fighting and nothing conclusive happens. We thought that having a third party make the plan would help us reach a solution."

"I couldn't agree more that you're in the right place," I said. "Do I have your permission to start picking at some pretty sensitive stuff? I'm about to ask you a bunch of touchy questions, so things could get a little charged. I need you both to promise there will be no blaming or shaming each other, okay? My office is a shade-free zone," I joked.

They laughed. "Agreed."

"Great," I said. "Now, when you sit down together to make plans, where does the conversation usually go off the rails?"

"When we talk about how much to put where," Karusia said. "We know about debt stacking, but we can never decide how to prioritize them."

"Let's start with you, Karusia," I said. "How would you prioritize these debts?"

"I would pay them off in order of highest interest to lowest. That's the smartest way to do it, right?"

"Smart has nothing to do with it," I said. "But most efficient, yes, that's likely." I turned to Clay. "Clay, how would you prioritize things?"

"I'd pay off the CRA first. I am totally scared that I didn't pay my tax bill on time. I'm on an installment plan with them now and it's driving me nuts. This year felt like a major blow, and, if we're being honest"—he paused and looked at Karusia—"you often throw my tax payments in my face during a fight. So I want it gone."

She didn't say anything. I thought there was truth to what Clay was saying, so I just let it be.

"So, have you guys thought about paying the income taxes first and then tackling the rest of the debts from highest to lowest interest?" I asked.

"We thought of that and we've tried before," Clay said.

"Why didn't it work?" I asked.

Clay raised his hands in mock surrender. "Okay, I'm not trying to throw shade here, but Karusia often puts so much of her paycheque onto the line of credit—'in secret'—that we run out of cash between cheques. And then we end up using the credit cards for things like groceries, gas and . . . life."

"I'm missing something," I said. "Why don't you consolidate the credit cards with the line of credit?"

"Whenever I go to do that, we end up in a huge fight," he said. "So we're locked into this pattern."

I looked at Karusia and she blushed. "Tell me how you see it, Karusia," I said carefully.

She looked down. "Yes, it's true, I do throw money at the line of credit. But it's not like I'm trying to put us into more credit card debt. I just can't look at that line of credit anymore. It stresses me out so much."

"Is that why you keep making secret payments on it?" I asked.

"I guess," she said. "I just hate it so much."

Ahh, yes. The old panic-and-throw-money-at-a-problem tactic. "I have a theory about the emotional cost of debt," I said. "I think you guys are proving it correct."

They didn't say anything. A swing and a miss. I was tap-dancing pretty hard. "Basically, there are times when certain debts make us so upset, so resentful, afraid or angry, that it's best to pay them down first, even if the interest rate is lower than for other debts."

"That's basically what I'm doing, but without a plan," Karusia said, daring a bit of a laugh.

"So let's examine this for a second," I said. "It looks like each debt has a different meaning for both of you. I'm going to ask that you each rank your debts on a scale of 1 to 5, 1 being 'It doesn't bug me, happy to pay it down over time' and 5 is like 'I hate it and looking at it makes me feel so hopeless and resentful.'" I had them each rank the debts at the same time before sharing their lists with one another.

212

				Emotional Cost (out of 5)	
Emotional Cost of Debt					
Debt	Amount	Interest Rate	Minimum Payment	Clay	Karusia
Line of credit	$20,000	3.39%	$250	2	5
Credit card A	$13,000	24.99%	$390	5	4
Credit card B	$15,000	19.99%	$450	4	3
Taxes owing	$5,000	5.00%	$450	5	5
Total	**$52,000**		**$1,540**		

Interesting—they agreed on the income taxes. They were as surprised as I was.

"So, Clay, the most upsetting debts for you are the income taxes owing and the 24.99 percent credit card."

He nodded. "The tax stuff freaks me out because it's my business and I don't want to piss off the taxman. The credit card makes me angry because 24.99 percent is so high that I just feel like a chump."

"And Karusia," I said, "earlier you said you'd prefer to pay the income tax later because of the lower interest rate, but here you've marked it a 5 out of 5. Tell me about that."

She shifted in her seat. "Normally I wouldn't have, but I've realized today that I do really resent it. We fight about it, a lot, and I don't want to fight about money anymore. Getting rid of the income taxes would help Clay feel better, and it would be good for me too, because it wouldn't be hanging around pissing me off."

They both chuckled. That was good.

"Okay, so income taxes take the win for agreed-upon highest emotional cost," I said. "Karusia, tell me why the line of credit is a 5 out of 5 and why you keep going off the plan to throw money at it."

She sighed deeply. "We borrowed on the house the first time to pay for our eldest son to go to university. Then he dropped out about six months ago. For me the debt represents a huge mistake on my behalf."

"Why on your behalf?" I asked.

"Because our son wasn't sure and I feel that I pushed him to go. Clay suggested that we let him take on a student loan, but I wouldn't hear of it. My parents paid for my schooling and I wanted to do the same for him. Anyway, now I just feel stupid, and the $20,000 puts me in a bad mood every time I look at our banking."

"Clay, how do you feel about it?" I asked.

"Well, I rated it a 2. Obviously having a $20,000 line of credit isn't ideal, but it's a low rate, and in the end we made the decision together to borrow on the house. We couldn't have known that our kid would drop out. I don't like it either, but I definitely wouldn't prioritize it over the credit cards."

There was the problem: they couldn't agree on how to pay off their debts because they had warring emotional costs of debt. But now at least we knew that paying back the income taxes should be their first order of business, because both had scored it 5 out of 5 on the emotional-cost-of-debt scale. Where they went in completely different directions was with the line of credit and the credit card. The 24.99 percent interest rate on the credit card was enough to make Clay rate it 5 out of 5, while Karusia scored the line of credit at 5 out of 5. If you ever find yourself in a situation where two people have warring emotional costs of debt, it's best to default to the debt with the higher interest rate.

"Okay, so we'll start with the income taxes."

"I would be happy to have the income taxes gone," said Clay.

"And I'd be happy to fight less once the income taxes are gone," said Karusia.

"After that, it looks like credit card A and the line of credit rate really high for both of you. Since you each labelled a different debt as 5 out of 5, we'll have to default to prioritizing by highest interest. So next we should tackle credit card A, then the line of credit, and then credit card B."

"That sounds great," Karusia said.

"Okay, but there'll be a cost to this, so let's see what it is," I said.

If Clay and Karusia stacked their debt from highest interest to lowest, here's how it would play out with a very large Magic Amount of $650:

Clay and Karusia's Debt Stack, Prioritized by Interest Rate					
Debtt	Amount Owing	Interest Rate	Minimum Payment	Magic Amount	Payments Made
Credit card A	$13,000	24.99%	$390	$650	$1,040
Credit card B	$15,000	19.99%	$450		$450
Income taxes	$5,000	5.00%	$450		$450
Line of credit	$20,000	3.39%	$250		$250
Total	$52,000		$1,540	$650	$2,190

Predicted Results			
Debt	Paid Off By	Interest Paid	Amount Freed Up
Income taxes	Month 12	$130.32	$450*
Credit card A	Month 15	$2,193	$1,490 ($390 + $650 + $450)
Credit card B	Month 22	$4,097	$1,940 ($450 + $1,490)
Line of credit	Month 30	$1,296	$2,190 ($250 + $1,940)

---

* Note: The taxes owing would be paid off within 12 months even without the additional Magic Amount, because $450 per month is enough to pay it all back within a 12-month period.

On the other hand, if they prioritized by emotional cost, it would play out like this:

Clay and Karusia's Debt Stack, Prioritized by Emotional Cost					
Debt	Amount Owing	Interest Rate	Minimum Payment	Magic Amount	Payments Made
Income taxes	$5,000	5.00%	$450	$650	$1,100
Credit card A	$13,000	24.99%	$390		$390
Line of credit	$20,000	3.39%	$250		$250
Credit card B	$15,000	19.99%	$450		$450
Total	$52,000		$1,540	$650	$2,190

Predicted Results			
Debt	Paid Off By	Interest Paid	Amount Freed Up
Income taxes	Month 5	$59.01	$1,100
Credit card A	Month 15	$2,684	$1,490 ($390 + $1,100)
Line of credit	Month 25	$1,053	$1,740 ($250 + $1,490)
Credit card B	Month 30	$5,497	$2,190 ($450 + $1,740)

The Comparison		
	Traditional Debt Stack	Emotional Cost Debt Stack
Time to pay off	30 months	30 months
Interest paid	$7,716	$9,293

"So how does this work for you both? Is prioritizing the debts that make you feel the worst worth the extra month and the additional $1,577 in interest?"

They sat on it for a moment. Then Karusia spoke. "That actually makes me feel worse."

"Me too," said Clay.

"Why?" I asked.

"I mean, $1,577 is a lot to throw away because I have a thing about the money we spent for our son's schooling," Karusia said. "When I see it like this, it's not worth it. In fact, it actually makes me resent it more, because it's costing me an extra $1,577 for nothing."

"I couldn't agree more," Clay said. "I feel good about the taxes, though. I'm glad we're both on the same page there."

This is common. Sometimes it feels good to prioritize certain debts by emotional cost but not others. There does come a point when it stops making financial sense to everyone, but that is up to the individuals involved. If Clay and Karusia were willing to pay the extra $1,577, I wouldn't have stopped them, but it's not about what I think they should do, it's about what they want to do and, more important, what they will do. If paying the extra $1,577 would help them feel excited and motivated all the way to the end of their Debt Game Plan, I would have given them permission to do so. In this case, however, it didn't work like that.

Clay and Karusia's Debt Stack, Prioritized by Emotional Cost and Interest Rate					
Debt	Amount Owing	Interest Rate	Minimum Payment	Magic Amount	Payments Made
Income taxes	$5,000	5.00%	$450	$650	$1,100
Credit card A	$13,000	24.99%	$390	0	$390
Credit card B	$15,000	19.99%	$450	0	$450
Line of credit	$20,000	3.39%	$250	0	$250
Total	$52,000		$1,540	$650	$2,190

Predicted Results			
Debt	Paid Off By	Interest Paid	Amount Freed Up
Income taxes	Month 5	$59.01	$1,100
Credit card A	Month 15	$2,684	$1,490 ($390 + $1,100)
Credit card B	Month 22	$4,097	$1,940 ($450 + $1,490)
Line of credit	Month 30	$1,296	$2,190 ($250 + $1,940)
Total interest paid		$9,224.48	

"That feels like a good compromise," Clay said.

"I agree," said Karusia.

In the end we prioritized the income taxes first and then paid the rest in order from highest interest rate to lowest. This was a plan that they had made together, one that felt good, doable and motivating.

I checked in with them in Year 2. "So, how's it going?" I asked.

"We've just started tackling what's left on the line of credit, now that the credit cards are paid off. And of course the income tax has been paid up for some time now."

"Congrats! How does the line of credit make you feel today?" I asked.

Karusia spoke first. "Good. Once I realized why I was so scared of it, it helped me see that, no matter what I do, that $20,000 has been spent. I can't really do anything about it except be smart with our money now."

"Actually," Clay added, "we celebrated when we'd paid off the first $20,000 in our Debt Game Plan. Once the income tax was paid, we just pretended that the $13,000 and $7,000 on the other credit card represented the money we had paid for Kevin's university."

"That's great. How did you celebrate?" I asked.

"We had a 'Big Bad Debt Be Done' party, just for us," he said. "We had wine and I actually got balloons."

They laughed.

"Associating the first $20,000 of credit card debt with the money we'd spent on school felt good," he continued. "It was a huge emotional relief. Even though technically the money we spent for our son's schooling was on the line of credit, paying off the equal value was freeing."

"It felt like we had accomplished something—together," Karusia said.

"That's wonderful," I said. "I'm so happy you found a way to work together to stay not only financially but also emotionally motivated with your debt-repayment plan. You're so close to the end now."

"We know. We can't believe it," Clay said. "Less than a year to go!"

"Then look out, retirement savings," I said.

"Oh, totally," Karusia agreed. "The $2,190 that we'll be freeing up is going to go straight to retirement."

"After a trip, maybe?" I said.

Karusia laughed. "Definitely."

▶

It's okay to slightly defy the Debt-Repayment Gospel in order to figure out the best way for you to prioritize your debt, especially if it means you'll stay motivated to see your debt-repayment plan through until the very last payment. I hereby give you permission to prioritize paying off the debt that is costing you the most emotionally if that will keep you motivated. If your debt has a high emotional cost, your Debt Game Plan will be packed with strong emotional wins along the way. It makes paying down your debt more meaningful, more motivating and way more likely to happen.

How to Prioritize Your Debt by Emotional Cost

1. Revisit your Debt Map from Chapter 5.

2. Rank your debts in order of emotional cost. Which debt makes you feel frustrated, stuck, bad with money, guilty? Which debt gives you the most emotional strife?

3. Calculate how long your Debt Game Plan would take and how much additional interest you'd pay if you prioritized by highest interest rate. Compare the results to prioritizing by emotional cost.

4. If the extra time and money feel worth the emotional relief, you have my permission to prioritize your debt stack by highest emotional cost of debt.

CHAPTER 13

Free Up Money Fast

If you've been living in a Debt Loop for some time, it's very possible that a large portion of your income is going towards minimum debt payments each month. You've done it all: reduced Fixed Expenses as much as possible and cut all other savings. There's no Magic Amount and the Spending Money you have left over is already unrealistically low.

If this is you, the first order of business is to stop going into more debt. That's your most important job—always. No matter what. None of the strategies for debt repayment matter if you are taking on more debt. Not sinking into more or at least controlling how much debt you take on, is a huge part of the battle to break the Debt Loop and give you control over your finances.

When There's No Extra Money: Stack and Swap

Sometimes when money is tight and you're up against the wall financially, you can break the Debt Loop by paying off the lowest amount owing first, so you can free up cash flow for other things besides debt repayment. Yes, I just said that. Sometimes it's okay to pay off the lowest amount owing, even if it doesn't have the highest interest rate, so that you can free up money as soon as possible.

Meet Vanessa

Age: 28

Relationship status: dating

Kids: 0

Annual gross household income: $50,000

Assets: $2,000 coming in from a one-off contract

Liabilities: $12,000 credit card debt; $4,000 car loan; $3,000 consolidation loan

Vanessa's Debt Map			
Debt	Amount	Interest Rate	Minimum Payment
Credit card A	$7,000	22.00%	$210
Credit card B	$5,000	19.99%	$150
Car loan	$4,000	4.90%	$470
Consolidation loan	$3,000	3.39%	$250
Total	**$19,000**		**$1,080**

Vanessa had reached out to me as a last-ditch effort to get control and pay down her debt.

"It's getting ridiculous. I'm not a stupid woman, but for the life of me I can't seem to make a dent," she said in her wonderfully thick Cape Breton accent.

Vanessa was a self-employed side-hustle queen with three businesses—as a virtual assistant, a bookkeeper and a ride-share driver. "I live in Sydney. I do what I gotta do. Jobs can be hard to find out here."

Her three businesses kept her extremely busy and the income was relatively consistent, about $50,000 a year before taxes. But that was no longer enough. About three years ago Vanessa had paid for retraining as a bookkeeper ($3,000) at the same time that she was stuck with an unexpected move ($5,000) and an emergency car replacement ($20,000). For the first time, Vanessa had taken on debt.

The new minimum payments were so high (especially for the car payment) that she couldn't afford daily life anymore. The spike in debt restricted her cash flow so severely that she had started taking on even more credit card debt just to make ends meet. Now, three years later, her car loan was almost paid off, but she still had ever-increasing credit card debt. She was in a deep Debt Loop.

"I've been trying to get it under control but failing again and again," she said. "I need help."

"Tell me about what you've been doing," I said. "What plans haven't been working?"

"Well, I read all these books and blogs and articles that told me I'm supposed to consolidate my debt where I can and pay off the highest interest rate first. But it never helps. I've tried a bunch of plans so far."

"Tell me about the last one."

"I was trying to pay down all my debt over two years. It meant putting an extra $200 a month towards my debt on top of the minimum payment, starting with the 22 percent credit card. That felt doable— on paper."

I looked at her financial snapshot and scrunched up my face.

Vanessa's Financial Snapshot	
Monthly After-Tax Income	**$3,020**
FIXED EXPENSES	
Rent	$1,055
Business subscriptions	$100
Renters' insurance	$20
Car insurance	$125
Cellphone	$50
Cable/Internet	$40

(continued on next page)

Minimum debt payments:	
Credit card A	$210
Credit card B	$150
Car loan	$470
Loan	$250
Total Fixed Expenses	**$2,470**
SHORT-TERM SAVINGS	
Big purchases	0
Emergencies	0
Total Short-Term Savings	0
SPENDING MONEY	$550
TOTAL COST OF LIFE	**$3,020**
Meaningful Savings (Magic Amount)	**0**

"Let me get this straight," I said. "You were trying to pay an additional $200 a month on top of your minimum payments?"

"Yes."

"But based on what I see here, your Spending Money is only $550 per month, without putting anything extra to debt. If you took an additional $200 from that, you'd have only $350 per month left for literally everything that wasn't a bill. Including groceries and gas."

"Yeah, but I don't spend money. I'm broke. My only splurges are a five-dollar trivia night and a beer every now and then. I don't buy fancy clothes or go to expensive coffee shops. I should be able to do this."

This sounded like a typical situation where someone assumes they can be on their best spending behaviour for far too long. "Let's take a look at your past expenses to see what you spend on average. If you're taking on more and more debt, you probably need to spend more than $550 a month just to feel human."

We downloaded three months' worth of Vanessa's credit card history, pulled out the Fixed Expenses and averaged out the rest. Here's how it looked:

Average Monthly Spending				
Category	May	August	September	Average
Groceries	$225	$260	$250	$245
Toiletries	$25	$40	$40	$35
Gas	$130	$200	$150	$160
Car repairs	$600	0	0	$200
Trivia night/fun	$100	$130	$115	$115
Clothes	0	$80	$40	$40
Ferry	0	$45	0	$15
Grooming	$70	0	$50	$40
Alcohol	$40	$60	$50	$50
Gifts	0	$20	$100	$40
Total	**$1,190**	**$835**	**$795**	**$940**

"Vanessa, your life costs more than $550 per month, let alone $350. It may be that there just isn't enough money coming in to pay your bills and live your normal life. See? On average you're spending $940 per month."

"Well, May looks really bad because I had to get my brakes fixed. Driving in the Highlands is hard on your car."

"Totally, but that's exactly my point. That's something you'll likely have to spend money on again; you need to expect it and plan for it. Three hundred and fifty dollars a month for spending money is totally unsustainable. I'd argue that $550 a month, which is what you currently have left after covering your Fixed Expenses, is also too low for you."

She shifted. I could see she didn't like that. "I don't feel like I live beyond my means."

"You don't," I was quick to add. "It's just that the minimum payments going towards your debt are leaving you with too little spending money. Check it out." I grabbed my calculator. "Your total minimum debt payments add up to $1,080. That's 35 percent of your take-home pay each month. Most people budget 35 percent of their income for housing, but your minimum debt payments are actually more than your rent! If we delete your minimum debt payments, you are actually living well below your means."

"Well, that's a relief," she said.

"All we have to do is get those debts paid off and then you can redistribute the amounts to savings and spending."

"That's why I'm here. I've tried everything—applied for consolidation loans, haggled with the bank, sold stuff. I'm maxed out."

"You mentioned in your notes that you have $2,000 coming in from a part-time job last month, right?"

"Yep. I helped out with this music festival a few months ago, so I have a cheque waiting to be cashed."

"And your income taxes and business taxes are all paid up?" I asked.

"Yep, I remit quarterly. Didn't even include it here. I'm a bookkeeper, so I know what's up," she joked.

I laughed. "Perfect. So I can use that $2,000 for your Debt Game Plan, right? It's not earmarked for anything?"

"Well, I was going to put it to my credit card."

"I have a different idea. It may be better used elsewhere."

"Twenty-two percent interest is so high."

"Just hear me out. I think I want to try something I call the Stack and Swap."

"The what now?"

"Stack and Swap. It's where we pay off the debt with the lowest amount owing first, to free up that minimum payment as fast as possible. Then you swap the minimum payment into Spending Money so you can realistically afford your life and stop going into debt."

"I'm confused. Aren't I supposed to pay off debt with the highest interest rate first? That's the smartest thing to do financially, right?"

"On paper, yes. But you're fighting a different battle right now. The bigger issue here is that your Spending Money is unrealistically low.

Putting the $2,000 onto your $7,000 credit card debt won't free up the minimum payment completely; it will still take you some time to pay it back. Your immediate problem is that you need to stop sinking into more credit card debt. The only way to do that is to loosen the purse strings and give yourself more Spending Money so you can realistically get groceries and pay for gas. That will help you stop taking on more debt, which is your first priority. The *second* is to pay back debt with high interest."

"Okay, I'm listening," she said, slightly suspiciously. That wasn't surprising, considering that my suggestion ran contrary to all conventional wisdom. But conventional wisdom had put her in this situation. We needed a completely different approach. You may be thinking that I'm out to lunch, since 22 percent is so high. But I'm telling you after years on the front lines, the first order of business is to *stop taking on more debt*. It's paramount to everything. For Vanessa, freeing up as much money as possible was the only way to do it, and that meant paying down the lowest amount owing first, regardless of interest rate.

"Watch this," I said. "If we put the whole $2,000 cheque on your loan, you'll only have $1,000 left to pay back." I pulled up the Debt-Payoff Calculator. "If you just keep paying the minimum $250 each month, you'll have it all paid off in four months. Then you can keep that $250 per month as Spending Money. That will put $250 back in your pocket, taking you from $550 to $800. Way more sustainable!"

She looked at me incredulously. "So you're saying I should pay off the lowest-priority debt just so I can nab the minimum payment? But instead of putting it towards other debt, I spend it?"

"Yes. I want to get your Spending Money up to $800 per month and also add $200 to Short-Term Savings for repetitive spikes in spending, such as brakes and rust repair for your car. If we can do that, I believe you can finally sustainably pay down all your debt—because you'll be able to stick to a plan. That's been the missing link."

"What if I start with the 22 percent credit card?" she asked.

"If you start with the $7,000 credit card debt, you won't be able to free up the full $210 minimum payment for over four years. We've already seen that you can't live off $550 per month for the next five years. And the last thing you want to do right now is take on more debt."

"Okay, this is actually starting to make sense," she said. "Can't pay back debt if I keep going into it."

"Exactly."

In order to get Vanessa's Spending Money up to $800, she needed to free up an extra $250. That would happen quickly if she paid down the loan. Then she would need to free up an additional $200 per month to put towards her Short-Term Savings, for a total of $450. So we turned to the next smallest amount owing, which was the car loan. Paying off the loan and the car loan would free up $720 ($250 from the consolidation loan plus $470 from the car loan), which was actually $270 more than she needed to create a sustainable living situation. As a result, once those two debts were paid off, she could again prioritize her debt repayments from highest to lowest interest rate.

Vanessa's Debt-Stacking Plan, Prioritized by Lowest Amount					
Debt	Amount	Interest Rate	Minimum Payment	Magic Amount	Payments Made
Loan	$1,000	3.39%	$250	$650	$900
Car loan	$4,000	4.90%	$470		$470
Credit card A	$7,000	22.00%	$210		$210
Credit card B	$5,000	19.99%	$150		$150
Total	**$18,000**		**$1,080**		**$1,730**

After putting the $2,000 towards the loan, Vanessa would have only $1,000 left to go. Here's how her plan worked out:

Vanessa's Predicted Results			
Debt	Paid Off By	Interest Paid	Amount Freed Up
Loan	Month 4	$7	$250*
Car loan	Month 9	$79	$470†
Credit card A	Month 24	$2,041	$480 ($210 + $270)
Credit card B	Month 30	$807	$630 $150 + $480)

---

* Vanessa does not add the $250 freed up to her debt stack. Instead she keeps it for herself to take her Spending Money from $550 to $800. Woot!

† Vanessa keeps $200 of the freed-up $470 to put towards Short-Term Savings for car emergencies and other spikes in spending that used to put her in debt. That means she would finally have a Magic Amount of $270 that she could use to attack the rest of her debt.

Once her Spending Money was a sustainable $800 per month and she was prepared for short-term emergencies, Vanessa would no longer be at risk of falling back into the Debt Loop because of unsustainably low Spending Money. At that point she could implement a Debt-Stacking Plan to attack the credit cards, prioritizing by interest rate. All in all, it would take Vanessa just under three years to pay everything off and would cost $3,934 in interest. She could do all this without making an unrealistic Debt Game Plan that would reduce her Spending Money to where she was doomed to go back into a Debt Loop.

"How do you feel about this?" I asked after I showed her the stats. "You'll have sustainable living in only four months, an emergency fund ready in nine, and everything paid off in 30 months."

"That feels like a relief, which makes me think it's the right thing to do." She looked at me. "You're right, I can't keep scraping by. It's not realistic."

"It's not."

"Once I clear up that last card, I'll have $630 I can save towards retirement, right?"

"One hundred percent," I said. "The first four to nine months are touch and go, because there's no emergency savings until Month 9 and you'll have to live off that unsustainably low $550 for four months. You'll have to make cuts to your spending money that would probably not be realistic in the long term. But it's only four months, not four years. Basically the first four months of your plan will suck because you have to stick to this unrealistic budget and live off $550 a month."

"Don't worry, I'm a Caper," she said.

"Sorry?"

"I'm from Cape Breton," she explained. "We're a tough bunch. Hard to kill."

I laughed. "Well, as long as you can make it through the next four months without going into debt, this will work. You just need to pay off that consolidation loan as fast as possible so you can swap the minimum payment for more spending money."

"I can do it for four months. I'll probably still go to weekly trivia, but I'll reduce expenses elsewhere. Maybe I'll try to live off turnips."

I laughed again. "However you manage, just remember that it's only four months. This is not forever. You're just racing towards the finish line of that consolidation loan. Then you can breathe."

I checked in with Vanessa in Month 9 to see how it was going.

"Consolidation loan and the car loan are done!" she exclaimed.

"And did you use them for Spending Money and Short-Term Savings?" I asked.

"Yes, but it took every ounce of strength I had not to start putting it towards debt. After making it through the first four months on $550, I thought you were wrong and I could just keep going like that. I did it for one more month and then I wanted to go see my family out in Newfoundland. That trip cost me $300, which all went on credit. I felt so guilty about it, but then I remembered that if I had stuck to our plan I would have had an extra \$250 a month to spend and the trip wouldn't have been an issue. That motivated me to just relax. Once I had \$800 a month to spend, I felt like I was rich. I've been so used to scraping and scrimping and failing. Now, with \$200 a month going to emergency savings as well, I don't have to be afraid of potholes and rust. It's a huge relief. I smile more."

"Can you see the light at the end of the tunnel?" I asked.

"Definitely. I'm starting on that 22 percent credit card now with the extra money from the car loan. I haven't felt this in control in a long time. I'm not stressed about it. Now it's just a matter of time."

I was so happy. Vanessa was well on her way to living debt-free and happily paying down debt. It was no longer a constant struggle. By paying down the smaller amount owing first and using the freed-up minimum payment to add to Spending Money instead of using it as a new Magic Amount, she became much more motivated, because the plan was realistic. She could live and pay down debt at the same time. That's why it worked.

▶

If you don't have enough money to realistically live your life and pay your bills, pay down the lowest amounts of debt first so that you can free up the minimum payments fast. First use the freed-up minimum payments to increase your Spending Money and Short-Term Savings to where life is sustainable and then start paying down debt, prioritizing by highest interest rate. It may seem counterintuitive, but the first order of business is to keep you out of the Debt Loop so you don't fail. It may take longer and you may pay more in interest, but this approach will keep you motivated to stick with your plan and see it through to the end, because you know you can live and pay down debt at the same time. That's what I call a win.

How to Effectively Stack and Swap

1. Prioritize your debt stack from smallest amount owing to largest amount owing, regardless of interest rate. That way you'll clear the smaller debts sooner and be able to take the minimum payment for yourself (instead of the debt stack) to spend each month.

2. Don't add the freed-up minimum payment to the debt stack as your Magic Amount until you reach a point where you have enough Spending Money and Short-Term Savings to stay out of debt.

3. Once your Spending Money and Short-Term Savings are at a sustainable level, you can prioritize your debt stack by interest rate and keep paying off debt in a normal fashion.

Controlled Debt Burn: When Debt Is Inevitable

Sometimes debt is inevitable. There's literally no other option; it's happening. If debt is happening, does that mean you are financially screwed? No! There are still a ton of really important, financially awesome things you can do even if you are going into debt.

When I was battling my own Debt Loop during the Barter Babes Project, I wish in hindsight that I hadn't given up. I wish I'd found a way to feel hope and had made a plan. Perhaps I would have ended up with only $4,000 worth of credit card debt instead of $9,000.

I know now that I should have planned on going into debt from the get-go instead of fooling myself into thinking that somehow I could live off $35 a week. Because I wasn't being honest with myself, every purchase felt scary. The guilt was palpable and the fear was real. I was mired in the Shame-and-Blame Mentality, and that's why I hid my debt from Matt, stopped logging in to my banking and stuck my head in the sand. If I had just admitted to myself that for that year debt was supposed to happen, I wouldn't have carried around so much shame. I could have kept it in check, not been afraid of it, dealt with it and made a plan. I could have been in control and gone into debt with my eyes wide open. Planning for debt allows you to have it happen to you. You plan for it and, by accepting it, you control it.

This is something I call a Controlled Debt Burn. It's when you know you're playing with fire and that it's dangerous, but you've actually got it under control. It's a financial harm-reduction plan.

If you've got debt already, there may be something coming down the pipeline that you know you may have to take on more debt for. A Controlled Debt Burn can help you survive and come out on the other side with as little debt as possible. This is a helpful strategy for surviving post-secondary education, parental leave or periods of unemployment.

A simple example of a Controlled Debt Burn is my client Farah. She was a law student living off a massive student line of credit—she had access to $80,000. Without a plan in place, she might just have borrowed from that line of credit whenever she felt she should. In the end she could have wound up maxed out. But she came to me to make a plan, and a Controlled Debt Burn was necessary.

Here's how to manage a Controlled Debt Burn:

Step 1: Calculate your financial needs over the time period.

Farah's Controlled Debt Burn needed to last 24 months. She needed to pay $20,000 a year for tuition for the last two years of school and she needed $2,500 per month to pay her rent and bills and live.

Financial Needs over 24 Months	
Tuition	$40,000 ($20,000 × 2 years)
Living	$60,000 ($2,500 per month × 24 months)
Total	**$100,000**

Step 2: Tally up all money that is realistically due to you over the time period.

Farah knew that she would be getting $10,000 from her family over the next two years. In addition, she would get a placement for one summer with a law firm, where she would make $1,100 (after tax) per week for 13 weeks. She also had a part-time job as a teaching assistant that would pay her $2,850 (after tax) each year.

Money Coming in Over the Next 24 Months	
Help from family	$10,000
Summer placement	$14,300 ($1,100 × 13)
Teaching assistant job	$5,700 ($2,850 × 2)
Total	**$30,000**

Step 3: Calculate the total shortfall.

Farah would be short $70,000 ($100,000 – $30,000). That's how much debt she would be taking on during her Controlled Debt Burn. She would use the $20,000 from her jobs and the $10,000 from her family, plus $10,000 from her line of credit, to pay the $40,000 tuition. For her day-to-day life she would need to borrow $2,500 a month from the student line of credit. I suggested that she take out $2,500 every month and put it into her chequing account like a paycheque, so she could stick to the budget once she runs out of savings and income from her jobs. Farah could have borrowed $80,000 on her student line of credit, but with her Controlled Debt Burn, she'd graduate only $70,000 in debt. Future Farah will be stoked!

Do the same for future you. A Controlled Debt Burn can help you stay in control if life has thrown you a curveball and debt is inevitable. It is a strategy that will ensure you come out the other side with as little debt as possible.

Farah's situation was fairly simple. My clients Maya and Kellen are a perfect example of how life can throw you curveballs and plunge you into debt when it's really inconvenient.

Meet Maya and Kellen

Ages: 35 and 37

Relationship status: married

Kids: 1, age 2, and 1 on the way

Annual gross household income: $65,000 (Maya) + $65,000 (Kellen) = $130,000

Assets: $2,000 in emergency account; $16,000 in vested stock options at Maya's work

Liabilities: $22,000 in loans; $8,500 line of credit

Maya and Kellen's Debt Map			
Debt	Amount Owing	Interest Rate	Minimum Payments
Department store loan	$1,000	24.00%	$150
Consolidation loan	$12,000	7.80%	$266
Student loan (Maya)	$9,000	5.56%	$350
Line of credit	$8,500	5.00%	$50
Total	**$30,500**		**$816**

"I'm pregnant," Maya said, and held her breath to wait for my reaction.

Maya and Kellen lived in Toronto and had had a financial session with me about a year before. At the time they had just come out of a maternity leave, and during the previous year they had taken on an additional $20,000 worth of debt between credit cards and lines of credit. We made a Debt Game Plan that included a consolidation loan for their high-interest credit cards, setting up Short-Term Savings and reducing their Fixed Expenses and Spending Money as low as they could go. Since then, things had been on track, with the exception of a recent $2,500 splurge on department store credit for a home gym. Another change was that $16,000 worth of Maya's stock options at work had been vested, which meant she could now access them for the first time.

"A new baby!" I said. "How exciting!"

"And expensive and terrifying—a total 'oops-a-baby,'" Maya said with a smile. "I mean, we're happy and stoked and all that, but it happened *way* earlier than we anticipated. We were going to wait for Sophie to be in full-time public school before a second baby came, so we wouldn't have to do the daycare and mat-leave thing."

"We are only partway through the Debt Game Plan we made with you last year, and we still have so much debt," Kellen said. "We're scared," he added with a nervous laugh. "Like, I don't actually know how we can afford to make it through."

"Well, let's map it out," I said.

Maya and Kellen's Financial Snapshot	
MONTHLY AFTER-TAX INCOME	
Maya	$4,000
Kellen	$4,000
Total Monthly After-Tax Income	**$8,000**
FIXED EXPENSES	
Rent	$2,500
Utilities	$100
Childcare	$1,290
Renters' insurance	$25
Transit pass (Kellen)	$110
Cellphones (both)	$180
Cable/Internet/subscriptions	$100

Bank fees	$14
Minimum debt payments:	
Department store credit	$150
Consolidation loan	$266
Student loan (Maya)	$350
Line of credit	$50
Total Fixed Expenses	$5,135
SHORT-TERM SAVINGS	
Slush fund	$125
Vacations	0
Emergencies	$200
Total Short-Term Savings	**$325**
SPENDING MONEY	$2,390
TOTAL COST OF LIFE	**$7,850**
MEANINGFUL SAVINGS	
RRSP contributions	0
TFSA contributions	0
Magic Amount	$150
Total Meaningful Savings	**$150**

Maya's income would drop from $4,000 to $1,980 per month (after tax) in 10 months, once she started her maternity leave. That's a reduction of $2,020, which was more than their monthly Spending Money. It meant they'd take on $24,240 worth of new debt ($2,420 × 12 months) over her mat leave.* Ouch!

I totally understood why they were terrified. "Is it possible to reduce the childcare expense while you're on mat leave?" I asked them.

They looked at each other. "Not really," Maya said. "We would lose her spot, which is a whole can of worms in itself. It's so hard to get one in Toronto."

"It's basically a fixed expense," Kellen said.

I knew from our first meeting that all their other expenses had

---

* See "EI Maternity and Parental Benefits" in Additional Reading (page 311).

already been reduced to their lowest realistic level. "The only other thing to do," I said, "is aggressively pay off debt in the next 10 months to free up enough cash flow from what you pay off so you can survive." This was another case where prioritizing debt by the lowest amount owing over the highest interest rate could be helpful in order to free up cash flow.

Once Maya's mat leave started, they would be $2,040 short every month, so I wanted them to pay off as much debt as possible before Maya's income was reduced to ensure that they wouldn't have to make as many minimum payments. I started by mathing it all out.

Maya and Kellen's Debt Map, Prioritized by Lowest Amount/Fastest to Pay Off			
Debt	**Amount**	**Interest Rate**	**Minimum Payment**
Department store credit	$1,000	24.00%	$150
Student loan	$9,000	5.56%	$350
Line of credit	$8,500	5.00%	$50
Consolidation loan	$12,000	7.80%	$266
Total	**$30,500**		**$816**

"Okay, guys. I've figured out a way to reduce the amount of debt you'll have to go into from $24,240 to $11,940."

"What? Really?" Maya asked. "How?"

"Yes. Here's the plan: Maya, cash in the $16,000 in vested stock options. After putting aside 25 percent for taxes, this will give you a lump sum of $12,000. With this $12,000, you'll pay $1,000 to the department store and $9,000 towards your student loan. That will pay both of them off completely, freeing up $500 ($150 + $350). Then put the final $2,000 on your line of credit so the balance owing is only $6,500 ($8,500 − $2,000)."

She was furiously taking notes.

"After you do that, you'll be able to add the $150 original Magic Amount, the $150 from the department store credit card and the $350 minimum payment from the student loan to the $50 minimum payment that currently goes towards your line of credit. Your total monthly payment will then be $700 per month ($150 + $150 + $350 + $50). At that rate you'll have the line of credit paid off within 10 months, freeing up $700 per month before your mat leave starts!"

"Seriously?" Kellen said.

"Yes! Plus you can continue to save $200 per month for the next 10 months for emergencies, taking your emergency account to $4,400. And you can continue putting in $125 a month for the next 10 months for spikes in spending, leaving you with $1,250. If you do this," I said, "here's what your finances will look like on maternity leave."

Maya and Kellen's Maternity Leave Financial Snapshot	
MONTHLY AFTER-TAX INCOME	
Maya	$1,980
Kellen	$4,000
Total Monthly After-Tax Income	**$5,980**
FIXED EXPENSES	
Rent	$2,500
Utilities	$100
Childcare	$1,290
Renters' insurance	$25
Transit pass (Kellen)	$110
Cellphones (both)	$180
Cable/Internet/subscriptions	$100
Bank fees	$14
Minimum debt payments:	
Department store	0

(continued on next page)

Consolidation loan	$266
Maya student loan	0
Line of credit	0
Total Fixed Expenses	**$4,585**
SHORT-TERM SAVINGS	
Slush fund	0
Vacations	0
Emergencies	0
Total Short-Term Savings	**0**
SPENDING MONEY	$2,390
TOTAL COST OF LIFE	**$6,975**
MEANINGFUL SAVINGS	
RRSP contributions	0
TFSA contributions	0
Magic Amount	0
Total Meaningful Savings	**0**
TOTAL SHORTFALL	**$995**

"But we'll still be short," Kellen said.

"You will, by $995 per month," I agreed.

Maya's chest fell as she let out a sigh. "Sh*t."

"It's okay," I assured them. "This is a Controlled Debt Burn."

"A what?" Maya asked.

"A Controlled Debt Burn. You're going to have to go into debt, but you're planning for it."

"Shouldn't we try to reduce our Spending Money even more, or something?" Kellen asked.

"Do you think your family can live without debt for 12 months with a spending limit of $1,395 ($2,390 – $995)?" I asked.

He shook his head and let out a laugh. "No. We have tried."

"Well then, let's just be real about it. Last year you were positive that $2,390 was your realistic non-extravagant household Spending Money for everything from diapers and kids' clothes to groceries and gas. I'm going to hold that constant, even though you're bringing a new human into the fold. You're already going to have to adjust your regular living expenses to make it work on $2,390. Going lower rather than doing it in a controlled way is likely to lead to more debt for your family."

"What do you mean?" Kellen asked.

"Last year when you came in, you both said you had given up halfway through maternity leave and just started spending money because you felt like there wasn't any way out of the debt."

"We definitely made it rain," Maya joked.

"Yes, but not in the beginning," I pointed out. "That happened near the end."

"Totally," she agreed. "We were just like 'f*ck it' all the time."

"Exactly. So this time I want to be realistic about it so you don't reach a point where you just throw in the towel. Fine, you're going into debt, so let's make it the smallest amount of debt possible. You feel me?"

They nodded.

"Since you'll have paid off all your debt except the consolidation loan, your line of credit will be at zero. You can borrow back $995 per month for the 12 months. Every month, just move $995 from the line of credit into your joint household chequing account to offset your fixed expenses. That's it. No more. Everything else runs as usual."

I did some more calculations. "By the end of the 12 months you'll have racked up $11,940 on the line of credit and you'll have a new minimum debt payment of $50. But Maya will be back at work, Sophie will be in public school, and perhaps more of your work shares will be vested. So you will free up one child's daycare but have to swap it for the second," I said and smiled. "It's a good thing babies are cute."

They laughed. "Yes, because they are hella expensive," Kellen said.

Maya and Kellen came in for a financial checkup once Maya was back at work. "I'm very proud of you," I said after looking over their finances.

"We controlled that burn," Kellen said.

"You sure did!" I exclaimed.

Maya and Kellen's Post-Mat-Leave Debt Map, Prioritized by Interest Rate			
Debt	Amount	Interest Rate	Minimum Payment
Consolidation loan	$6,148	7.8%	$266
Line of credit	$11,940	5.0%	$50
Total	**$18,088**		**$316**

"So how did knowing you couldn't borrow more than $995 each month help to keep your debt under control?" I asked.

"I think it just gave us permission to borrow without guilt. That helped make it feel like we weren't constantly screwed. I didn't panic this time. It felt like we were being financially responsible even though we were using our line of credit to live. What about you, babe?" Maya said.

"Totally," Kellen said. "The panic is what led to our just ignoring the debt and not being responsible with it the first time. I felt in control this time."

"Awesome," I said.

▶

If you're in a situation where there's simply not enough money for you to survive financially for a set (short) period of time, a Controlled Debt Burn will help you feel in control of your finances even as you sink into debt. You'll be sinking on purpose and with purpose, and only for a limited time. Feeling in control will help keep you out of the Shame-and-Blame Mentality, which will help you stay on track, stay hopeful and keep the debt that you do need to take on as low as possible.

How to Do a Controlled Debt Burn

1. Before you start your burn, try to aggressively pay off debt with as many Debt-Slammers as possible. Prioritize which debts you pay by smallest amount owing rather than highest interest rate, so that you can free up as much cash flow as possible.

2. Calculate your shortfall by subtracting your projected financial needs from the total amount of money that will be coming in over the set time period.

3. Try to space out the borrowed money over the time. For example, borrow only what you need each month and put it into your chequing account like a salary, to supplement any other income.

How to Navigate Love and Money

Love and debt. This is a doozy of a topic. Combining finances when one or both partners have debt is tricky and can often bring up feelings of dread for everyone involved. I'm not saying you have to show someone your credit card statement on the first date, but if you've got debt and you're serious about starting a life with another person, at some point it's got to be talked about. In this chapter I'm not talking about people who are newly dating and aren't really sure about their potential partner. I'm speaking to people who are in a committed relationship and planning to build a future together, because that's when debt becomes a household financial issue.

When both people in a relationship have debt, Debt Game Plans aren't as ripe for disagreement, resentment and secret fears. Many of my clients have a joint home equity line of credit that's maxed out, shared credit cards that are carrying a balance, and student loans they've been battling together for years. But what happens when one person has debt and the other person doesn't? I've been working with couples, from dating to divorced, for a long enough time to know that this is an area that is emotionally, financially *and* legally complicated.

I've also seen an increase in the scenario where both parties aren't on the same financial playing field, especially over the past 10 years. People are getting married later and coupling up later as well. Back in the day, you'd marry someone straight out of high school or post-secondary and possibly start your life together with two incomes from the get-go. But now people may live their own financial lives for a long time before they get involved in a relationship. That means there is more opportunity for someone to come to the table with debt or savings. Each person has been doing their own financial thing.

Is the person with debt dragging the other down? Is the person without debt a judgy jerk? Should the person with debt carry the burden alone or should their partner help? It's all very complex.

More than a decade of front-line financial planning has consistently proven one thing with Debt Game Plans: two incomes are better than one. Love it or hate it, if you can tag-team the household savings you're both better off than each of you acting in your own financial silo. Regardless of debt, it's always better to work as a team. Planning for a down payment? Best to combine forces and save up. Saving for kids? Form a united front when it comes to your RESP strategy.

It's the old "What's mine is yours and what's yours is mine," only with money. Did your heart just skip a beat? If so, that likely means you're in a situation where not all savings goals are shared. But I know that, mathematically, working alone slows everyone down. Meeting every goal takes longer, whether that's debt repayment, a wedding, a down payment or retirement planning.

Big-deal alert! This book makes recommendations for debt management for couples from a financial perspective only and is not intended to provide legal advice. Every situation is unique. Therefore, it is important to get legal advice from a family lawyer when you are considering combining finances. There could be financial ramifications down the road if you break up. Before you make a decision to combine finances, you should seek independent legal advice to see if a cohabitation agreement or marriage contract is appropriate. Every couple in the stories below had the proper legal protections for themselves in place when it was necessary.

Take my clients Adam and Avery, for example. Adam had student debt but Avery did not, as her schooling had been paid for by her parents. As a result, in her early twenties she'd had no minimum debt payments to meet. When she got her first job, she was actually able to save instead of pay down debt. Now, at age 30, she had $30,000 saved up. Adam graduated with $30,000 worth of student debt. He'd been dutifully paying that back and had only $13,000 left at 5 percent, with a minimum payment of $575. He'd been very financially responsible, but he wasn't debt-free and had no savings. As a team, they could save $900 a month ($450 each). Let's assess their financial situation after two years, to see if they would be better off working alone or saving together.

With his current Debt Game Plan, Adam would pay $1,025 each month towards his debt ($575 minimum payment + $450 Magic Amount). At that rate his student loan would be paid off in 14 months. During that 14 months, he'd pay $384 in interest. After that, for the next 10 months he could save the $1,025 that had been freed up, at a 2 percent interest rate, giving him $10,344 at the end of the two years, including $94 in interest.

Avery had $30,000 saved and was also getting 2 percent interest in her savings account. If she continued to save $450 per month, after 24 months she'd have $42,251, including $1,451 in interest. Together, in two years they'd have $52,595.

"It's my debt. I don't want her paying back my debt," I remember Adam saying. But then I had shown them something.

If we put the $900 a month ($450 from each of them) towards Adam's student debt as a household Magic Amount, it would make each payment to his student loan $1,475 ($575 minimum payment + $900 Magic Amount). At that rate they'd be done with the student loan in 9 months instead of 14 months and pay only $272 in interest. Then they'd free up $1,475 that they could save at 2 percent for the next 15 months.

If Avery's $30,000 accrued interest at 2 percent for the first nine months, with no additional contributions it would be worth $30,453 by the end of Month 9, including $453 in interest. Then they would be adding $1,475 per month for the next 15 months. At that rate, their combined savings after two years would be $53,645, earning another $1,067 in interest. Let's review:

Adam and Avery's Debt Game Plan		
	ALONE	AS A TEAM
Avery	$10,800 ($450 × 24 months)	$22,125 ($1,475 × 15 months)
Adam	$10,250 ($1,025 × 10 months)	
Total contributions	**$21,050**	**$22,125**
Interest earned	$1,545	$1,520
Savings in 24 months	**$52,595**	**$53,645**
Interest paid	$384	$272
Total savings	**$52,211**	**$53,373**

"You'll have $1,160 more in your pockets if you work as a team to pay down the debt first and then save together," I said.

"How is that possible?" Adam asked. "I don't want her to carry that burden."

"Well, if you look at the numbers, she'll carry more of a financial burden if you put $1,025 to debt every month and not to your joint savings plan."

Avery agreed. "Get over it, babe. I want us to save more—together."

Tag-teaming the household finances is almost always a financial win for the household. But not only is it a financial win, it's usually a big emotional win too.

Secret Debt: Confessing Debt to Your Teammate

Meet Jared and Willow

Ages: 29 and 30

Relationship status: engaged

Kids: 0

Annual gross household income: $50,000 (Jared) + $55,000 (Willow)
   = $105,000

Assets: $10,000 in wedding account

Liabilities: 0?

Jared and Willow came to see me for some household financial planning, as they were getting married. Willow had a job as an executive assistant and Jared was in the third year of his freelance photography business. When I asked them what they wanted to get out of their financial planning session, they told me they wanted to learn how to combine finances once they were married and save for a house. Awesome, right? At the time, I didn't know Jared had debt; it wasn't listed on their liabilities chart.

We made a plan together. They needed $13,000 for their wedding, so they had to put $400 a month towards that ($200 each) and to save $60,000 so they could have a down payment in five years ($500 each per month). If they could do that, they could afford a home and be debt-free after their wedding.

We hugged, I said congrats, and they left my office hand in hand, on the way to a celebratory dinner. About a week later I got an email from Jared:

Hey Shannon,

I'm kind of freaking out. This is really hard for me to say, but I have debt from my business that I haven't told Willow about. It's

$47,000. I don't know what to do now that we've made all these plans. I can't afford to save the amounts you told us to save for the down payment and pay down debt. Please help?

Jared

That's when sh*t got super real. My response? "Come by tomorrow and let's chat about it. I just need 30 minutes of your time."

The next day Jared came in to meet with me. He was nervous. My first order of business was to ensure that he knew he was not about to be judged or shamed. Obviously this was a big secret, and the last thing I wanted to do was make him feel like he should have kept it that way. It was a big deal that he had opened up to me. I was reminded of the anxiety I felt when I had to confess my debt to Matt after my laundry-room meltdown.

"So, tell me what's going on," I said.

He took a deep breath. "I started my photography business three years ago, and in the first two years I had to spend a lot of money on equipment, gear, courses and travel to try to make money. We live in the suburbs, so I have to drive a lot to get to gigs, and I needed to use debt to get the equipment I needed." He paused. "I know what you're thinking."

"What am I thinking?" I asked.

"That $47,000 is a ton of money and that profitable businesses shouldn't need to go into debt."

I waited a moment to see if there was anything else he wanted to get off his chest. Then I said, "I'm not thinking that at all. In fact, there's an entire industry dedicated to giving loans to new businesses, because many do need to borrow in the first few years. Especially those that require equipment."

"Yeah, I guess. I just feel so stupid." He put his hands over his eyes and leaned his head back. "People say things like 'You need to spend money to make money,' but how do you know what the right amount of debt is?"

"What do you think is the right amount of debt for your business?" I asked.

"Some, but not this much. I mean, I literally had to start from scratch. The problem is that I totally spiraled. In the beginning I had a credit card with a $10,000 limit on it that I was going to use just for business. I spent $4,000 on a website and $5,000 for equipment, and before I knew it I had maxed out the card before I even had all the stuff I needed. So I paid it off with my line of credit."

"Then what?"

"Well, I was terrified at first. Ten thousand dollars is a lot of money and I had never had debt before, but I didn't have even half the equipment I needed in order to get well-paying gigs. And I also needed money to pay subcontractors to help. So I ended up maxing out my credit card again and borrowing even more on the line of credit. So much debt, so quickly. When I hit $25,000 owing, I think something just snapped."

"Snapped?"

"I just stopped thinking about it. Every time I used my credit card, I would think about it as the business's debt, not mine. I justified my spending that way every time I swiped, and then I ignored it."

"Why didn't your debt feel real to you?"

"Hmm, that's interesting. You're right, I guess it didn't feel real." He paused. "I'm not sure. Maybe because I kept convincing myself that at some point I'd get my sh*t together and deal with it then, you know? I knew I'd have to pay it back eventually, but it never seemed like the right time to do it, so I'd just pay the minimum amount and forget about it until the next month when the payment was due. Now I'm left with $47,000 owing and I can't save for our wedding or down-payment plan. It's such a disaster." He sighed.

"Jared, why doesn't Willow know?" I ventured.

"Because I don't want her to worry about marrying me and I don't want her to think I'm stupid." He stared at the table, unable to look me in the eyes.

I leaned in and made eye contact. "You're not stupid, Jared. Tell me, what do you say when money stuff comes up between you guys?"

He took off his baseball cap and put it on the desk. "I tell her the business is fine and that I'm just stressed out about a client issue."

I sat back. "Jared, you need to tell Willow."

"I can't. I'm actually worried that she won't want to marry me because I've been lying to her for so long."

Oh, man, this was all so familiar. I had been exactly where Jared was. Taking a line from my laundry-room fairy godfather, I asked, "What would you do if your roles were reversed?"

"I don't know. Give her a big hug and tell her it's okay?" He laughed nervously.

"Do you mean that?"

"Yes, a hundred percent," he said with conviction.

"So is it possible she would do the same for you?"

"For sure." He smiled. "I need her to expect less from me, as terrible as that sounds. I can't keep bringing in the same amount and save the way she needs me to save if I'm actually going to pay this debt down. I just don't want to disappoint her."

"Well, Jared, you cannot do this alone. You're absolutely right. To get it paid off, you need to divert the money you earn from your savings plan to the debt."

"How do I even begin to tell her?"

"You have to tell her and show her your Debt Game Plan. That's the best way to tell someone," I said, and we got to work.

Jared's Secret Debt Map (shhh)			
Debt	Amount	Interest Rate	Minimum Payment
Credit card	$15,000	19.5%	$450
Line of credit	$32,000	5.0%	$160
Total	**$47,000**		**$610**

Jared was already paying $610 towards his debt each month. I worked out that if he diverted the $500 he was supposed to contribute to the down-payment fund to his debt and the $200 that was supposed to go to the wedding (after the wedding happened), he could pay $1,310 per month towards his debt. At that repayment rate, he would be debt-free in 39 months. Meanwhile, he could still contribute $200 a month to their wedding fund for the next seven months. Here's what would happen:

Jared's Predicted Results			
Debt	Paid Off By	Interest Paid	Amount Freed Up
Credit card	Month 17	$2,295	$1,150 ($450 + $500 + $200)
Line of credit	Month 40	$4,048	$1,310 ($160 + $1,150)

"Tell Willow that you can be debt-free in three and a half years and can continue to save $200 to the wedding fund for the next seven months. Once the debt is paid off, you can save the $1,310 freed up to the down-payment fund for 20 months, for a total of $26,200 in savings. If she keeps saving her $500 a month as well, you'll have $56,200 towards a house. It will take you three additional months to save up your $30,000 portion, but the entire household net worth will be much better off. You're much more likely to be able to get a mortgage if you have no debt. Show her this plan. I promise you, this is the best thing you can do for you both, and for your future together."

Let's review where the household will be five years (60 months) from now, assuming that Jared could pay only an additional $200 per month to his debt after the wedding, while continuing to save $500 towards the down payment.

Jared and Willow's Financial Picture in 60 Months		
	ALONE	AS A TEAM
Credit card	0	0
Line of credit	$11,651	0
Total debt (Jared)	**$11,651**	**0**
DOWN-PAYMENT FUND		
Jared	$30,000 ($500 × 60)	$26,200 ($1,310 × 20)
Willow	$30,000 ($500 × 60)	$30,000 ($500 × 60)
Total savings	**$60,000**	**$56,200**
Household net worth	**$48,349** **($60,000 − $11,651)**	**$56,200** **($56,200 − 0)**

When he left my office, I knew Jared was bummed and afraid, but also hopeful. Having the plan to show Willow gave him the courage to explain where he was at but also the plan of attack. Having a Debt Game Plan already worked out when you tell someone is so important, because it shows the person you're telling that you mean business about paying it back.

A week or so later, I heard from Jared and Willow.

"Soooo, how are things?" I asked playfully.

"Good, actually." Willow laughed. "I mean, obviously scary, but your plan seems solid."

"So, Jared, how'd that go for you?"

"The worst! Willow was terrified."

She smiled. "No, I wasn't!"

They were goofing around. I knew all was fundamentally well. "So how do you feel now that everything is out in the open?" I asked.

"Relieved, to be honest. And she didn't leave me." He laughed and she pretended to be offended. "For real though, knowing that I don't have to keep pretending things are okay is a huge weight off my shoulders. Plus, making plans about having a house in the future doesn't freak me out with stress anymore, because Willow knows what's going on and I don't have to pretend I can afford to pay for it."

"What's changed for you?"

"It's the first time I feel truly accountable for the debt. Like, it's mine and I actually want to do something about it. And because Willow knows I can't put as much money into savings, for the first time I believe I can actually do something about it and it's not going to throw us way off course forever with our plans."

"What about you, Willow?"

She got a bit misty-eyed. "I just feel so bad that he felt he couldn't tell me. I almost feel guilty for constantly pushing us to make these expensive plans, because I had no idea of the financial stress he was under. I'm so happy I know now too, so that I can help instead of hinder."

"And how do you feel about the house fund? I know that was hugely important to you."

"I still want to buy a home, but now I know this is actually the best way for us to tackle our household finances together. As long as we divert that money from debt to savings when it's done, we'll come out on top in the long run. I'm good with it, for real. The plan really helped to show that. Hearing that he has $47,000 in debt was scary, but knowing that it won't hold us back from our goals was huge."

"Awesome," I said. I was grinning from ear to ear.

I'm happy to report that Jared and Willow are midway through their Debt Game Plan. Jared hasn't taken on more debt because he doesn't have to generate additional income and they pulled in their spending together. Jared and Willow have had their wedding, which was totally paid for with savings—no debt hangover. They are well on their way.

The key here was that Jared broke through the Shame-and-Blame Mentality by telling Willow about his debt. That made his debt real; he couldn't ignore it anymore, because he wasn't the only person who knew it existed. He was accountable to someone else. As a result, they made their plans together for him to pay it off. She lightened her expectations of what he was supposed to "bring home" as income, because she understood what he couldn't afford to do, and they adjusted their lifestyle together to make ends meet.

Jared wasn't alone anymore. That was the single most important gift they gave themselves—a way to better their financial lives now and to stay motivated in the long run. Sharing your debt secret can help take the load off you, set realistic expectations of what you can do financially in the household, and give you the accountability you need to make your debt real and motivate you to keep taking action. Jared was lucky that Willow was so supportive and understanding. It allowed them to create a plan together instead of his shouldering the burden alone.

I can't emphasize the importance of having your partner onside with debt plans. It helps to create a supportive home where you can be financially honest and vulnerable. In order to work as a team, map it out first. Make a plan and compare it to one where you keep going your own ways. Most times, both people are better off if they combine forces and tag-team the household finances and savings together.

But that's not always the case, as with my clients Kelsey and Alex.

Paying Someone Else's Debt

Meet Kelsey and Alex

Ages: 36 and 42

Relationship status: married

Kids: 0

Annual gross household income: $35,000 (Kelsey) + $75,000 (Alex)
= $110,000

Assets: Kelsey: 0 / Alex: condo worth $650,000; $50,000 in TFSA

Liabilities: Kelsey: $5,000 credit card debt; $15,500 personal loan /
Alex: $250,000 mortgage

Kelsey's Debt Map			
Debt	Amount Owing	Interest Rate	Minimum Payment
Credit card	$5,000	19%	$250
Personal loan	$15,500	6%	$360
Total	**$15,500**		**$610**

Kelsey and Alex lived in Vancouver and had been married for five years. Right after they got married, they moved into Alex's condo, which Alex had owned long before they got together. When I looked at their forms before they came in, they read almost as if two completely different people were coming in to two completely different meetings.

Kelsey	Alex
What are your short-term financial goals?	
• Make a budget	• Make lump-sum payment to mortgage
• Pay down debt	• Renovate bathroom

• Go on a trip	• Keep travelling
What do you want to get out of our financial session?	
• Plan to get and stay out of debt	• Road map: retirement savings vs. mortgage • Start investing

The only thing these two had in common, financially speaking, was that they both wanted to go on a trip. How was it possible that a couple in love, married and living together could have two such completely different financial lives? I see this a lot.

This happens, and when it does, I have to respect it and work around it, especially when debt is involved. As you know by now, debt can be an emotionally charged topic that brings up a whole bunch of feels in people.

Alex and Kelsey came in for their session, both a little nervous (I could tell).

"This is a question for both of you. What do you want to get out of today so that when you leave here, you're like, 'Hell, yes, that was the best!'?" I asked.

Kelsey spoke first. "Just what we put on the forms."

"Okay, so Kelsey, you'd like"—I read from her answers—"a plan to get out of debt."

She nodded.

"Great!" I said. Neither of them was smiling. This was a bit like pulling teeth. I just needed to keep going so I could take the edge off for them both.

"Alex, what about you?" I asked her.

"Well, as the form says, I have a pension at work, but I'm not sure how best to prepare for retirement outside of that. Do I invest? Do I put money into my mortgage? I just have a lot of questions and need a roadmap."

Okay. So next came the part where I needed to step it up and make things uncomfortable—for the greater good. "I'm sure this comes as no surprise, but you two have extremely different financial goals," I said, pointing to the elephant in the room.

They shifted awkwardly for a moment. I said nothing and just kept smiling, waiting to see who spoke first. That's important. It's usually the person who feels most strongly about keeping finances separate who speaks first.

And then Kelsey weighed in. "Well, we're in two totally different financial situations, so we can't really have the same goals. I have debt and Alex doesn't. It's Alex's house—she bought it, so the whole mortgage versus RRSP thing isn't really something I need to know about. We run our finances separately."

"Alex, what do you think?" I turned to her, not wanting to let her off the hook.

"Well, yeah, I guess when we got together, we each had our own thing going on financially and we never really officially merged finances."

"Do you want to merge them?" I asked. "That's a question for you both."

They looked at each other. Kelsey shifted in her chair again and Alex put her hand on Kelsey's knee, a gesture of support. Obviously money stuff brought up a ton of feels for them. I imagined that either they had had some big arguments about it or maybe it was something that just never came up at all.

"I think we're good with things separate, but I don't want to speak for Alex," Kelsey said.

"I mean, it works for us," Alex said.

I let them off the hook and out of the hot seat for a moment. The tension had to be lifted. I knew we'd eventually have to circle back to financial teamwork, but I didn't want them to think I had a hidden agenda to get them to share chequing accounts. *It's totally possible to work as a financial team and still keep finances separate.*

"Great!" I said cheerfully. Their relief was palpable. "Let's have a look at the finances."

Kelsey and Alex's Financial Snapshot		
Monthly After-Tax Income	KELSEY	ALEX
	$2,320	$4,200
FIXED EXPENSES		
Mortgage		$1,000
Utilities		$300
Property tax		$350
Home insurance		$100
Cellphones	$60	$100
Cable/Internet	$80	
Bank fees	$10	$15
Minimum debt payments:		
Credit card	$250	
Consolidation loan	$360	
Total Fixed Expenses	**$760**	**$1,865**
SHORT-TERM SAVINGS		
Slush fund		$250
Vacations	$200	$200
Emergencies	0	$300
Total Short-Term Savings	**$200**	**$750**
SPENDING MONEY	$1,360	$1,230
MEANINGFUL SAVINGS		
RRSP contributions	0	0
TFSA contributions	0	$355
Magic Amount	**0**	**0**
Total Meaningful Savings	**0**	**$355**

"So, Alex, it looks like you cover all the housing bills," I said.

"Yep, everything but the cable and Internet," she said.

"I cover those," Kelsey said, quickly adding, "and I cover all the household groceries, toiletries and stuff instead of paying rent."

"Okay, great. Kelsey, let's start with you. Tell me about the debt. Is it rising, going down or just kinda hanging out where it is?"

"Hanging out," she said in a defeated tone. "I can't seem to get the credit card under control. I've always had a credit card balance. I work at a non-profit, so my income has grown only slowly over time, but it doesn't make sense to me why I can't pay it down. I feel like I barely spend any money. Seeing the numbers laid out like this really confuses me. Like, I don't spend $1,360 a month . . . but I must?" She looked at Alex. "That doesn't make sense, right? That my spending money is more than yours?"

"No, definitely not. I spend way more on clothes and going out than you do," Alex confirmed.

Interesting, right? Alex felt that she spent way more than Kelsey. Kelsey didn't even pay rent and yet was struggling to keep her head above water.

"Well, let's take a look at the spending," I said, and pulled up their average spending.

Kelsey and Alex's Average Monthly Spending		
	KELSEY	ALEX
Household groceries, pet stuff	$900	
Household toiletries	$100	
Household alcohol (wine)	$120	
Coffee shops	$50	$125
Clothes	$40	$200
Grooming	$30	$130
Dining/going out	$100	$425
Fitness classes	$10	$50
Rock climbing		$200
Entertainment	$10	$100
Total	**$1,360**	**$1,230**

At an initial glance, you might not see an issue of inequity between them. But I immediately knew why Kelsey couldn't stay out of debt and why Alex was totally in control—and it had nothing to do with bad financial habits.

"So I think I know what's going on here," I said. "The shared expenses aren't really being split fairly." A provocative thing to say, to be sure. I had done it on purpose.

"It's totally fair," Kelsey said immediately and defensively.

"Well, it looks like you're shouldering all the household groceries and trips to the wine shop and pharmacy, right?"

"Yes, but I don't pay rent. Those are my contribution," she said.

Alex jumped in. "Yes, but I make more money than you. Maybe that's why?"

"Part of it," I said.

"Wait," Kelsey said to Alex. "The amount I pay for groceries and stuff is less than the bills. Look, the cable and Internet, groceries, toiletries and wine only add up to $1,200, and your housing costs are $1,650. It's not you, Alex, it's me. I'm just sh*tty with money."

"Is that why you don't want to merge finances?" I ventured.

"Well, obviously. I don't want to bring her down. It's my sh*t and I want to deal with it. I don't want Alex to have to pay for my past mistakes."

And there it was. Kelsey was the one pushing back on the team-effort front. She didn't want handouts; she didn't want to feel even more guilt about her finances. I believed that the thought of Alex taking on her financial goals would stress her out even more. But she obviously needed help. I was going to have to do some fancy footwork.

"I'm going to say some things that both of you may not like or maybe both of you will. But either way, I ask that you hear me out, okay? Even if it makes you really dislike me for the moment."

They nodded.

"Okay, so when I look at how you're running the shared bills, I see inequity. Here's why. First off, all shared bills should be shared *equitably*, not equally. I know you've tried, but the portions of your incomes are off.

261

Kelsey, your contributions to shared household expenses are 52 percent of your after-tax income, whereas Alex, yours are only 39 percent."

"I knew something was off," Alex said.

I nodded. "Second, and more important, the *type* of expenses that Kelsey covers are harder to plan around."

"What do you mean?" Kelsey asked.

"Groceries, toiletries, wine—these are all fluctuating expenses." I pointed to their spending over the past months.

Expense	January	July	September	Totals
Groceries	$850	$1,050	$800	$900
Toiletries	$80	$120	$100	$100
Wine	$85	$150	$135	$120
Total	**$1,015**	**$1,320**	**$1,035**	**$1,120**

"In some months your contributions to these expenses are less than $1,120, but in others, you're over. These types of expenses vary frequently depending on what you both do that month. It's almost impossible to predict with accuracy what you'll need to spend. Alex's bills, however, are the same every month, no matter what's going on in your lives. She knows exactly what she needs to put aside in her budget for them. You don't. That's why some months you feel like there's extra money to save towards your debt and in others you're using debt to pay for stuff."

"I never even thought of that," Alex said.

"Neither did I," Kelsey added.

"I see this a lot. It's not fair to the person trying to guess what they'll need to spend each month. That usually leads to debt, especially if it's a large portion of their income. Which in your case, Kelsey, it is. It's why you feel that you don't spend money but you're still always broke. You don't really spend anything on yourself, while almost half your income is going to fluctuating household expenses."

"That makes sense," she said.

"So what do we do to fix it?" Alex asked.

"Without getting joint chequing accounts and without my finances affecting Alex's," Kelsey said.

"Just redistribute the shared expenses," I said. "Your shared household expenses are around $2,850 a month—$1,730 for Fixed Expenses and $1,120 fluctuating. Kelsey's income should handle 35 percent of the household expenses and, Alex, yours should handle the other 65 percent. So the shared expenses should be broken out this way."

Kelsey and Alex's Equitable Expense-Sharing Plan			
Expenses	Total	Kelsey (35%)	Alex (65%)
FIXED EXPENSES			
Mortgage	$1,000	$350	$650
Utilities	$300	$105	$195
Property tax	$250	$88	$162
Home insurance	$100	$35	$65
Cable/Internet	$80	$28	$52
Total	**$1,730**	**$606**	**$1,124**
FLUCTUATING EXPENSES			
Groceries	$900	$315	$585
Toiletries	$100	$35	$65
Wine	$120	$42	$78
Total	**$1,120**	**$392**	**$728**
OVERALL TOTAL	**$2,850**	**$998**	**$1,852**

"So Kelsey's total monthly contributions are now $998 instead of $1,200, which is $202 less, and Alex, yours are $1,852 instead of $1,650. How does that sit?"

Alex looked at Kelsey. Kelsey took a deep breath and looked back at Alex. "Does that still leave you with enough money to save and do all the things you want to do?" Kelsey asked.

"Alex," I said, "that's an extra $202 per month that you will now have to put towards the shared household expenses."

"If that's what's fair, then that's what it is," Alex said. "I've got room to lower my expenses. Maybe I can reduce my slush fund from $250 to $150 and reduce my spending money by $102. It all feels totally doable."

"And if it's not," I said, "we can always rejig. This is an experiment—nothing signed in blood." They both laughed. "We're just testing it out to see if we can make a win here for everyone."

"I have a question," Kelsey said. "How do we share the fluctuating expenses? I work from home a lot, so it makes sense that I go to the store."

"There are a few options. Ideally, my advice would be a joint chequing account just for the shared expenses. Then you'd each be responsible for depositing your share of the expenses each month. A lot of times couples will have one joint chequing account for all the shared fixed expenses and one for all the shared fluctuating expenses. Sometimes this can be a shared credit card with a low limit on it."

"I have a credit card with a $1,500 limit that I barely use," Alex said. "I could easily add Kelsey onto it and we could make it the household groceries and toiletries card."

"Kelsey, how do you feel about that?"

"I don't mind the low-limit joint credit card for shared groceries et cetera, but I think we should still keep everything else separate."

Alex agreed.

"Then, each month, Kelsey would transfer her share of the expenses to Alex."

"Like rent," Kelsey said.

"More like your fair share," Alex said.

"I definitely want to recommend that both of you sit down and talk things out with a lawyer, just to be careful. Since you're married but Alex owns the home, there could be some complicated family law issues there."

"We did that when we moved in together, and we do have a

cohabitation agreement in place. But now that we're shifting things around, it may be time to revisit that," Kelsey said.

"I think it would provide a lot of comfort to you both," I said. "Just, ya know, rip the romance right out of it and get real about money."

They both laughed again.

"So, to summarize, each month Kelsey transfers $606 to Alex for fixed expenses and $392 to the shared credit card. Alex will keep paying the house bills from her bank account and will put $728 per month into the shared credit card. If expenses go over that, you'll need to share the amount according to the 35:65 ratio."

Everyone was smiling and nodding now. Yay!

"Kelsey, this frees up $202 for you each month," I said. "I suggest we use $200 as your Magic Amount to pay back the debt and the other two dollars for Spending Money. Don't spend it all in one place, now," I joked.

She laughed. "Hey, two dollars is two dollars. But $200 towards my debt will be amazing!"

"This is so exciting!" Alex said.

Using $200 a month as Kelsey's Magic Amount would mean that all her debt would be paid back within 29 months, versus the 39 months it would have taken on her own, which would save her $1,482 in interest. And once she became debt-free, Kelsey could then save $810 a month to her TFSA.

Let's compare their household net worth 39 months from now.

	ALONE	AS A TEAM
Kelsey's interest	$2,852	$1,370
Total debt	0	0
Kelsey's TFSA	0	$8,250
Alex's TFSA	$48,965	$48,965
Total assets	**$48,965**	**$57,215**
Household net worth	**$46,113** ($48,965 – $2,852)	**$55,845** ($57,215 – $1,370)

The household is better off by $9,732, in the same amount of time it would have taken Kelsey to become debt-free without sharing the financial load. I showed them the math.

"Wow," Kelsey said.

"That's so exciting!" Alex said, and they squeezed hands.

"As a team, your household is able to save much more together," I said, "even if you don't open joint chequing accounts. Sharing the financial load equitably will help everyone." Giving Kelsey a predictable budget that was shared equitably freed up enough dependable cash flow that she could consistently put $200 towards her debt and break her Debt Loop.

▶

When debt is involved, working as a team is almost always the more financially fruitful strategy if you look at it from a household perspective. But you must do it in a way that feels good for all parties. Is it redistribution of household expenses? Using money from savings to pay off debt for another person? Whatever it is, if you tag-team the household finances together, your household will be better off.

Don't be shy about talking to a family lawyer. An unbiased third party who knows the law will be able to help you both navigate those murky waters so that everyone feels heard, understood and protected.

CHAPTER 15

Big Levers: Downsizing, Credit Counselling, Consumer Proposals and Bankruptcy

There are times when you're sinking into debt and you can't stop. The Debt Loop has you in its clutches, and all the consolidation tactics, Magic Amounts, money pulled from savings and Controlled Debt Burns just aren't cutting it. Something drastic needs to happen. These are tough situations to be in, both financially and emotionally.

It's the end of the road. You've exhausted all the options and you've exhausted yourself. You've reached the end of the line. This is when big levers such as selling your home and downsizing or getting help from credit counselling, consumer proposal or bankruptcy can be needed.

If you're in a situation where you think it's the end of the road for you, I'm going to hold your hand the entire way through this chapter. (Obviously I can't do that in real life, but I'd be doing it if we were in the same room and you wanted me to.)

Here's the positive thing about knowing that you've reached the end of the debt road—there's nowhere to go but up. It literally cannot get worse, which is kind of a relief.

My clients Heather and Elliot lived in Toronto. They were at the end of the line, financially speaking. With two kids, less than 15 years until retirement, a mortgage and more than their fair share of financial lemons, they were sinking in debt and running out of options.

Meet Heather and Elliot

Ages: 56 and 58

Relationship status: married

Kids: 2, ages 20 (in school, still living at home in the summer) and 23 (graduated, not living at home)

Annual gross household income: $12,000 (Heather) + $80,000 (Elliot) = $92,000

Assets: house worth $750,000; $35,000 RRSP (Elliot)

Liabilities: $300,000 mortgage; $33,000 credit card debt; $15,000 car loan; $164,000 lines of credit

Heather and Elliot's Debt Map, Prioritized by Interest Rate			
Debt	Amount	Interest Rate	Minimum Payment
Credit card A (Heather)	$18,500	19.99%	$560
Credit card B (Elliot)	$14,500	19.99%	$440
Car loan (joint)	$15,000	7.20%	$400
Line of credit 1 (Heather)	$24,000	7.00%	$150
Line of credit 2 (Elliot)	$30,000	6.00%	$150
Home equity line of credit (joint)	$110,000	4.8%	$410
Total	**$212,000**		**$2,110**

Heather and Elliot's Financial Snapshot	
MONTHLY AFTER-TAX INCOME	
Elliot	$4,660
Heather (average)	$1,000
Total Monthly After-Tax Income	**$5,660**

FIXED EXPENSES	
Mortgage	$1,625
Utilities	$300
Property tax	$400
Home insurance	$125
Family cellphones	$350
Cable/Internet/subscriptions	$100
Bank fees	$10
Minimum debt payments:	
Credit card A (Heather)	$560
Credit card B (Elliot)	$440
Car loan	$400
Line of credit (Heather)	$150
Line of credit (Elliot)	$150
HELOC	$410
Total Fixed Expenses	**$5,020**
SHORT-TERM SAVINGS	
Slush fund	0
Vacations	0
Emergencies	0
Total Short-Term Savings	**0**
SPENDING MONEY	$2,200
TOTAL COST OF LIFE	**$7,220**
MEANINGFUL SAVINGS	
RRSP contributions	0
TFSA contributions	0
Magic Amount	0
Total Meaningful Savings	**0**
TOTAL SHORTFALL	**$1,560**

Heather and Elliot were making $2,110 in minimum monthly payments and going into debt at a rate of $1,560 per month. Their combined income wasn't enough to cover even their Fixed Expenses. They were feeling really low; I could tell by their body language. You may be wondering how a couple with a house worth $750,000 could end up on the verge of bankruptcy. Let's back up a moment.

Heather had run a successful wedding planning and coordinating business for years; her annual income ranged between $50,000 and $65,000 (before taxes). Elliot and Heather had lived their regular life off his steady paycheque and used her income for vacations, retirement savings, extra mortgage payments and to help put their boys through university.

Five years ago, after a massive unexpected surge in housing prices, they borrowed $250,000 on their almost-paid-down mortgage to renovate their home. They redid the kitchen, put in a pool, dug out the basement to create an entire second rec room, and renovated their bathrooms.

"It was the first time we'd touched the house since we bought it in our thirties and it spiralled. But now we owe more on our mortgage than we bought the house for," Heather said. "At the time we figured we still had 15 working years ahead of us. Elliot's job was steady, he's got a pension and my business was doing well. We didn't feel at all scared about the future outlook. Boy, were we naive."

Four years ago, Heather developed an autoimmune disease that affected her health to a point where she could no longer work. "I didn't know what I had at the time, but I couldn't keep my eyes open, my hands were tingling, and I even fell asleep on the job during a wedding. Wedding planning and coordinating involves long hours, late nights and lots of stress. I couldn't physically do the work anymore, even though I wanted to," she told me. "It was like having the rug pulled out from underneath us."

She did not have disability or critical illness insurance to replace the income stream she would no longer be able to earn. "I just didn't think I needed it. I could never justify the expense. In hindsight, I wish I had. But hindsight is twenty-twenty."

That's when they began to borrow on their line of credit to make ends meet. "At first we assumed that I would heal quickly," Heather said. "I would change my diet, implement an exercise routine—we'd get through it."

"We must have bought a thousand books and tried hundreds of cures," Elliot added.

"Experimenting with your health is expensive," Heather said with a laugh. "Supplements, trainers, this type of healer, that type of healer. Most things weren't covered by Elliot's benefits. We must have spent $15,000 trying to get a proper diagnosis for me and a cure for the symptoms. When you're sick, you spend money looking for a cure. It's as if affordability doesn't even factor into the equation. You're sick—you try to find a way to fix it." She looked at Elliot and he nodded in agreement.

In the course of a year they had taken on more than $50,000 in debt on their line of credit. "We kept thinking I'd go back to work any day now and we'd be fine. I mean, I wanted—and still want—to work, but my body won't allow it. We didn't worry about the debt at first. We just kept living our normal life because I kept thinking that I'd get better and then I'd be working, and half my income could go to us and the other half to paying down the debt. After about a year and a half, we realized that I couldn't do my job anymore. That I wasn't getting better and I was going to have to retrain for something else that I could do, and work around my condition."

Heather and Elliot grabbed hands and I saw a squeeze. Solidarity. That simple gesture let me know that they operated as a united front. They had obviously been through a lot, but they were in it together. It wasn't anyone's fault; it was just life, complete with financial lemons.

"So then we spent another $20,000 training me in graphic design and web development," Heather said. "I've always been really great with that stuff and I thought it would be something I'd be able to do as a sole proprietor if I couldn't land a full-time job."

Smart, I thought.

"By that time our minimum payments had gone up by so much that my income could barely support our daily living. And then Ken, our eldest, went to university," Elliot said. Heather added, "And since I hadn't been able to work for two years at that point, we didn't have money saved up to help him. I think we've now spent more than $40,000 between the two boys, helping to offset school. They both have student loans and have used up what we had set aside in RESPs. But two kids living away from home during the school year is expensive. They've tried to get jobs too, but, like Mom, no luck."

Damn. This was tough.

"We still have our youngest son at home during the summers and I haven't been able to get nine-to-five work. Ageism is real," Heather said. "I've been actively looking for employment for two years now. I've had interviews, but I'm applying for entry-level positions. The interviewers are young enough to be my kids. I can tell they're just nodding along, thinking, *Okay, grandma*." She laughed wryly. "I've been able to do some freelancing, which has helped, but we need so much more at this point. I haven't been able to make more than $20,000 in any year. And so here we are today. We're tapped. Totally."

"That's a lot of lemons thrown your way, guys."

"Well, it hasn't been easy, that's for sure," Heather said.

"So how can I help today?"

"Do you have a winning lottery ticket?" Elliot asked.

"If I did, I'd sign it over to you right now," I said, and I meant it.

They looked at each other and Elliot let out a big sigh. "Well, we only have $25,000 left on our home equity line of credit. Our mortgage is up for renewal in a few months. We don't know what our next move is, or if we even have a next move. Are we on the brink of the Big B here?"

"I don't think so. There's still enough equity in the house to bring you to zero without having to go into bankruptcy. But I agree that the time to act is now. You're looking at the Big D—downsizing."

"You don't think we can just borrow on the mortgage again?" Elliot asked.

"If you roll the debt into the mortgage, your mortgage will go up to $512,000. With a rate of 3.3 percent, your monthly payment would go from $1,625 to $2,911—an increase of $1,286—if you amortized over 20 years. And even though that would clear up the $2,110 in monthly minimum payments, you'd really only free up $824 a month ($2,110 – $1,286).

"You're currently in a position where you're going into debt by $1,560 each month, almost $18,720 a year. Even if you put the $824 back into your pocket, you're still $736 short each month. Plus you want to retire in 15 years, so a 20-year mortgage isn't helpful either. I'm worried that if you keep sinking and refinancing, you're going to get to a point where there's only enough equity in the house to pay down the debt and your mortgage, with nothing left after that for retirement.

"If you sold the house right now for $750,000, you'd net about $200,500 after realtor fees ($37,500) and paying back all your debts ($212,000) plus the mortgage ($300,000). You can still do some damage with $200,500," I said.

"Is that the smartest thing for us to do? The house has been the only thing keeping us afloat over the past four years," Elliot said.

I understood his concern. If your house has bailed you out of sticky financial situations in the past, it's almost impossible to understand a universe where you don't have that emotional and financial safety net.

"Well, let me ask you this," I said. "Where would you live if you didn't live in your house now?"

"We've thought about this a ton," Heather said. "We can be a bit more flexible because the boys aren't in high school anymore, but John still lives at home in the summer and we'd like to stay in Toronto, or at least close to the subway. All our friends are here, our lives are here, and Elliot doesn't have to commute very far to work if we're near a subway line."

"The goal here is to get you to a safe retirement. If you can work for another 15 years and downsize to a two-bedroom condo some-where along the subway line for $460,000, you can use the $200,500 as a down payment. Your mortgage would be $259,500, but you'd be debt-free. With a mortgage rate of 3.3 percent, you could put $1,825 per month into the new mortgage and you'd be mortgage-free by the time you retire in 15 years. Plus, check this out: Heather, this is based on your income of only $1,000 per month after tax. It doesn't take into account any potential income above that. So that helps to take the pressure off you in case the health gods aren't on your side."

"That sure would take the pressure off," she said.

"I'm not saying you can't earn more than that each year, but I'd like it to be something you do when you're healthy enough to kick it up a notch, in order to relieve you of the financial worry when you cannot."

I showed them what their finances would look like if they down-sized to pay off their debt.

Heather and Elliot's Financial Snapshot after Downsizing	
MONTHLY AFTER-TAX INCOME	
Elliot	$4,660
Heather	$1,000
Total Monthly After-Tax Income	**$5,660**
FIXED EXPENSES	
Mortgage	$1,825
Utilities/condo fees	$500
Property tax	$200
Home insurance	$100
Family cellphones	$350
Cable/Internet/subscriptions	$100
Bank fees	$10
Minimum debt payments:	
Car loan payment	0

Elliot personal credit card	0
Heather line of credit	0
Elliot line of credit	0
Joint HELOC	0
Total Fixed Expenses	**$3,085**
SHORT-TERM SAVINGS	
Vacation fund	$170
Emergencies	$200
Total Short-Term Savings	$370
SPENDING MONEY	$2,200
TOTAL COST OF LIFE	**$5,655**
MEANINGFUL SAVINGS	
RRSP contributions	0
TFSA contributions	0
Magic Amount	0
Total Meaningful Savings	**0**
TOTAL SHORTFALL	**$0**

"Check it out!" I was excited. "If Elliot's income remains the same for the next 12 years, you'll be able to be mortgage-free and debt-free, spend $2,040 a year on vacations ($170 a month), put money aside for spikes in spending and emergencies, and keep your spending money the same as it is right now. Heather, that's if you earn $12,000 a year after tax."

"What about John, our youngest? He's still in school, with two more years to go. We paid a lot for Ken's education. It wouldn't be fair to John not to help him too," Heather said.

"How much do you anticipate needing to give him to make it even?" I asked.

"Probably another $30,000."

"Hmm." I thought for a moment. "What if he could take out student loans or borrow on a student line of credit to survive the last two years of university, while you keep up your job search and freelance? If you guys are debt-free and have downsized, any money Heather earns above the $12,000 a year can go into savings, since we know you've got a super-viable, safe financial plan with just the $12,000. Anything you earn above the $12,000 can be saved up and given to him when he graduates. Just don't tell him in the meantime, in case your health takes a hit again and you can't earn any more than the $12,000. How would that feel?" I asked.

"He's already got student loans, but they don't charge interest until six months after he graduates. So that could work," she said.

"Elliot?" I asked.

"Sorry . . . I'm still in shock that we can be debt- and mortgage-free and actually retire in 15 years."

Heather and I burst out laughing. "Have you even been listening?" Heather jokingly scolded him.

"No." He laughed, then said, "John will be fine. By the way, my pension won't be more than the equivalent of $35,000 a year, but it's indexed for inflation."

"Exactly. Since you'll be mortgage-free in 15 years, your cost of living will drop dramatically." I looked at his pension statement and their Canada Pension Plan statements of contributions. "Between your combined estimated CPP pensions ($15,000 in current-day dollars), Old Age Security (about $14,000 in current-day dollars) and your work pension ($35,000 in current-day dollars), you should have enough after tax to afford your daily life, pay your bills and still travel a bit. You're very lucky to have this pension," I said.

"We know," they said, almost in unison.

"You won't be yachting or anything like that in retirement, but you're safe. The key is being debt- and mortgage-free so that you can survive on the pensions and the retirement savings you have put away."

They laughed. "I don't want to yacht. I just want to sleep at night and stop stressing," Elliot said. He looked at Heather. "We'll get our lives back."

"I know."

"I can't even express the relief I feel right now," he said. "And we still have an asset in retirement. In case one of us needs care, we could sell the condo," he said.

"So, the hard part now will be actually selling your home," I said. "I've had downsizing conversations many times before, and most people don't go through with it in the end. Too emotionally charged."

"Well, it's not ideal," Heather said with a laugh, "but what else can we do? We have no other option. If we keep going this way, we'll end up broke, with no house at all. I'm just glad we're doing this now and not waiting until it's too late."

They left my office excited and nervous but full of hope, for the first time in a long time.

I'm happy to report that I had another meeting with Elliot and Heather two years later. This time it was a full-blown retirement planning session. They had assets and income! A totally different life, and they were a totally different couple.

"So, things look great on paper. How did it all play out on your end?" I asked.

"Way harder than we thought," Elliot said. "I thought I was totally into the downsizing. I mean, we did sell, but selling was hard. We were gutted. I didn't really appreciate how much life and love we'd put into that house. Saying goodbye was really tough. I moped around for the first few months in the condo, going, 'This place is too small. We have a postage stamp of a balcony.' Just, you know, generally being a downer."

"I cried the whole time the house was listed," Heather said. "When the real estate agent showed us the offers, I kept thinking, *No, that's not good enough!* Even though we actually got above asking."

"Above asking?" I was so happy for them.

"All the renos we'd done paid off a bit—we got about $50,000 above asking in a bidding war. We used the extra money right away for John's school costs."

"And Heather, how's the employment/freelance game going?" I asked.

"Still looking for a full-time job. But I've been earning about $15,000 to $20,000 through freelance work. That helped us afford a family vacation that was above our $2,000-a-year limit and we made some storage and cabinet renovations in our new condo without using debt to fund it. Imagine that!"

"Sounds like the plan is working well. I know it couldn't have been easy."

"Definitely hard. I think that if you had asked us to downsize even a year sooner, we would have laughed in your face. But I'm so glad we did. I haven't slept this well since before I got sick. Plus the fact that our lives and our retirement savings work now, given Elliot's income and me earning $12,000, is such a relief to us both. I didn't realize how deeply the anxiety was rooted in my body until we sold and paid off the debt. My shoulders were wrapped around my ears and there was a knot in my stomach that I didn't even know was there until it was gone. I was so used to living in panic mode, thinking that I needed to earn $50,000 or $60,000 to get us financially safe again. My health is improving, and I know that when my condition flares up again, any anxiety I have will be limited to my health wellness, not my health-and-financial wellness."

"We are happier and the boys are happier," Elliot said. "It was the best decision we've ever made. Thank you for the push."

"Hey, you both already knew what needed to happen. I just confirmed that it was the right choice," I said. "I'm so proud of you guys. Honestly, this is wonderful. And now we get to plan your savings strategy!"

"Woo-hoo!" We high-fived.

I was indeed happy for them. Downsizing is one of the hardest big levers to pull. As you get older, the stakes get higher and higher, and if you've got kids in school or friends in the area, they're potentially even higher. In addition, if housing prices go up, the downsizing is often a dramatic one. You might have to go from a house to a condo, or from owning a condo to renting an apartment. Either way, you'll likely feel the lifestyle adjustment keenly and may be blue or resentful from time to time. But that's normal.

All the downsizers in my practice have said the same thing—it was brutal. But, while there are still pangs of sadness and a bit of resentment, they never have regret. The freedom that comes from being debt-free cannot even be imagined from a place of panic and fear—which is where you may be living right now. It's easy to focus on all the things you won't have if you sell your home, but try to think about all the things you will enjoy without the debt. Relief. Freedom. The ability to build savings and live your life again. That's the dream—you just have to keep chasing that feeling.

Heather and Elliot were lucky in the eleventh hour that they still had their home to sell and a pension. They had equity they could use to keep them out of bankruptcy. But that's not the case for everyone. Many people don't have a house or condo to sell. What then do they do when they're sinking and can't stop? My client Victoria is a perfect example.

When You Need a Formal Credit Management Solution

There may come a time when you need help in a bigger way. When your regular Debt Game Plan isn't working on your own, things such as credit counselling, consumer proposals and bankruptcy may make sense. These are credit solutions that exist to help people, and there is nothing to be ashamed of if that's where you're at.

Maybe you're contemplating the Big B; maybe you've spent hours online at night researching "bankruptcy vs. consumer proposal" and you still don't know what to do. You don't want to make a move that feels so drastic, but you may also feel that there's no other option. If this is you, just breathe. There's always hope. Always. Even in the eleventh hour.

Victoria is a client who I will remember forever as the ultimate debt champion. She came to see me during the final moments of her epic financial battle. She had debt—lots of it. She was single, she rented, and she didn't have a great credit score. After a heartbreaking divorce, Victoria needed to start her life over.

Meet Victoria

Age: 42

Relationship status: divorced, single and online dating

Kids: 0

Annual gross household income: $70,000

Assets: $20,000 RRSP

Liabilities: $44,000 credit card debt; $40,000 line of credit

Victoria's Debt Map			
Debt	Amount Owing	Interest Rate	Minimum Payment
Credit card A	$25,000	22%	$750
Credit card B	$14,000	20%	$420
Line of credit	$40,000	8%	$250
Total	**$79,000**		**$1,420**

"I kind of always let someone else take care of my finances." Victoria cleared her throat. "I used to let my dad take care of my finances and then my ex; I just didn't want the responsibility. And I never really had to worry about money, so I didn't." She shifted in her chair.

"So tell me about the debt," I said. "Did it come all at once or was it a slow build?"

"I was in the start-up phase of my new business just before my ex and I split; I had left a well-paying marketing job to do my own thing. Then I got blindsided by the divorce. Once we separated, I didn't have a steady income, but I just kept living the same lifestyle that I always had, even though I didn't have enough income. At first it was a few hundred here and there—new shirt for a date, new furniture, personal development courses, retreats to heal my heart. Then I started investing in my business. That's when things went off the rails in a bigger way."

"What do you mean?"

"I guess I felt like life had thrown me some lemons and I deserved to feel happiness, y'know? I would be like, 'F*ck this, I'm gonna do what I want.' Totally harnessing my teen self." She giggled. "I guess I was rebelling against the logical side of me that knew I couldn't afford the life I wanted to keep living, so I just ignored it."

"That's pretty common, especially when debt has grown to a scary amount," I said.

"Totally. Whenever I would think about my debt or sit down to make a plan, my brain would literally shut down and I couldn't think of alternatives. It was like some sort of financial PTSD or something. Every time I tried to make a plan and get serious, the effort and the changes I would need to make seemed so drastic and felt so restrictive. I'd just had my heart broken and my life fall apart, so I needed to be in a place where I could think about growth and a future again. I needed to be able to feel that happiness was still possible. I felt like the debt-repayment plan that needed to happen was oppressive and would hold me back from what's possible. So I didn't start one—and here we are."

I could have listened to her all day. Victoria was so clearly able to articulate her battle with debt and what had happened and why she was there. She was just so wonderfully real. I felt lucky to be a person who gets to see people at their rawest, their most vulnerable. It's a privilege I do not take lightly.

"I have a question," I said.

"Shoot."

"When I had debt, and when many of my clients had debt, one common theme was that we believed something really big needed to happen in order to solve our debt problem. Until that happened, it was 'F*ck it, keep spending.' Did you have that experience?"

She thought for a moment. "Something similar. I heard an entrepreneur guru lecture and she had this amazing story about how she had only five dollars to her name and all this debt. You know, she was totally broke, and then three days before her rent was due, her business took off and she made all this money and she was rich. I was sitting in the audience, eyes wide, thinking, *That's like me!* I truly believed some sort of miracle would happen—a bailout, a massive overnight shift in income from my business—and eventually everything would just click into place. I remember joking to myself that one day this debt would be just a good story for my memoirs."

"So what made you make the appointment with me?"

Victoria let out a breath. "I'm totally maxed out." She shook her head. "I'm single, I'm 42 and I'm at a place where paying my rent is getting hard because of my minimum debt payments. I just got a full-time job that pays well. I can't keep running from it."

She looked at her Debt Map on the computer screen in disbelief. "It's strange to see it all laid out like this. It still doesn't feel real. I know that it is, but I can't believe that it is what it is." She looked at me. "Am I totally f*cked here?"

I looked her squarely in the eyes. "No, you're not. There is always hope. Even if the debt were to result in a bankruptcy, I don't believe that means you're f*cked. Bankruptcy, consumer proposals, credit counselling are all financial tools that exist for a reason—to be used."

She sort of half smiled, and I started through the list of possible solutions. "Okay, so let's go through the list of possible solutions first. Have you tried to lower interest rates on the credit cards?"

"Yep. Denied by my bank twice, and I also didn't qualify for any more balance transfers."

"Have you tried to consolidate your debt with a consolidation loan or line of credit?"

"Yep. Maxed out on my line of credit a while ago, paying off my credit cards. A few weeks ago my request for a consolidation loan was denied by a B lender, which left me feeling pretty vulnerable and ashamed."

"I'm so sorry to hear that. But I want to acknowledge how much amazing work you've already done on your own to sort through this.

I think you know more about managing your finances than you give yourself credit for."

"Maybe. I wish I had done something sooner, but I can't go back in time. I've literally done everything. I even asked my dad for a loan."

"I'm assuming that didn't turn out the way you anticipated," I said carefully.

She sighed. "No, which really surprised me. I didn't think he would want me paying this much in interest. I had a plan ready to pay him off every dollar plus interest over five years, you know? Not a gift this time, but a business transaction. Want to know what he said?"

I winced. "Lay it on me."

"He said, 'Even though we can, we aren't going to lend you the money. This is your debt and you need to dig yourself out of it.'"

"Ouch."

"Then he told me to go bankrupt." Her voice cracked. "It was like a punch to the gut."

I put my hand on hers. "Victoria, you *can* do this on your own. I know you can. There are still options."

She wiped tears from her eyes. "I feel like there must be an important lesson or gift for me in all this. Something about taking responsibility and ownership and not hoping another person will come along to save me."

"One hundred percent," I said, and she smiled.

"So what's next? Do I actually need to go bankrupt?" she asked, her tone back to business.

"Not necessarily. There are other options, but I do think it may be time for a more formal credit management solution. Right now you're at risk of not being able to pay your rent and you've missed some minimum payments. If you were to continue making just the minimum payments, this debt would take over 15 years to pay back and you'd be maxed out for quite some time. That would also mean that for the next couple of decades you'd be on an extremely tight budget."

"I know. I think I'm at the end of the road here. What are the options?"

"Well, three common credit management solutions are credit counselling from an accredited counsellor, consumer proposals with a licensed insolvency trustee, and then there's the Big B."

"Oh yes. I've spent many nights researching those online at three a.m. when I can't sleep. But I'm still confused."

"Essentially, depending on which solution is best for you, you get some outside help and set up a structured repayment plan. That may give you the motivation and the formal repayment structure you need to start digging out," I said.

She paused. "Those methods make me nervous."

"Why?"

"They feel extreme to me."

"What makes you say 'extreme'?"

"Don't they hurt your credit score for years? And aren't you not allowed access to any credit while you're paying them off? As a single woman, that's terrifying to me. I mean, if I had to get another apartment I'd be screwed. How am I supposed to pay for subscriptions like Netflix?"

"Those are fair points. Yes, your credit score will take a hit. You might be in R9 or R7 for all or some of the time, depending on which option you choose. But—"

She cut me off. "What is R7 and R9?"

"I'm so sorry for using jargon!" I said and took out a chart from the Financial Consumer Agency of Canada to show her. "On your credit report, each of your creditors and financial institutions that you owe money to assigns you a credit score on a scale from 1 to 9 and reports it to the credit bureau. R1 is the best credit rating and R9 is the lowest. See?"

R1   You paid that creditor's loan on time.

R2   Your payment is 30 days late.

R3   Your payment is 60 days late.

R4   Your payment is 90 days late.

R5   Your payment is 120 days late.

R6   [typically not used]

R7   You are in a consumer proposal, consolidation or debt-management plan offered through a non-profit credit counsellor.

R8   A secured creditor has taken steps to realize on their security, for example, repossessing your car. This rarely appears on a credit bureau report because, after they take your car, they generally commence legal or collection action, which is rated R9.

R9   A bad debt has been placed for collection or is considered uncollectible, or you are bankrupt.

"These are like Dante's nine circles of hell," Victoria said drily.

I laughed so hard that I snorted. "I'm definitely using that in a book one day," I told her.

"Go for it," she said with a smile.

"So yes, your credit score will take a hit, and likely a big one, for a period of time. But here's the thing: right now your credit score is already taking a hit every day, because you're starting to miss minimum payments and you are constantly maxed out. Sure, you're not in R7 or R9, but at your current rate of repayment it may take more than a decade for you to be debt-free. Your credit score might not improve for five to eight years anyway, because of your debt-to-income ratio.

"If you do decide to get some help through a more formal credit management solution, it's likely you'll be debt-free in five years or less. Even if your credit score takes a hit for three years after you've successfully completed your debt-settlement plan, it could go back up to normal in eight years. So you get to start fresh again. And it's much more likely you'll be able to break your Debt Loop forever, which for me is the big thing."

I showed her a chart comparing the the three common credit management options.[*]

---

[*] See "Credit Management Solutions" in the Resource Library (page 309).

"It would be so good to feel like I'm not drowning anymore," she said. "I'm just scared of living life without a credit card and with bad credit."

I understood. "That's exactly what makes credit management solutions like these feel extreme, even though they are tools for you to use. But with a bankruptcy or consumer proposal, the trustee may be able to negotiate with your creditors to lower the total amount of debt that has to be repaid, and with all three options you get one consistent monthly payment. The thought of bad credit and no credit is scary, but honestly, where you're at, there's no room for new credit anyway."

She actually laughed. "You're so right. I'm maxed out and basically living without credit right now. Will talking to a credit counsellor or a bankruptcy trustee hurt my credit score?"

"Not until you actually sign on to a debt-repayment program with them. You can talk to a credit counsellor or a trustee to weigh your options, and I strongly suggest that you do," I said.

She let out a long sigh. "Okay, so what do I do next?"

"You need to explore all your options, but be careful who you talk to. You want to ensure that you're dealing with a reputable, trusted, accredited person. Be careful of companies that may try to scam you. There are businesses out there that offer to help people pay off debt or repair their credit score, but they are misleading and potentially a scam. The best thing to do is check the Financial Consumer Agency of Canada website and ensure that the company or trustee you want to meet with is listed there. To explore your credit counselling options, make sure any agency you're working with is in good standing with a provincial or national association and that the credit counsellor is qualified.

"If you want to explore consumer proposals or bankruptcy, you need to speak to a licensed insolvency trustee (LIT). These are people who are licensed by the Office of the Superintendent of Bankruptcy (OSB) to administer the bankruptcy process."

I also gave Victoria links to the Government of Canada's "Find a Licensed Insolvency Trustee" and "Getting Help from a Credit Counsellor."

"This will help ensure that you're looking in the right places."[*]

"Got it. Is there anything I can do to prepare?"

"Absolutely. It's likely that you'll have to fill out some sort of intake form to give the credit counsellor or trustee your information, things like personal identification and spouse or dependant information. Also, business information if you're self-employed, details on any prior insolvencies or proposals, and possibly about your bank or who your accounts are with. They will likely want to see some proof of all this, things like bank statements, ID, agreements such as mortgages or leases, life insurance, savings accounts, pay stubs—that sort of thing."

"Well, it's a good thing I've got all that sort of info in a drawer some-where in the depths of my storage room." She laughed.

"I know it can seem like a lot, but they basically just need proof of your financial situation. A lot of the work you've done for our session will help you prepare, since you've already mapped out your income, expenses, assets and liabilities."

"Okay. Anything else?"

"In all cases when you sit down with someone, you need to ensure you know exactly what services they will provide and how much they will charge. Then compare the information with the Financial Consumer Agency of Canada to ensure that it's standard," I said. "And if something sounds too good to be true, it probably is."

She left my office prepared to talk to a credit counsellor and a licensed insolvency trustee to explore all her options. After she did, she checked back in with me.

"I'm going to go forward with a consumer proposal."

"What sealed the deal for you?"

"Well, I liked the credit counsellor option, because I really believe in the ongoing education and support part of a debt-repayment plan.

---

[*] See "Getting Help from a Credit Counsellor" in Additional Reading (page 311).

But I couldn't realistically pay off all my debt within 60 months, so that wasn't the best option. When I went to the trustee, they were able to negotiate a lower total amount owing for me, so I'll only have to pay back $46,000—still over five years. Payments are going to be similar to what I pay overall, and it will be actually paying off principal!" she exclaimed excitedly. (It's important to note that every credit counselling plan, consumer proposal and bankruptcy is completely unique. You must get customized advice from a qualified professional.)

"Amazing. How do you feel?"

"Relief. Fear. Excitement? Anxiety. Shame still, in low moments. But mostly relief."

"What did the trustee say about your credit rating and the fact that you can't use debt products?"

"I can try to apply for a credit card and I can use one, as long as I'm upfront with the creditor and they approve it. Or I may be able to get a prepaid or secured credit card. It's not ideal, but I'm hopeful that could be a good solution for my monthly subscriptions and things like booking online. We'll see if that works out."

"You seem happy."

"I am. This has all been really interesting to learn about. And the range of emotions! I go from feeling relieved and peaceful to scared and overwhelmed by all the things I need to get done and the unknown future. But all in, I'm positive it's the way forward."

"I think so too. Everything happens for a reason."

"Absolutely. I believe this will heal my relationship with money. It was a painful lesson from my dad, but now I know I can't pin any expectations on anyone but me. The debt is mine and I'm finally accountable for it, in a way that makes me feel peaceful rather than rebellious or resentful. It's weird. Adulting is scary."

We hugged on her way out. She was so strong, and I knew she'd be totally okay.

I checked in with Victoria in Year 4 of her consumer proposal. She had paid it off early!

"My credit score will take a hit for another two years. Then this whole thing is behind me!"

"Wonderful!" I said.

She had decided to keep up her side hustle so that the extra money could go into her consumer proposal. In only three years Victoria had become debt-free.

"Anything you wish you knew before going into it?" I asked.

She thought about it. "Well, I knew I couldn't use credit, but the logistics of that were annoying. Especially when you're a single person who can't rely on a parent's credit card to book stuff. It was hard at times if I wanted to book something or pay for a concert ticket, or just regular life stuff. But I'm surviving. This has really taught me how important it is to limit the amount of money you have access to. It's a bit suffocating at first, but after three years I've learned to work within it."

"Do you feel that you're in the possibilities mindset again? Like, things are possible?"

"Yes. The consumer proposal gave me my life back. I'm no longer living just to run up debt and then run away from it. Thank you for making it okay."

"What do you mean?"

"Well, I knew I had to do something like this, but my shame was so strong that I didn't have the guts. You made it feel like less of a judgment. And when I thought about it as a tool instead of a punishment for people who suck at money, I could get my sh*t together and do it. It was the best thing I've done for my finances in my whole life, and the first time I really took ownership of them."

I was so happy for her. Victoria had taken financial lemons and made lemonade.

How to Approach Credit Management Solutions

If you're in a situation where you feel like it's the eleventh hour and there's no other choice, don't be afraid to talk to someone about credit management solutions. Whether it's credit counselling, a consumer proposal or even a bankruptcy, exploring your options is important. It just may be the best financial decision you've ever made. It doesn't mean you're bad with money and it certainly doesn't mean you'll be bad with money forever. These services act like a lifejacket in a turbulent sea. Grab on to your opportunity to get ashore safely.

Here's how to tell if you should be speaking with an accredited credit counsellor or a licensed insolvency trustee:

- You have an income or some way to pay back the debt.
- You are unable to pay debts as they become due. This usually means you've been missing minimum payments or using payday loans. Your debt is rising but your income is not.
- You have unsecured debts such as credit cards, a line of credit, income taxes or HST (for sole proprietorships).
- You feel like you're sinking and cannot stop and you don't know who to pay.

Where do you start? Your first step is to explore your options with both an accredited credit counsellor to discuss debt-management plans and a licensed insolvency trustee to discuss consumer proposal and bankruptcy. Before you sit down with them, search the websites of the Government of Canada or provincial or national associations to ensure that the agency is in good standing. For insolvency trustees, go to the Government of Canada's "Find a Licensed Insolvency Trustee" and search there.[*]

You'll need to find out about the agency's services and costs, so ask the following questions to help find an agency that is right for you:

- Is the first consultation free?
- What services does the agency provide?
- Will the agency provide a written proposal describing how they will help?

---

[*] See "Credit Management Solutions" in the Resource Library (page 309).

- What type of support will the agency give to help you improve your money management skills?
- Will the agency provide you a monthly statement of payments?
- What are the counsellor's qualifications?

And here are some things to keep in mind so you can watch out for scammers:

- Companies or agencies cannot guarantee that they will repair your credit quickly.
- Improving your credit score will take time. It's not a quick fix.
- Do not take out a high-interest loan to pay off debts.

It will be scary, but you can do this. Think of how far you've already come. These consultations are just conversations for now. That said, you want to be prepared and to take them seriously. Here are some questions you'll want to ask:[*]

- How much of your debt will be repaid?
- What type of debts will be repaid?
- How long will you be making payments?
- How much will your monthly payment be?
- What happens if you miss a monthly payment?
- What will happen if your financial circumstances change and you need to reduce your payments or cannot make them?
- Can creditors or debt-collection agencies continue to contact you?
- What will happen to your assets?
- What will happen to your credit score?
- How much will you pay in fees?
- Can a creditor change their mind and withdraw from the agreement?

---

[*] These questions come from the Financial Consumer Agency of Canada (canada.ca/en/financial-consumer-agency.html).

291

Compare your answers from different agencies to figure out which is right for you. Remember, these are tools for you to use so you can move forward with your life. Focus on what it will mean for your future, not what it means about your past.

Trust Yourself—
You're Not "Bad with Money"

I always hear things like "I'm just the worst person when it comes to money." I think one of the worst things about debt has nothing to do with minimum payments or interest—that's just math. It's the Shame-and-Blame Mentality that haunts us, robbing us of our ability to trust our gut when it comes to our ability to handle money. You see, if you have debt and enough people make you feel bad about it, eventually you'll start to believe that you are, in fact, "bad with money."

Let me set the record straight. No one—and I mean no one—is bad with money. Sure, some people have the information they need to succeed earlier. Or maybe they're just luckier. A lot of times I see people mistaking luck for financial savvy. Things like *My brother bought his house for, like, nothing and just sold it for a ton of money. He's so good with money*, or *My friend made so much on that marijuana stock. I should have invested too. I'm so bad with money*. Think about it. Whether it's housing prices or the stock market, no one knows exactly what's going to happen. It's all risk. Everyone just plays the hand they're dealt the best way they can and life plays out one way or another. Financial luck does not equate with financial savvy. Don't confuse the two. If someone has had more financial luck than you, that doesn't make you bad with money.

If you're reading this book, you have debt. But debt does not represent financial failure. Remember Chapter 2? Debt was likely the only option in the beginning. As soon as you catch yourself thinking that you're bad with money, you have to stop. Why? Because once you believe that you're someone who's "just bad with money," you risk becoming that. If you say it to yourself often enough, eventually your actions will follow. I've seen it so many times.

"Bad with Money"—a Self-fulfilling Prophesy

"So, how do you feel about this Debt Game Plan?" I asked.

"Good," Brent said. Then his shoulders sort of shrank, giving away his insecurity.

"But . . ." I said, raising an eyebrow.

"No, it's fine. All good."

"I'm not buying. Spill it," I said.

He waved away my concern, but I've always been the persistent type. "Look, Brent, there's no point in your leaving here with a plan that you can't—or won't—implement." Sometimes I get super-real with people really quickly.

He shifted, obviously a bit uncomfortable with my directness. "It's not that I don't want to. I'm just afraid that I can't."

"Is the Magic Amount too much? We can tone it down if it doesn't feel realistic."

"No, no, it's totally doable. Everything is doable and I want to do this. I want to make it work. I've just been so burnt by attempts to get my debt under control. I've failed so many times."

"It sounds like you've lost faith in your ability to feel confident about your money."

"Yes!" he said. "Exactly. That's exactly it! I'm just so bad with money, I guess I don't trust myself."

"Have you always thought you were bad with money, or is this recent?" I asked.

The question surprised him. "I don't know."

"Tell me about a time when you were good with money."

He laughed uncomfortably. "Ah, I don't know."

I didn't say anything right away; I didn't want to let him off the hook.

"I guess . . ." He paused. "I guess never? God, that's sad."

"What do you mean, never?"

"Well, I've always been bad with money. I graduated from university with $40,000 worth of student loans and I really struggled to get my first full-time job. My parents are from Manitoba, but there was no work in my field there, so I couldn't live at home after school. I had debt and I could barely make ends meet during my early twenties. I didn't file taxes for a few years. I've just always had debt or made bad choices."

"How do you think your feeling that you're bad with money has affected how you manage your finances?"

"I *don't* manage them," he said with a bit of a laugh.

"What do you mean?"

"I think I either ignore them or let someone else deal with them. Like, because I didn't file my taxes a few times, now I just let my mom's accountant deal with them. Here I am in my mid-thirties and my mom's accountant still handles my taxes! I just send off the documents and have no idea what happens to them after that. My girlfriend does all the household finance stuff. She even made this appointment."

"Why do you think you defer your finances to others to manage?" I asked.

"Because I don't want to screw up again."

"Fear," I said.

"Fear," he agreed.

"Do you *want* to believe you're bad with money?"

"Obviously not."

"So what needs to happen for you to believe that you're good with money?"

He thought about that for some time and then let out a sigh. "I guess I'd have to be able to stick to this plan we just made for six months straight."

"How would that convince you?"

"I've never been able to stick to any financial plan, budget or debt-repayment plan for longer than two paycheques. If I made it to six months, I think it would feel like I've broken the curse."

"You can do this," I assured him. "And you *will* do this, because I believe that you want to."

"I do."

"So, six months—twelve paycheques."

"Yes."

"Okay." I put a note in my calendar. "I'm going to call you in six months, but I also want you to email me every payday."

"What do I send you?" he asked.

"Just a note that you've followed through on the banking plan. Like a buddy system."

Brent agreed and went home to implement his plan. On his first payday I got an email with a checkmark emoji. I wrote back with a fireworks emoji. It was a deep conversation.

Every 15 days I'd get the same email from Brent, until the six months were finally up. I couldn't wait to call him.

"From the looks of your emails, things have been going well," I said, excited to see how he felt about things.

"I haven't missed a payment and I used the strategic banking plan. The money I've been putting towards debt has actually been paying the principal. I can't believe it."

"Yay!" I squealed with excitement. "You see?"

He let out a big sigh. "It feels so good. I'm going to have my first credit card paid off in another five months."

"How has making it to six months affected your outlook?" I asked.

"I think I'm just more motivated," he said. "Is that weird?"

"Not at all. I think it's made you feel confident in your own abilities, and that confidence is what's helping keep you motivated."

"Totally. I've begun to daydream about being debt-free again. Like, now I believe it's possible for the first time in a long time, even though there's almost two years left until I'm done."

This was great. Brent's confidence was up. "Do you still think you're bad with money?" I asked.

"Ask me again in 20 months," he said, and I laughed.

"Oh, you know I will. I'm putting a reminder in my calendar to email you then."

He laughed.

"Do you still want to email me on paydays?" I asked.

"No, I think I've got this. Or at least I want to try."

"Awesome," I said.

When that calendar reminder popped up 20 months later, let me tell you, I was stoked. I went to my computer to shoot him an email, but there was already a message waiting in my inbox. The subject line was 10 checkmark emojis. I clicked it excitedly.

Nailed it was all it said.

I smiled, picked up the phone and called him. "Congrats!"

"I can't believe I did it," he said. "I'm debt-free, for the first time in my adult life!"

"Woo-hoo!!!"

"I can't even express the relief. I've already started a savings plan to move the money I was putting towards debt into retirement savings. It feels so good to feel productive. It was hard, for sure, especially when I had to say no to spending on things I really wanted to do. But the more I paid off, the more confident I got, and then the more excited I got. It built up. Now I feel totally addicted to this plan."

"Now I'm supposed to ask you something. Do you still think you're bad with money?"

"I do not," he said proudly.

"When did the switch happen?"

"Good question." He thought for a moment. "Last year I had to spend $300 when I broke my phone. I didn't have anything in Short-Term Savings, so it went straight onto my credit card. Before, something like that would have thrown me right off course. It would have made me feel that the whole plan was stupid and I was doomed to be a person who lived with debt. But this time I kept going with my plan. I didn't get sidetracked by the panic of not having enough money. I was like, *Brent, you've paid off so much. This is just a minor setback. You'll be fine.* I kept going! It was wild. I've never done something like that."

"And now you don't have debt anymore," I said.

"I don't."

"How are you celebrating?" I asked.

"By starting that RRSP," he said, with such a hearty laugh I couldn't help but laugh too.

"Well, you know, you can spend a small amount on yourself if you want to. You deserve to recognize this achievement."

"Oh, I know. But honestly, feeling good about my finances for the first time in my life is a bigger deal. I've promised myself that when I've saved $5,000 to my RRSP, I'll book a trip."

It was like speaking to a different person. I could not have been happier for Brent. He had spent his whole adult life believing that he was bad with money. As a result, his finances had suffered. Gaining confidence in himself and his ability to make good financial choices on his own had made him way more motivated to stick to his plans and see them through until the end.

Stop believing you're bad with money. You're not. No matter how you got to where you're at, regardless of what happened or how much you owe, there is hope and you can take action.

You've Got This

You made it—all the way through. Yay! I'm so excited for you.

Let's reflect for a second. You took stock of your debt, mapped it out, got organized, made a plan and implemented a banking strategy that will keep you living within your means without hating your life. What an accomplishment! This is the start of your amazing debt repayment plan that will have you living debt-free. It *is* possible to live your life and pay down debt.

Believing in your plan is half the battle. The other half is the doing part. All you have to do now is take the first step and implement all the juicy strategies in this book. It will work, I promise. Harness your inner tortoise. Forget the hare—slow and steady wins the race here.

Regardless of what happened before, whatever setbacks you faced or how you used to manage your finances, that's all in the past now. You get to choose what happens tomorrow.

- Choose to stop carrying around shame and blame.
- Choose to be motivated to pay back your debt, beyond the math.
- Choose to make a realistic Debt Game Plan so you can live your life.
- Choose to spend money strategically and avoid your Financial Tripwires.
- Choose to start believing that you are good with money.

Be kind to yourself, be realistic and, above all else, trust yourself. You can do this. You *can* be living debt-free. You're ready.

You've got this.

XO
Shannon

Resource Library

NOTE: The following calculations are all based on estimates. Results cannot be guaranteed and are only approximations. In addition, many of these resources are housed online at worryfreemoneybook.com, so they can remain relevant (the financial industry and regulations tend to change over time).

Debt-Payoff Calculator

If you want to figure out how long it will take you to pay off your debts at your current payment rate, use the Debt-Payoff Calculator at worryfreemoneybook.com/calculators.

Example

Line of credit loan	$4,500
Annual interest rate	3%
Monthly payment	$100

It would take you 48 months (4 years) to pay down this loan at the current monthly payment rate. You would pay $279.88 in interest.

Your Credit Score

See worryfreemoneybook.com/creditscore for information on where to get a free credit score, what affects your credit score, how to fix it and my thoughts on credit monitoring services.

Debt Types

See worryfreemoneybook.com/debttypes for more information.

Tax Estimator

You can estimate after-tax income from your job, sole proprietorship or side hustle by using this tool: simpletax.ca/calculator.

Example

You live in British Columbia and earn $1,700 a year from self-employment income (sole proprietorship). Your employment income is $41,616 per year. When you enter these figures into the tax calculator, you find that your marginal tax rate is 22.7 percent. Therefore, 22.7 percent of that $1,700 will go to income tax and CPP, which comes to $385.90. You get to keep $1,314.10 of your self-employment income.

Debt Stacking

Using Paul as an example, let's walk you through the step-by-step process that you will use to work out your Debt-Stacking Plan, using the Debt-Payoff Calculator.

Step 1: Take stock and organize your Debt Map (Chapter 5).

Step 2: Prioritize your debt and stack it in order of importance. Paul's debts are prioritized by interest rate.

Step 3: Calculate your Magic Amount. Paul's Magic Amount is $300.

Paul's Debt Map			
Debt	Amount Owing	Interest Rate	Minimum Payment
Credit card A	$5,350	19.99%	$160
Credit card B	$12,000	18.00%	$360
Personal loan	$3,500	5.60%	$70
Line of credit	$10,000	4.00%	$35
Total	**$30,850**		**$625**

Paul's Debt-Stacking Plan, Prioritized by Interest Rate ($300 Magic Amount)					
Debt	Amount Owing	Interest Rate	Minimum Payment	Magic Amount	Payments Made
Credit card A	$5,350	19.99%	$160	$300	$460
Credit card B	$12,000	18.00%	$360		$360
Personal loan	$3,500	5.60%	$70		$70
Line of credit	$10,000	4.00%	$35		$35
Total	**$30,850**		**$625**	**$300**	**$925**

Step 4: Apply the new Magic Amount to the next debt.

Step 4a: Use the Debt-Payoff Calculator at worryfreemoneybook.com/debt-payoff-calculator/ to see how long it will take to pay off the first debt and how much it will cost in interest.

Credit Card A

Loan amount $5,350

Annual interest rate   19.99%

Monthly payment $460

Results: Paid off in Month 14; interest paid of $646. This frees up $460, which becomes the new Magic Amount in the Debt-Stacking Plan.

Step 4b: For each of the other debts, enter the amounts and note the balance of the debt that corresponds with how long the first debt will take to pay off—in our example, 14 months.

Credit Card B

Loan amount $12,000

Annual interest rate   18%
Monthly payment $360

You will see that credit card B will have a balance of $9,218 at the end of Month 14 and have cost $2,258 in interest so far.

Personal Loan
Loan amount $3,500
Annual interest rate   5.6%
Monthly payment $70

Paul's student loan will have a balance of $2,725 by the end of Month 14 and have cost $205 in interest so far.

Line of Credit
Loan amount $10,000
Annual interest rate   4%
Monthly payment $35

The line of credit will have a balance of $9,976 by the end of Month 14 and have cost $466 in interest so far.

Paul's Debt-Stacking Plan at the End of 16 Months ($460 Magic Amount)					
Debt	Amount Owing	Interest Rate	Minimum Payment	Magic Amount	Payment Made
Credit card A	0	19.99%	0	0	0
Credit card B	$9,218	18.00%	$360	$460	$820
Personal loan	$2,723	5.60%	$70		$70
Line of credit	$9,976	4.00%	$35		$35
Total	$21,919		$465	$460	$925

Step 5: Repeat for each loan, starting with the next debt to be paid off with the new Magic Amount and total payment.

Step 5a: Put the second credit card debt into the Debt-Payoff Calculator at worryfreemoneybook.com/debt-payoff-calculator/.

Credit Card B

Loan amount $9,218

Annual interest rate   18%

Monthly payment $820

The credit card B balance will be zero (paid off) in 13 months, with $954 paid in interest. However, recall that this is 13 months *after* the first 14 months. So this is actually Month 27. So the card will be done in Month 27, with $3,212 paid in interest, freeing up $820 ($360 minimum payment + $460 Magic Amount). This makes the new Magic Amount $820.

Step 5b: For each debt, enter the amounts and note the balance of the debt that corresponds with how long the previous debt will take to pay off—in our example, 27 months.

Personal Loan

Loan amount (original debt amount) $3,500

Annual interest rate   5.6%

Monthly payment $70

The loan will have a balance of $1,959 by Month 27 and will have cost $1,501 in interest.

Line of Credit

Loan amount (original debt amount) $10,000

Annual interest rate   4%

Monthly payment $35

The line of credit will have a balance of $9,952 by Month 27, with $897 paid in interest.

Paul's Debt-Stacking Plan at the End of 27 Months ($820 Magic Amount)					
Debt	Amount Owing	Interest Rate	Minimum Payment	Magic Amount	Payment Made
Credit card A	0	19.99%	0		0
Credit card B	0	18.00%	0		0
Personal loan	$1,959	5.60%	$70	$820	$890
Line of credit	$9,952	4.00%	$35	0	$35
Total	**$11,911**		**$105**	**$820**	**$925**

Step 5c: Put the next debt into the Debt-Payoff Calculator at worryfreemoneybook.com/debt-payoff-calculator/.

Personal Loan

Loan amount $1,959

Annual interest rate   5.6%

Monthly payment $890

Paul's student loan balance is zero (paid off) in three months with a final $15 in interest. However, recall that this is 27 months into the plan, so this is actually Month 30. The loan will be done in Month 30 with $1,516 in interest paid, freeing up $890 ($70 minimum payment + $820 Magic Amount).

Step 5d: Enter the amount and note the balance of the next debt that corresponds with how long the previous debt will take to pay off—in our example, 43 months.

Line of Credit

Loan amount (original debt amount) $10,000

Annual interest rate   4%

Monthly payment $35

The line of credit will have a balance of $9,947 by Month 30, with $997 paid in interest.

Paul's Debt-Stacking Plan at the End of 30 Months ($890 Magic Amount)					
Debt	Amount Owing	Interest Rate	Minimum Payment	Magic Amount	Payment Made
Credit card A	0	19.99%	0	0	0
Credit card B	0	18.00%	0	0	0
Personal loan	0	5.60%	0	0	0
Line of credit	$9,947	4.00%	$35	$890	$925
Total	**$9,947**		**$35**	**$890**	**$925**

Step 5e: Put the line of credit into the Debt-Payoff Calculator at worryfreemoneybook.com/debt-payoff-calculator/.

Line of Credit

Loan amount $9,947

Annual interest rate   4%

Monthly payment $925

Paul will pay off the final bit of his line of credit in 11 months, with $199 in interest paid. Keep in mind that this is 11 months after the first 30 months, so the real time is 41 months. The total interest paid will be $1,196. The line of credit will be done in Month 41, freeing up $925.

For Paul, this is how his debt stack played out:

Paul's Predicted Results			
Debt	Paid Off By	Interest Paid	Amount Freed Up
Credit card A	Month 14	$646	$460
Credit card B	Month 27	$3,212	$820 ($360 + $460)
Personal loan	Month 30	$1,516	$890 ($70 + $820)
Line of credit	Month 41	$1,196	$925 ($35 + $890)

Extra Paycheques

If you are paid biweekly, you get two additional paycheques a year. These can help to offset the amount you need to save to Short-Term Savings.

Example

Your regular paycheque is $1,500 every other week. You have budgeted for 24 paycheques a year because, 10 months of the year, that's what you get. But there are two months in which you receive an additional paycheque. Let's say that one comes on March 30 and the other on August 31. Assume that your total amount set aside (money you cannot spend) is $2,100 and your Spending Money is $900 per month, or $450 per payday.

Step 1: The $1,500 goes into Bills and Savings, then $450 goes into your Spending Money account and $1,050 stays in Bills and Savings for Fixed Expenses and savings.

Step 2: Calculate how much extra you can put towards your debt each year from your extra paycheques.

For the paycheques on March 30 and August 31, you'll move $450 to Spending Money and put the remaining $1,050 towards your debt. This works because you've already left $1,050 in the Bills and Savings account twice that month, with the first two paydays. This gives you an extra $1,050! So twice a year $1,050 goes towards your debt, for a total of $2,100 per year.

You can use exactly the same process for weekly paycheques, only with four additional paycheques a year.

Consolidation Methods

Go to worryfreemoneybook.com/debtsteps for more information on this subject.

Long-Term Savings Calculator

Use this calculator to estimate how much your savings will be worth over time: worryfreemoneybook.com/long-term-savings-calculator/.

Example

You have a gross annual salary of $50,000 and want to save $5,000 per year (10 percent). This means monthly contributions of $416 ($5,000 ÷ 12 months). You'd like to know how much you will have saved up over 30 years if your income increases by 2 percent per year for inflation, and therefore your retirement contributions as well.

Input the following into the online calculator:

Initial amount 0

Annual rate of return   5%

Annual savings amount $5,000   ($416 × 12)

Increase yearly with inflation?   yes

Inflation rate   2%

The result? In 30 years, you will have a nest egg of $439,351.

Credit Management Solutions

Check out worryfreemoneybook.com/creditmanagement.

Additional Reading

Canada Pension Plan—How Much Could You Receive

canada.ca/en/services/benefits/publicpensions/cpp/cpp-benefit/amount.html

Old Age Security—Overview

canada.ca/en/services/benefits/publicpensions/cppold-age-security.html

EI Maternity and Parental Benefits—Overview

canada.ca/en/services/benefits/ei/ei-maternity-parental.html

GST/HST Credit—Application and Eligibility

canada.ca/en/revenue-agency/services/child-family-benefits/goods-services-tax-harmonized-sales-tax-gst-hst-credit/gst-hst-credit-application-eligibility.html

Find a Licensed Insolvency Trustee (Consumer Proposal/Bankruptcy)

ic.gc.ca/app/osb/tds/search.html?lang=eng

Getting Help from a Credit Counsellor

canada.ca/en/financial-consumer-agency/services/debt/debt-help.html

Acknowledgements

This book would not have been possible without the love, support and brainpower of many people. I appreciate you all so much. Thank you!

Mom – Thank you for always being my sounding board. I love you. Thank you especially for the endless cups of tea and brainstorming sessions.

Matt – Thank you for being the best partner in crime and always encouraging my dreams and Capricorn drive.

My family – Thank you for being endlessly supportive throughout the entire writing process and always cheering me on.

Kate Cassaday, my brilliant editor – For being such a boss. I heart your brain. Thank you for all of your hard work and hustle.

Martha Webb, my agent – For also being such a boss. I won the jackpot with you on my team.

To HarperCollins Canada – Debt books are so important. Thank you for believing in this project as much as I do.

I'd also like to thank the following people for sharing their expertise and letting me pick their brains:

Patricia White, executive director of Credit Counselling Canada, and Bryan Gelman, licensed insolvency trustee and managing director of Albert Gelman – Thank you for helping me show Canadians that credit counselling, consumer proposals and bankruptcy can be helpful services and a tool in our financial toolkits.

Alexa Turner, collaborative family lawyer at Victoria Smith Collaborative Professional Corporation – Thank you for helping me show Canadians who are coupling up how to tag-team their household finances in a safe and protected way.

Index

SHANNON LEE SIMMONS is a certified financial planner, an author, a life coach, a speaker and the founder of the award-winning New School of Finance. She is a personal finance writer for *The Globe and Mail*, and she is the personal finance expert on CBC's *Metro Morning* and CTV's *The Marilyn Denis Show*. She is also the bestselling author of *Worry-Free Money*. She lives in Toronto with her husband and son.